# International Firms and Modern Imperialism

**Selected Readings**

Hugo Radice

Penguin Books

Penguin Books Ltd,
Harmondsworth, Middlesex, England
Penguin Books Inc.,
7110 Ambassador Road, Baltimore, Maryland 21207, U.S.A.
Penguin Books Australia Ltd,
Ringwood, Victoria, Australia
Penguin Books Canada Ltd,
41 Steelcase Road West, Markham, Ontario, Canada
Penguin Books (N.Z.) Ltd,
182–190 Wairau Road, Auckland 10, New Zealand

First published 1975

This selection copyright © Hugo Radice, 1975
Introduction and notes copyright © Hugo Radice, 1975

Copyright acknowledgement for items in this volume will
be found on p. 255.

Made and printed in Great Britain by
Cox & Wyman Ltd, London, Reading and Fakenham
Set in Monotype Times

To the Memory of
György Ádám (1911–1974) and
Steve Hymer (1935–1974)

# Contents

# Introduction

At first sight there is nothing especially difficult to understand about international firms[1] and their activities. That firms should attempt to extend their
activities regardless of any natural or political boundaries; that they should
take advantage of their trans-national scope to undermine the organizations
of labour or the restrictions of government; that they should have a centralized direction which embodies certain private interests, not any pretended
national or global interest – all these matters are readily seen in the activities
of Ford or ICI by the average worker as well as the 'expert'. He sees for
himself the costs and benefits of their activities. In this respect the international firm cannot be mystified so readily as, for example, the international
monetary system, which impinges only in a very mediated way upon day-to-
day life.

However, this only means that the essential features of the activities of
international firms can be easily *described* (as in Tugendhat, 1973); there are
still crucial problems of *analysis*, if we seek an adequate understanding of
why they have developed and what implications follow for the development
of society in general and for capitalism in particular. Thus, why are international firms of such importance to us when they account for such a small
proportion of employment?[2] What is the real difference between internationalized production and international trade or financial flows as forms
of world economy? Why is it that international firms appear to undermine
nation-states, and yet rely increasingly on state support? What are the
implications of these new economic empires for the non-industrialized or
underdeveloped countries? Or for class struggle (or class collaboration) in
the advanced countries? Is it necessary and possible for trade unions to 'go
international'? All these questions demand that we go much deeper than the
surface appearances of international firms, and *locate* them within an analysis of the capitalist system as a whole.

The main thrust of this collection of readings is that this analysis can only
be adequately provided by the theory of imperialism. Although no doubt
some might regard this as self-evident, some clarification is necessary.

1. The term usually used to describe companies with production facilities in more
than one country is 'multinational corporation (firm, enterprise)'. I use the term
'international firm', partly because it is more accessible, and partly because it emphasizes the movement of capital *across* and *between* 'nations' in the world economy, while
'multinational' has a quite incorrect connotation of 'more than one nationality'.

2. Only 8·7% in the USA., 7% in Great Britain, and 3–4% in France and Germany
according to Altvater (1973), p. 4.

First, it does not follow that the general viewpoint is 'against' international firms. Certainly, it is against the continued existence of capitalism as a social system, but it recognizes that capitalism is in a certain sense historically progressive even today; it is not a Luddite view. But because the general tenor is against capitalism, orthodox (or bourgeois) social science regards such a viewpoint, especially when explicitly derived from Marx, as ideological and unscientific. The response of Marxism *and* of radical social science is that the orthodoxy is itself ideological: it implicitly treats fundamental aspects of the status quo as eternal and natural, and falsely claims neutrality and objectivity for its views in consequence. The historical materialist method of Marx goes further than this, arguing that the social sciences as ideological formations are part of the development of society along with the economic and social formations to which they correspond, and that a truly scientific social science, equally product and agent of the transformation of society, must be critical, must seek to transcend these formations'. Neutrality and objectivity as eternal criteria do not exist: the only real human knowledge or science is gained through *praxis*, the unity of theory and practice in social action, not by detached observation, and the theoretical component of praxis is inseparable in the final analysis from 'political' practical activity.[3] It must be emphasized that *within* the methodological framework of orthodox social science the charge of bias against the system is irrefutable: Marxists can only insist that man in history shall be the judge, not abstract ideas.

Second, and linked to this: I am not arguing that *only* self-proclaimed Marxists have anything useful to say about capitalism. On the contrary, precisely because it starts from appearances, orthodox social science gathers a great deal of descriptive material in summary form, and develops a large number of working hypotheses about economic and social phenomena which are perfectly acceptable to everybody. But in uncovering the nature of society we have to go behind outward appearances, including those of our own ideological and political formations, and this an ahistorical, uncritical, fetishized[4] social science simply cannot do. To carry out the task, we have to draw on a very wide range of material by writers of every hue, and study them critically in relation to our own method, to what we ourselves observe, and to our own social practice.

Third, by imperialism I understand capitalism in its simultaneously

3. Needless to say, not all Marxists would share this view by any means. For fuller discussion, see Marx, *Grundrisse*, Introduction section 3, 'The method of political economy'; and also Blackburn (1972).

4. For understanding this term, there is no substitute for Marx, *Capital*, Vol. 1, chapter 1, section 4; see also the references in footnote 3 above (in particular Geras's article in Blackburn, 1972).

extensive (towards a world-wide system) and intensive (socialization of the forces of production) development, at once phase and moment of the path of capitalism in history. By capitalism I understand that mode of production based on a free labour force and the private appropriation of surplus labour; by a world-wide system I mean production and exchange relations on a world scale; by socialization of the means of production I mean those trends loosely summarized in the term 'monopoly capitalism': increasing inter-dependence of workers in production, internalization of market relations by capitals, concretion of the spheres of circulation of productive, commodity and money capital as finance capital, and the re-emergence of the state as a vital overarching institution supporting the continued reproduction of the system.

The remainder of this introduction will first briefly survey different approaches to international firms, and then examine orthodox economic theory and the theory of imperialism in relation to them.[5]

## Approaches to international firms[6]

Let us first summarize some of the most important generally agreed facts about international firms, defining them as firms which command production facilities in more than one country.

IFs are large both in general and in relation to national firms in their own industries. They tend to be found in more concentrated or oligopolistic industries. They are mostly rather national in terms of ownership and still more in terms of control, and whatever the extent of observable 'decentralization' are subject to highly centralized strategic decision-making through complex management structures and information systems (which is not to say that these systems necessarily work very well in practice). They vary in incidence as foreign or home-based firms from country to country, and between industries, and they include raw material, production goods and consumption goods firms, often highly diversified or even conglomerate. They are supported by a growing internationalization of banks and of service companies of all kinds. A historical shift is embodied in IFs from a portfolio to a direct form of foreign investment flow: they increasingly internalize flows of goods and money. The weight of IF investments has also been shifting since the second world war from raw materials to manufactured goods and from less developed to developed countries, although world-wide sourcing (Reading 4) indicates a partial reversal of the latter trend. Finally, the private interests and centralized direction of IFs clash at least potentially with economic and other goals of states and classes in both less developed and developed countries, and the consequence is

5. For a more detailed development of the next two sections, see Radice (1973).
6. Hereafter often abbreviated to IFs.

responses from governments, trade unions, international agencies, consumers, etc.[7]

We can separate broadly supportive and critical views on IFs and their activities. Ádám (1971), in a survey of views, distinguishes two varieties of 'apologetics'. The first is a pure, global neo-classicism: the market mechanism must reign supreme in order to develop a 'fully rational international division of labour that will "optimize" the productive resources of the world' (Business Week, 1970). Nation-states must not get in the way: they have been replaced by the IF, both in theory and in reality, as the agent of world-wide Pareto-optimality. The second, more moderate in tone, is the prevailing orthodoxy, typified by the work of Vernon (1971), Dunning (1970 and 1972), or Rolfe (1969). The basic intellectual framework, neo-classical trade and welfare theory, remains the same, but the need for state activity to correct imperfections and achieve agreed goals is explicitly recognized. IFs are seen as providing host countries with a package deal of new products, technology, capital and management skills (especially technology) which can be evaluated in terms of its contribution to national economic welfare. They can thwart governmental controls which have been adequate for national firms, and they may also harm the positions of national firms, so that there are costs as well as benefits. The same potential dangers apply to home countries, who reap a benefit in the form of repatriated profits, linked export orders and competitive advantage in world markets, but a cost in outflow of funds and transfer of production. All these costs and benefits are seen as the subject of implicit or explicit bargaining between IFs and governments. However, while in the short term states must exercise their powers to avoid dislocation and damage to their national economies, in the long run freedom of action for IFs is seen as generally desirable. Since less developed countries are weaker in bargaining power, i.e. in what they have to offer in return for the benefits, and in their ability to threaten, they are allowed more latitude in interfering with world market forces, but are cautioned against impossible attempts to do without IFs. Supra-national cooperation in developing policies towards IFs is seen as useful so long as it does not create an unwieldy regulative structure; out-and-out internationalism, like nationalism, is unrealistic and harmful. A good deal of time and energy is put into providing statistical and other evidence for these arguments.

The body of critical writing also falls into two categories, although again the distinction is blurred: explicitly Marxist and more generally radical. The latter rejects the neo-classical framework surrounding the orthodox view, and sees the oligopolistic nature of international business as a necessary

7. Vernon (1971) is the best single source of information, statistics and further references. See also the bibliography to these readings.

cause and effect of a world-wide hierarchy of economic dependence, power and welfare. Although I Fs bring benefits to host countries, these could be improved on by developing public, non-market structures at national and world level, and their costs involve increasing political and economic dependence for the host, whether industrialized like Canada or underdeveloped, leading to economic backwardness in the long run. Much of the evidence adduced by orthodox writers is rejected as based on meaningless criteria. The activities of I Fs require rigorous control, if not exclusion, and particular emphasis is placed on the independent generation of technological progress.

Whereas this view tends to give a rather 'flat' picture of a strict hierarchy of exploitation, to emphasize problems of market monopoly rather than class relations in production, and to lead often towards nationalist and 'third-worldist' policies and attitudes, Marxist views seek to bring out the contradictory nature of capitalist world economy: the historically *progressive* aspect of capitalism in developing the means of production and breaking down outmoded political and social formations; the contradictory relation between capital and the nation-state rather than simple opposition; the class nature of both capital and the state; the need for an international, working-class socialist movement as the only solution. For all 'critical' writers, indeed, any moves to counter the activities of I Fs through governments or through trade unions only make sense in a long-run perspective of world socialism.

## International firms and economic theory

Orthodox economics since Keynes has been an uneasy amalgam of neoclassical economics (an all-embracing analysis of the economic system of capitalism incorporating a particular methodology, theory of value, theory of markets and prices, of the state, etc.) and Keynesian macro-economics, an essentially *operational* body of descriptive analysis and policy prescription (O'Connor, 1969). This dichotomy is expressed clearly in the terms 'microeconomics' and 'macro-economics' which confront the student in the world of textbooks and economics lectures, and serve to make the real world, not divided so conveniently, often harder to understand for him than for the 'unenlightened'.

Because 'macro-economics' is basically operational, its scope is limited to its original tasks: the management of the national economy through government economic policies. It is therefore not surprising that the orthodox economist approaches international firms from the only available body of orthodox theory on the world economy, the neo-classical (and classical) theory of international trade and factor movements. Since it is only too obvious that I Fs make it impossible to use a model of a world market economy with independent, individual economic actors (countries

A and B), what approach can be adopted? Lacking any alternative theoretical framework, the neo-classical one is maintained, but IFs are added to, or substituted for, nation-states as actors in the market, and the latter is seen as subject to many distortions and imperfections which are approached in the manner of neo-classical welfare economics. The theoretical difficulties are then set aside quickly as the economist turns to the familiar solid ground of *the facts* (the specialist theoreticians are free to apply their skills to these difficulties: see for example Aliber, 1970). Here the economist picks up the Keynesian operational approach to the economic functions of the state, and couples it to the pragmatism of industrial economics. The former gives him a framework for assessing the impact of IFs on national economies (in uneasy harness with welfare theory); the latter, for analysing the structure and market behaviour of IFs.

Unfortunately, in any field of social inquiry even the self-proclaimed pragmatist cannot avoid using and developing a body of theory, at least implicitly. Partly it orients and organizes the internal structure of his work, and partly it justifies the selection of a particular field of inquiry in the first place. And it is plain since the great capital-theory controversy unleashed by Sraffa (1960)[8] that neo-classical economics is no longer adequate: it is not just apologetic and irrelevant, it is also internally inconsistent. Although it is undergoing something of a resurgence as an applied economics tool for studying social problems in the USA (the marginal analysis of pollution, racial discrimination, unemployment of economists, the decline in baseball, etc.), and although it will inevitably hold sway in the classrooms of the 'civilized' world for years to come[9], no academic bourgeois economist can rely on a Samuelson to provide a theoretical framework and justification as well as tools.

This would be serious enough for the orthodox economist studying IFs; but perhaps worse still, even pragmatic, operational Keynesianism no longer seems to deliver the goods. Not only do poverty and underdevelopment persist at the world-economy level at which he is forced to operate, but at home, even as GNP continues to rise, inflation becomes rampant, economic instability increases, inequalities get worse, and monetary and fiscal policies become ever more unpredictable in effect; government economic strategies oscillate wildly, with the economists panting to keep up with them and justify the latest change of line; and the international monetary system, subject of a thousand learned PhDs, falls apart in front of his eyes. There is a growing

8. For a full analysis of this see Harcourt and Laing (1971) and Hunt and Schwartz (1972). For a much earlier, explicitly Marxist critique of neo-classical economies, see Bukharin (1919).

9. Thirteen years after the publication of Sraffa's work, we at last have one anti-neoclassical university-level textbook, by Robinson and Eatwell (1973)

mood of unease in the profession,[10] not helped by the resurgence of Marx's critique of political economy.

What is loosely termed the 'Cambridge School', or 'left-Keynesianism', can provide an alternative framework for studying I Fs without adopting a Marxist approach. Left-Keynesianism recognizes the class nature of capitalist society: the role of class struggle in the distribution of income, the state as agent of class rule, the 'political trade cycle', etc. It also sees the relation of nation-states in the world economy as a non-market one of power and rivalries, in which, e.g., devaluation is a competitive weapon, and international monetary chaos a struggle by Europe and Japan to cut the USA down to size. There are clear affinities to this in the work of Levitt (1970), for example. But although there is increasingly an implicit acceptance of much of the Cambridge School's approach (for example in regard to incomes policy – see Jones, 1973), it would be expecting too much for this school of thought to become a 'new orthodoxy' except in a castrated form, and then only given a major lurch towards social democracy in the advanced capitalist countries. The prognosis is, rather, still more pragmatism – the academic as business journalist – and continued failure by orthodox economists to relate I Fs in any coherent or illuminating way to the many general problems of the continued development or approaching demise of the capitalist system.

### International Firms and the Theory of Imperialism

Can we then turn to the Marxist theory of imperialism as providing a fully developed framework for studying international firms? Not at all; as Ken Tarbuck puts it:

... there seem to have been very few attempts to develop the theory of imperialism since the first quarter of this century, by Marxists of any particular hue. In large measure, this has been due to the raising of Lenin's ideas into canonical dogma during the period of Stalin's sway within the world Communist movement. (1972, p. 42).

In recent years this picture has, however, been changing somewhat, as Tarbuck acknowledges. If we restrict ourselves to English-language Marxist work, first Rosa Luxemburg's *Accumulation of Capital* (1913, English ed. 1951), then Nikolai Bukharin's *Imperialism and World Economy* (1918, English re-issue 1972) and now the debate between them (Tarbuck, 1972) has been rediscovered[11] (Trotsky is an awkward case; unfortunately only

10. To take just one major periodical, the *Economic Journal*, see Phelps Brown (1972), Kaldor (1972) and Wiles (1973).

11. We *still* await an English translation of Rudolf Hilferding's *Das Finanzkapital* (1910) – available in French, Italian, Spanish, etc. – which was extremely important in the development of both Bukharin's and Lenin's ideas.

'Trotskyists' take him seriously). The work of the Monthly Review school, notably Baran (1957), Baran and Sweezy (1966) and Magdoff (1969), and Barratt Brown (1963, 1974), Kemp (1967), Mandel (1968), Frank (1969) and Emmanuel (1972), have all raised the level of debate. Apart from these, there is now a wealth of material on imperialism, both theoretical and empirical, for example in the collections by Rhodes (1970) and Owen and Sutcliffe (1972). But beyond accepting fundamental descriptive definitions of imperialism (for example, Lenin's five points[12]), major problems remain. All I can do here is to go over some points especially relevant to the study of international firms.

First, what do we understand by internationalization or world economy in relation to national economy? It is widely accepted that for Marx the analysis of a closed national economy was a simplifying assumption only, especially for Vols. I and II of *Capital*; in Vol. III, where the analyses of production and of circulation are brought together in studying the accumulation of capital, we find that world markets, foreign investment, colonialism (all given sporadic mention in Vols. I and II) are systematically located, if only briefly analysed, along with banking, the stock market, etc. But it is apparent from the *Grundrisse* and from Marx's correspondence, as Nicolaus (1973) shows, that international trade and the world market, and the state as well, were subjects of the unwritten later sections of his great project: they represented further *concretizations* of his theory, necessary developments towards determining political practice and strategy because they are among the concrete historical trends of capitalism.[13] Of Marx's successors, it is Bukharin who develops the concept of world economy most clearly (see Reading 1), but the relation between national and world economy is a major difficulty (as Palloix (1971) stresses, for example). The tendency is to take the national economy – the developed, monopoly capitalist system in which the capitalist mode of production is universal, the development and socialization of the means of production has gone furthest, and the dominance of capital and its movement is most clear – and then to analyse the *forces projecting out from* this system into the outside world. In this view, 'capitalism' is the system operating within the national economy, and 'imperialism' is the relation between the national economy and other national economies. It may instead be argued, following Bukharin (Reading 1), that while initially capital only encompasses small areas within a national economy as a domi-

12. These were: concentration of production and capital; emergence of finance capital; export of capital as a major feature; formation of international capitalist combines and complete territorial division of the world by the great powers. (Lenin, 1917, p. 86 of 1970 edition.) It should be noted that Lenin is no longer accorded automatic obeisance – see especially Barratt Brown (1963).

13. The methodological issue of the relation of the abstract to the concrete in Marx's approach has been the basis of a lot of the criticism of Luxemburg: see Tarbuck (1972).

nant social relation, and impinges on other areas of the world as an alien and intruding force, there is a general trend of *internationalization* inherent in the expansive nature of capitalism which tends to create a specifically capitalist world economy. Increasingly, this capitalist world economy is subject *as a whole* to the laws of motion of capitalism; national economies both influence and are influenced by it. Hence we may say that capital has both an international and a national moment; or that there is an international law of value which is more than just a simple average of national values, in fact value being determined at an international level.[14]

Leading on from this, the mechanisms of imperialism represent the working-out of the process of capital accumulation as a whole in the world economy. On the one hand, this means that the appropriation and redistribution of surplus value cannot be understood solely in terms of the circulation of commodities (trade), nor of the circulation of money (financial flows), nor of the production process (international division of labour); the accumulation of capital involves *all* these. On the other hand, the 'function' of imperialist relations for capital in an advanced capitalist country has to be seen in terms of the adequacy of the national economy as a basis for continued accumulation and the reproduction of capitalist social relations, within the world economy. There is a 'surplus of capital', or 'surplus value cannot be realized', in relation to the accumulation of capital on a national basis, and hence capital must reconstitute itself at a world level, incorporating resources, labour and produced commodities in other areas of the world under its sway, pushing the internationalization process further.

Secondly, the law of 'uneven development', so often cited and so rarely explained, demands some clarification. At the world economy level, this is linked to the concept of underdevelopment (cf. Frank, 1969, for example) and the prospects for capitalist development at the periphery. Murray (1972) has interestingly analysed underdevelopment and the activities of international firms in terms of laws of spatial location within an increasingly unified world economy, while Warren (1973) has strongly challenged the widely-held view that independent capitalist development is no longer possible in underdeveloped countries. Again in relation to underdevelopment, we are analysing basically the capitalist mode of production, and we must be quite clear on the relation of it to other modes of production, and the nature of the mode or modes of production at the 'periphery' (cf. Laclau, 1971). Finally,

14. Palloix (1971, 1973) sees internationalization as a three-stage process, in relation to the three circuits of capital analysed in Vol. II of Marx's *Capital* (see also Reading 3). First there is internationalization of commodity-capital (development of international trade), then of money-capital (export of capital as in Lenin), finally of productive capital (the international firm). The last stage makes the world economy the basic arena for capital and thus also the only adequate level for its analysis.

it is still not appreciated sufficiently the extent to which Marx rightly saw capitalism as progressive, and the sense in which he meant it: the system forced, not necessarily against the will of its ruling capitalist class, but precisely *unconsciously* by its own contradictions, to seek to transcend those contradictions, thereby laying the material basis for conscious control in a classless society.[15] Under monopoly capitalism, Marxists have so loosely spoken of the decay, bankruptcy and imminent collapse of the system (almost as if it would collapse by itself), but does not this progressive element remain? Thus industrialization of any sort to any degree in the less developed countries does develop the forces of production in very many ways. In any case, a *purely* unidirectional trend of 'underdevelopment' requires establishing in terms of the *world* economy (see above).

The important point is that if international firms are a basic institutional form of imperialism today, first, they must be understood as bearers of forces at work within the system which are themselves the object of theoretical work; and secondly, the study of these concrete forms is essential if the theory of imperialism is to be united with the practice of the struggle for socialism. Analysis of international firms and development of the theory of imperialism go hand in hand.

### Selection of the readings

The chief consequence as regards international firms is that they must be understood in terms of the *internationalization of capital* and the *accumulation of capital*. The subject matter of the study of IFs starts to take on a different shape; it is no longer determined by the 'facts' alone. In this collection of readings, I have chosen material around four different themes. The collection does not try to supply systematic information on the activities of international firms: for this, the reader can make use of the bibliography at the end.

The first theme is the internationalization of capital and the overall development of the capitalist world economy in relation to the spread of IFs, their structure and their behaviour. This allows the broadest issues – the international division of labour, underdevelopment – to be broached.

The second is the relation of capital to the state. The chief point I would stress here is that it is quite wrong to see this as a *clash between* the IF and the nation state. Although in concrete terms such clashes do occur, they reflect the conflicts between the national and international moments of capital itself.

The third theme is linked to the second but is broader: the conflicts between different national groups of capitals. Accepting that capitals have

15. And not just the technical basis in nuts and bolts; see for example the discussion on education in *Capital*, Vol. 1, chapter 15, section 9.

a nationality, does the growing internationalization of economic life imply that imperial rivalries become more acute, or that a dominant imperialist power can penetrate and subdue others, or that super-states are required now to resolve the national/international contradiction?

The fourth theme is one particular aspect of the activities of IFs in less developed countries, the question of technological dependence. Many writers have argued that the control by IFs over technology and technical progress binds the recipients to them in a variety of ways and forms the basis of an exploitative control, which can only be broken by seizing control over the knowledge needed for industrial development. Is this view justified, what are the prospects for less developed countries of gaining technological independence, and what do we understand by this?

I am well aware that these are only some of the themes that can be pursued with regard to international firms, and that their treatment here leaves a large number of unanswered questions. There is a great deal more work to be done in developing our understanding of imperialism in order to struggle against it.

## References

Ádám, G. (1971), *The World Corporation Problematics: Apologetics and Critique*, Hungarian Scientific Council for World Economy.

Aliber, R. Z. (1970), 'A Theory of Foreign Direct Investment', in C. P. Kindleberger (ed.), *The International Corporation*, MIT Press.

Altvater, E. (1973), 'Multinational Corporations and the Working Class', in K. P. Tudyka (ed.), *Multinational Corporations and Labour Unions*, SUN, Nijmegen.

Baran, P. (1957), *The Political Economy of Growth*, Monthly Review Press; Penguin, 1970.

Baran, P. and Sweezy, P. (1966), *Monopoly Capital*, Monthly Review Press; Penguin, 1970.

Barratt Brown, M. (1963), *After Imperialism*, Heinemann.

Barratt Brown, M. (1974), *The Economics of Imperialism*, Penguin.

Blackburn, R. (ed.) (1972), *Ideology in Social Science*, Fontana.

Bukharin, N. (1918), *Imperialism and World Economy*, Merlin Press (1972 edition).

Bukharin, N. (1919), *The Economic Theory of the Leisure Class*, Martin Lawrence (1927 edition).

Business Week (1970), 'The Multinationals Ride a Rougher Road', *Business Week*, 19 December.

Dunning, J. (1970), *Studies in International Investment*, Allen & Unwin.

Dunning, J. (ed.) (1972), *The Multinational Enterprise*, Allen & Unwin.

Emmanuel, A. (1972), *Unequal Exchange*, New Left Books.

Frank, A. (1969), *Capitalism and Underdevelopment in Latin America*, Monthly Review Press; Penguin, 1970.

Harcourt, G. C., and Laing, N. F. (eds.) (1971), *Capital and Growth*, Penguin.

HILFERDING, R. (1910), *Das Finanzkapital*. French edition, *Le capital financier*, Editions de Minuit, 1970.

HUNT, E. K., and SCHWARTZ, J. G. (eds.) (1972), *A Critique of Economic Theory*, Penguin.

JONES, A. (1973), *The New Inflation*, Penguin.

KALDOR, N. (1972), 'The Irrelevance of Equilibrium Economics', *Economic Journal*, December.

KEMP, T. (1967), *Theories of Imperialism*, Dobson.

LACLAU, E. (1971), 'Feudalism and Capitalism in Latin America', *New Left Review* no. 67, May–June.

LENIN, V. I. (1917), *Imperialism, the Highest Stage of Capitalism*, Progress Publishers (1970 edition).

LEVITT, K. (1970), *Silent Surrender*, Macmillan.

LUXEMBURG, R. (1913), *The Accumulation of Capital*, Routledge (1951 edition).

MAGDOFF, H. (1969), *The Age of Imperialism*, Monthly Review Press.

MANDEL, E. (1968), *Marxist Economic Theory*, Merlin.

MARX, K. (1857–8), *Grundrisse*, Penguin (1973).

MARX, K. (1867), *Capital*, Vol. I, Lawrence & Wishart (1970).

MURRAY, R. (1972), 'Underdevelopment, International Firms and the International Division of Labour', in *Towards a New World Economy*, Rotterdam University Press.

NICOLAUS, M. (1973), 'Foreword', in Marx, *Grundrisse*, Penguin.

O'CONNOR, J. (1969), 'Scientific and Ideological Elements in the Economic Theory of Government Policy', *Science and Society*, Fall–Winter. (Also in Hunt & Schwartz, 1972).

OWEN, R., and SUTCLIFFE, B. (1972), *Studies in the Theory of Imperialism*, Longmans.

PALLOIX, C. (1971), *L'Économie mondiale capitaliste*, Maspero.

PALLOIX, C. (1973), *Les Firmes multinationales et le procès d'internationalisation*, Maspero.

PHELPS BROWN, E. H. (1972), 'The Underdevelopment of Economics', *Economic Journal*, March.

RADICE, H. K. (1973), 'International Firms and Economic Theory', in K. P. Tudyka (ed.), *Multinational Corporations and Labour Unions*, SUN, Nijmegen.

RHODES, R. I. (ed.) (1970), *Imperialism and Underdevelopment*, Monthly Review Press.

ROBINSON, J., and EATWELL, J. (1973), *An Introduction to Modern Economics*, McGraw-Hill.

ROLFE, S. E. (1969), *The International Corporation*, International Chamber of Commerce.

SRAFFA, P. (1960), *Production of Commodities by Means of Commodities*, Cambridge University Press.

TARBUCK, K. (ed.) (1972), Rosa Luxemburg and Nikolai Bukharin, *Imperialism and the Accumulation of Capital*, Allen Lane.

TUGENDHAT, C. (1973), *The Multinationals*, Penguin.

VERNON, R. (1971), *Sovereignty at Bay*, Longmans.

WARREN, B. (1973), 'Imperialism and Capitalist Industrialization', *New Left Review* no. 81, September–October.

WILES, P. (1973), 'Cost Inflation and the State of Economic Theory', *Economic Journal*, June.

# Prologue

The central theme of Nikolai Bukharin's classic work, first published in 1918, is that imperialism is the combined effect of two trends at work in capitalism: the trend towards *internationalization* – the extensive and intensive growth of capitalist economic relations in the world economy – and the trend towards *nationalization* – the centralization of capital, emergence of finance capital, and tendency to fusion of capital and the state, in the national economy.

To Bukharin, writing in 1915 at the height of an inter-imperialist war, the latter dominated the former: the tendency to internationalization acted only *through* that of nationalization, in the form of the drive for control over sections of the world economy and for annexations; hence the formation of international cartels and trusts (forerunners of international firms) was hesitant and unstable if it *cut across* the hardening division of the world between imperial powers.

Granted that 'nationalization' was exaggerated by Bukharin as a trend, and that growing internationalization – reversed at such a cost to capitalism in the 1930s – forced a limitation of inter-imperial rivalries under American tutelage after 1945, the forces analysed so perceptively by Bukharin can explain internationalization of capital in the form of international firms as they appear today: centralization of capital on a world scale regardless of national boundaries, and interpenetration of national capitals.

# 1 Nikolai Bukharin

## World Economy and National Economy

Extracts from Nikolai Bukharin, *Imperialism and World Economy*, Merlin Press, 1972, Chapters 1, 2, 3, 4, and 8 (first published 1918; first English edition, Martin Lawrence, 1927).

### 1 World economy defined

We thus observe a peculiar distribution of the productive forces of world capitalism. The main subdivisions of social labour are separated by the line that divides two types of countries; social labour proves to be divided on an international scale.

International division of labour finds its expression in international exchange.

Since the producers do not come into social contact with each other until they exchange their products, the specific social character of each producer's labour does not show itself except in the act of exchange. In other words, the labour of the individual asserts itself as a part of the labour of society, only by means of the relations which the act of exchange establishes directly between the products, and indirectly, through them, between the producers.[1]

The social labour of the world as a whole is divided among the various countries; the labour of every individual country becomes part of that world social labour through the exchange that takes place on an international scale. This interdependence of countries brought about by the process of exchange is by no means an accident; it is a necessary condition for continued social growth. International exchange thereby turns into a process of socio-economic life governed by definite laws ...

Any connection between producers who meet in the process of exchange presupposes the individual labours of the producers having already become elements of the combined labour of a social whole. Thus production is hidden behind exchange, production relations are hidden behind exchange relations, the interrelation of producers is hidden behind the interrelation of commodities. Where connections established through the process of exchange are not of an accidental nature, we have a stable system of production relations which forms the economic structure of society. Thus we may define world economy as *a system of production relations and, correspondingly, of exchange relations on a world scale*. One must not assume,

1. Marx (1867), p. 73.

however, that production relations are established solely in the process of commodity exchange. '. . . from the moment that men *in any way* work for one another, their labour assumes a social form'[2] (*Italics ours – N.B.*); in other words, whatever the form of connections established between producers, whether directly or indirectly, once a connection has been established and has acquired a stable character, we may speak of a system of production relations, i.e. of the growth (or formation) of a social economy. It thus appears that commodity exchange is one of the most primitive forms of expressing production relations. Present-day highly complicated economic life knows a great variety of forms behind which production relations are hidden. When, for instance, the shares of an American enterprise are bought at the Berlin stock exchange, production relations are thereby established between the German capitalist and the American worker. When a Russian city obtains a loan from London capitalists and pays interest on the loan, then this is what happens: part of the surplus value expressing the relation that exists between the English worker and the English capitalist is transferred to the municipal government of a Russian city; the latter, in paying interest, gives away part of the surplus value received by the bourgeoisie of that city and expressing the production relations existing between the Russian worker and the Russian capitalist. Thus connections are established both between the workers and the capitalists of two countries. Of particular significance is the role of the ever-growing movements of money capital, which we have noted above. A number of other forms of economic relations may be observed, like emigration and immigration; migration of the labour power; partial transfer of the wages of immigrant labour ('sending money home'); establishment of enterprises abroad, and the movement of the surplus value obtained; profits of steamship companies, etc. We shall still return to this. At present we only wish to note that 'world economy' includes all these economic phenomena which, all in all, are based on the relations between human beings engaged in the process of production. By and large, the whole process of world economic life in modern times reduces itself to the production of surplus value and its distribution among the various groups and sub-groups of the bourgeoisie on the basis of an ever widening reproduction of the relations between two classes – the class of the world proletariat on the one hand and the world bourgeoisie on the other.

## 2 Growth of world economy

The growth of international economic connections, and consequently the growth of the system of production relations on a world-wide scale, may be of two kinds. International connections may grow in scope, spreading over territories not yet drawn into the vortex of capitalist life. In that case we

2. Marx, *loc. cit.*

speak of the extensive growth of world economy. On the other hand, they may assume greater depth, become more frequent, forming, as it were, a thicker network. In that case we have an intensive growth of world economy. In actual history, the growth of world economy proceeds simultaneously in both directions, the extensive growth being accomplished for the most part through the annexationist policy of the great powers.[3]

The extraordinarily rapid growth of world economy, particularly in the last decades, is due to the unusual development of the productive forces of world capitalism . . .

Corresponding to the movement of labour power as one of the poles of capitalist relations is the movement of capital as another pole. As in the former case the movement is regulated by the law of equalization of the wage scale, so in the latter case there takes place an international equalization of the rates of profit. The movement of capital, which from the point of view of the capital exporting country is usually called capital export, has acquired an unrivalled importance in modern economic life, so that some economists (like Sartorius von Waltershausen, 1907) define modern capitalism as export capitalism (*Exportkapitalismus*). We shall touch upon this phenomenon in another connection. At present we only wish to point out the main forms and the approximate size of the international movement of capital which forms one of the most essential elements in the process of internationalizing economic life, and in the process of growth of world capitalism. Export capital is divided into two main categories. It appears either as capital yielding interest, or as capital yielding profits.

Inside of this division one can discern various sub-species and forms. In the first place, there are state and communal loans. The vast growth of the state budgets, caused both by the growing complexity of economic life in general, and by the militarization of the entire 'national economy', makes it ever more necessary to contract foreign loans to defray the current expenses. The growth of large cities, on the other hand, demands a series of works (electric railways, electric light, sewage system and water supply, pavements, central steam heat, telegraph and telephone, slaughter houses, etc., etc.), which require large sums of money for their construction. These sums are also often obtained in the forms of foreign loans. Another form of capital export is the system of 'participation', where an enterprise (industrial, commercial, or banking) of country A holds stocks or bonds of an enterprise in country B. A third form is the financing of foreign enterprises, creating of capital for a definite and specified aim; for instance, a bank

3. The Colonial system and the opening out of the markets of the world, both of which are included in the general conditions of existence of the manufacturing period, furnish rich material for developing the division of labour in society. Marx (1867), pp. 353–4.

finances foreign enterprises created by other institutions or by itself; an industrial enterprise finances its branch enterprise which it allows to take the form of an independent corporation; a financing society finances foreign enterprises.[4] A fourth form is credit without any specified aim (the latter calls for 'financing') extended by the large banks of one country to the banks of another country. The fifth and last form is the buying of foreign stocks, etc., with the purpose of holding them (compare activities of banks of issue), etc. (The last of the enumerated forms differs from the others in that it does not create a lasting community of interests.)

In various ways there thus takes place the transfusion of capital from one 'national' sphere into the other; there grows the intertwining of 'national capitals'; there proceeds the 'internationalization' of capital. Capital flows into foreign factories and mines, plantations and railroads, steamship lines and banks; it grows in volume; it sends part of the surplus value 'home' where it may begin an independent movement; it accumulates the other part; it widens over and over again the sphere of its application; it creates an ever thickening network of international interdependence . . .

'Participation', and 'financing' as a further step in participation, signify that industry is being moulded to an ever growing degree into one organized system. The most modern types of capitalist monopoly in their most modern centralized forms, like the trusts, are only one of the forms of 'participating companies' or 'financing companies'. They enjoy a more or less monopolistic ownership of the capitalist property of our times, and they are looked upon and classified, from the point of view of the movement of securities, as a specific expression of the capitalist property of our times.

We thus see that the growth of the world economic process, having as its basis the growth of productive forces, not only calls forth an intensification of production relations among various countries, not only widens and deepens general capitalist interrelations, but also calls to life new economic formations, new economic forms unknown to the past epochs in the history of capitalist development.

The beginnings of the organization process that characterizes the development of industry within 'national' economic boundaries become ever more evident also against the background of world economy relations. Just as the growth of productive forces within 'national' economy, on a capitalist basis, brought about the formation of national cartels and trusts, so the growth of productive forces within world capitalism makes the formation of international agreements between the various national capitalist groups, from the most elemental forms to the centralized form of an international trust, ever more urgent.

4. For more about such companies see Liefmann (1913).

### 3 Organization forms of world economy

World economy in our times is characterized by its highly anarchic structure. In this respect the structure of modern world economy may be compared with the structure of 'national' economies typical till the beginning of this century, when the organization process, briskly coming to the fore in the last years of the nineteenth century, brought about substantial changes by considerably narrowing the hitherto unhampered 'free play of economic forces'. This anarchic structure of world capitalism is expressed in two facts: world industrial crises on the one hand, wars on the other . . .

Still, notwithstanding the fact that modern world economy as a whole represents an anarchic structure, the process of organization is making strides even here, expressing itself mainly in the growth of international syndicates, cartels, and trusts . . .

Behind all these cartels and trusts, as a rule, stand the enterprises that finance them, i.e. primarily the banks. The internationalization process whose most primitive form is the exchange of commodities and whose highest organizational stage is the international trust, has also called into being a very considerable internationalization of banking capital in so far as the latter is transformed into industrial capital (by financing industrial enterprises), and in so far as it thus forms a special category: finance capital.

It is finance capital that appears to be the all-pervading form of capital, that form which, like nature, suffers from a *horror vacui*, since it rushes to fill every 'vacuum', whether in a 'tropical', 'sub-tropical' or 'polar' region, if only profits flow in sufficient quantities . . .

Colonial enterprises, and the export of capital to other continents, railway construction and state loans, city railways and ammunition firms, gold mines and rubber plantations, all are intrinsically connected with the activities of international banking trusts. International economic relations are extended through countless threads; they pass through thousands of cross-points; they are intertwined in thousands of groups, finally converging in the agreements of the largest world banks which have stretched out their tentacles over the entire globe. World finance capitalism and the internationally organized domination of the banks are one of the undeniable facts of economic reality.

On the other hand, one must not overestimate the significance of international organizations. Their specific weight compared with the immensity of the economic life of world capitalism is by no means as great as would appear at the first glance. Many of them (i.e. of the syndicates and cartels) are only agreements concerning the division of markets (*Rayonierungs-kartelle*); in a series of large subdivisions of social economy they embrace only very specific branches of production (such as the bottle syndicate which is one of the strongest); many of them are of a highly unstable nature. Only those international agreements which are based on a natural monopoly are possessed of a greater degree of stability. Still, there is a tendency towards a continuous growth of international formations, and this growth cannot be ignored when analysing the development of modern world economy.[5]

We have pursued the main tendencies in the growth of world economy from the exchange of commodities up to the activities of international banking syndicates. This process in all its ramified forms is the process of the internationalization of economic life; the process of bringing separate geographic points of economic development closer to each other; the process of reducing capitalist relations to one level; the process of the growing contrast on the one hand between concentrated property in the hands of the world capitalist class and, on the other, the world proletariat. It does not follow from this, however, that social progress has already reached a stage where 'national' states can co-exist harmoniously. For the process of the internationalization of economic life is by no means identical with the process of the internationalization of capital interests. A Hungarian economist was perfectly right when he remarked concerning the works of the English pacifist, Norman Angell, that

he [*i.e.* Norman Angell] forgets only one thing: that there are classes both in Germany and England, and that the thing that may be superfluous, useless, even harmful, for the people as a whole, can be of very great benefit (*sehr gewinnbringend sein kann*) for individual groups (large financiers, cartels, bureaucracy, etc.).[6]

This proposition can, of course, be applied to all states, for their class structure is beyond any doubt, at least from a purely scientific point of view. This is why only those who do not see the contradictions in capitalist development, who good-naturedly assume the internationalization of economic life to be an *Internationale der Tatsachen*, i.e. those who assume anarchic internationalization to be organized internationalization – can hope for the possibility of reconciling the 'national' capitalist groups in the 'higher unity' of peaceful capitalism. In reality things take place in a much more complicated way than appears to the opportunist optimists. The process of the internationalization of economic life can and does sharpen, to a high degree, the conflict of interests among the various 'national' groups of the bourgeoisie. Indeed, the growth of international commodity exchange is by

5. Sartorius von Waltershausen (1907) puts a very low estimate on the part played by international organizations. Compare: 'That there should be created, and there should exist, international companies with centralized [*einheitlicher*] management of production appears unlikely. But, of course, one may expect that there would be agreements between large national companies concerning the distribution of the selling markets' (p. 100). The opposite point of view is maintained by Harms.

6. Szabo, pp 647–8.

no means connected with the growth of 'solidarity' between the exchanging groups. On the contrary, it can be accompanied by the growth of the most desperate competition, by a life and death struggle. The same is true of the export of capital. 'Community of interests' is not always created in this field. Competitive struggle for the spheres of capital investment may here, too, reach a highly acute state. There is only one case in which we can say with assurance that solidarity of interests is created. This is the case of growing 'participation' and financing, i.e. when, due to the common ownership of securities, the class of capitalists of various countries possesses collective property in one and the same object. Here we actually have before us the formation of a golden international;[7] there is apparent here, not a simple similarity or, as one is wont to say at present, a 'parallelism' of interests; there is actual unity here; but the course of economic development creates, parallel to this process, a reverse tendency towards the nationalization of capitalist interests. And human society as a whole, placed under the iron heel of world capital, pays tribute to this contradiction – in unbelievable torment, blood and filth.

The perspectives of development can be pointed out only after analysing all the main tendencies of capitalism. And since the internationalization of capitalist interests expresses only one side of the internationalization of economic life, it is necessary to review also its other side, namely, that process of the nationalization of capitalist interests which most strikingly expresses the anarchy of capitalist competition within the boundaries of world economy, a process that leads to the greatest convulsions and catastrophes, to the greatest waste of human energy, and most forcefully raises the problem of establishing new forms of social life.

We are thus confronted with the task of analysing the process of the nationalization of capital.

## 4 The inner structure of 'national economies'

World economy, as we have seen above, represents a complex network of economic connections of the most diverse nature; the basis of this are production relations on a world scale. Economic connections uniting a great number of individual economies are found to become more numerous and more frequent as we proceed, within the framework of world economy, to analyse 'national' economies, i.e. economic connections existing within the

7. How the ideologists of the present-day bourgeoisie view this golden international (we do not speak, of course, of the contradistinction between the 'top' and the 'bottom') may be seen from the following statement by von Waltershausen (1907), p.14: 'The "golden international" can never be an ideal for a man who has a fatherland, and who believes that in that fatherland are sunk the roots of his existence.' This in turn shows the *comparative weakness* of the process of the internationalization of capitalist interests.

boundaries of individual states. There is nothing mysterious about this; we must not attribute that fact to an alleged creative rôle of the 'state principle' that is supposed to create from within itself special forms of national economic existence; neither is there a predestined harmony between society and state. The matter has a much simpler explanation. The fact is that the very foundation of modern states as definite political entities was caused by economic needs and requirements. The state grew on the economic foundation; it was only an expression of economic connections; state ties appeared only as an expression of economic ties. Like all living forms, 'national economy' was, and is, engaged in a continuous process of internal regeneration; molecular movements going on parallel with the growth of productive forces, were continually changing the position of individual 'national' economic bodies in their relation to each other, i.e. they influenced the interrelations of the individual parts of the growing world economy. Our time produces highly significant relations. The destruction, from top to bottom, of old, conservative, economic forms that was begun with the initial stages of capitalism, has triumphed all along the line. At the same time, however, this 'organic' elimination of weak competitors inside the framework of 'national economies' (the ruin of artisanship, the disappearance of intermediary forms, the growth of large-scale production, etc.) is now being superseded by the 'critical' period of a sharpening struggle among stupendous opponents on the world market. The causes of this phenomenon must be sought first of all in the internal changes that have taken place in the structure of 'national capitalisms', causing a revolution in their mutual relations.

Those changes appear, first of all, as the formation and the unusually rapid spread of capitalist monopoly organizations: cartels, syndicates, trusts, bank syndicates. We have seen above how strong this process is in the international sphere. It is immeasurably greater within the framework of 'national economies'. As we shall see below, the 'national' carteling of industry serves as one of the most potent factors making for the national interdependence of capital ...

All parts of this considerably organized system, cartels, banks, state enterprises, are in the process of growing together; the process is becoming ever faster with the growth of capitalist concentration; the formation of cartels and combines creates forthwith a community of interest among the financing banks; on the other hand, banks are interested in checking competition between enterprises financed by them; similarly, every understanding between the banks helps to tie together the industrial groups; state enterprises also become ever more dependent upon large-scale financial-industrial formations, and vice versa. Thus various spheres of the concentration and organization process stimulate each other, creating a very strong tendency towards transforming the entire national economy *into one gigantic combined enterprise under the tutelage of the financial kings and the capitalist state, an enterprise which monopolizes the national market and forms the prerequisite for organized production on a higher non-capitalist level.*

It follows that world capitalism, the world system of production, assumes in our times the following aspect: a few consolidated, organized economic bodies ('the great civilized powers') on the one hand, and a periphery of undeveloped countries with a semi-agrarian or agrarian system on the other. The organization process (which, parenthetically speaking, is by no means the aim or the motive power of the capitalist gentlemen, as their ideologists assert, but is the objective result of their seeking to obtain a maximum of profit) tends to overstep the 'national' boundaries. But it finds very substantial obstacles on this road. First, it is much easier to overcome competition on a 'national' scale than on a world scale (international agreements usually arise on the basis of already existing 'national' monopolies); second, the existing differences of economic structure and consequently of production-costs make agreements disadvantageous for the advanced 'national' groups; third, the ties of unity with the state and its boundaries are in themselves an ever growing monopoly which guarantees additional profits.

## 5 World economy and the 'national' state

We have laid bare three fundamental motives for the conquest policies of modern capitalist states: increased competition in the sales markets, in the markets of raw materials, and for the spheres of capital investment. This is what the modern development of capitalism and its transformation into finance capitalism has brought about.

Those three roots of the policy of finance capitalism, however, represent in substance only three facets of the same phenomenon, namely of the conflict between the growth of productive forces on the one hand, and the 'national' limits of the production organization on the other.

Indeed, overproduction of manufactured goods is at the same time underproduction of agricultural products. Underproduction of agricultural products is in this case important for us in so far as the demand on the part of industry is excessively large, i.e. in so far as there are large volumes of manufactured goods which cannot be exchanged for agricultural products; in so far as the ratio between those two branches of production has been (and is more and more) disturbed. This is why growing industry seeks for an agrarian 'economic supplement' which, within the framework of capitalism, particularly its monopoly form, i.e. finance capital, inevitably expresses itself in the form of subjugating agrarian countries by force of arms.

We have just discussed the exchange of commodities. Capital export, however, does not represent an isolated phenomenon, either. Capital export, as we have seen, is due to a certain overproduction of capital. Overproduction of capital, however, is nothing but another formulation for overproduction of commodities:

Over-production of capital is never anything more than over-production of means of production – of means of labour and necessities of life – which may serve as capital, i.e. may serve to exploit labour at a given degree of exploitation ... capital consists of commodities, and therefore over-production of capital implies over-production of commodities.[8]

Conversely, when the overproduction of capital decreases, there is also a decrease in the overproduction of commodities. This is why capital export in decreasing overproduction of capital, aids also in decreasing the overproduction of commodities. (Let us note parenthetically that if, for instance, iron beams are exported into another country to be sold there, we have commodity export pure and simple; if, however, the beam-producing firm establishes an enterprise in another country and exports its commodities to equip the enterprise, we have capital export; obviously, the criterion is whether the transactions of purchase and sale take place or not.)

But even aside from simply 'relieving the congestion' by exporting capital in commodity form, there is also a further connection between capital export and the decrease in the overproduction of commodities. Otto Bauer has very well formulated this connection:

Thus the exploitation of economically backward countries by the capitalists of a European country has two series of consequences: directly, it creates new spheres of investment for capital in the colonial country, and at the same time more selling opportunities for the industry of the dominating power; indirectly, it creates new spheres for the application of capital also inside of the dominating country, and increases the sale of the products of all its industries.[9]

If we thus consider the problem in its entirety, and take thereby the objective point of view, i.e. the point of view of the adaptation of modern society to its conditions of existence, we find that there is here a growing discord between the basis of social economy which has become world-wide and the peculiar class structure of society, a structure where the ruling class (the bourgeoisie) itself is split into 'national' groups with contradictory economic interests, groups which, being opposed to the world proletariat, are competing among themselves for the division of the surplus value created on a world scale. Production is of a social nature; international division of labour turns the private 'national' economies into parts of a gigantic all-embracing labour process, which extends over almost the whole of humanity. Acquisition, however, assumes the character of 'national' (state) acquisi-

8. Marx (1894), p. 255–6.
9. Bauer (1907), p. 464.

tion where the beneficiaries are huge state companies of the bourgeoisie of finance capital. The development of productive forces moves within the narrow limits of state boundaries while it has already outgrown those limits. Under such conditions there inevitably arises a conflict, which, given the existence of capitalism, is settled through extending the state frontiers in bloody struggles, a settlement which holds the prospect of new and more grandiose conflicts.

The social representatives of this contradiction are the various groups of the bourgeoisie organized in the state, with their conflicting interests. The development of world capitalism leads, on the one hand, to an internationalization of the economic life and on the other, to the levelling of economic differences – and to an infinitely greater degree, the same process of economic development intensifies the tendency to 'nationalize' capitalist interests, to form narrow 'national' groups armed to the teeth and ready to hurl themselves at one another any moment. It is impossible to describe the fundamental aims of present-day politics better than was done by R. Hilferding:

> The policy of finance capital pursues a threefold aim: first, the creation of the largest possible economic territory which, secondly, must be protected against foreign competition by tariff walls, and thus, thirdly, must become an area of exploitation for the national monopoly companies.[10]

The increase in the economic territory opens agrarian regions to the national cartels and consequently, markets for raw materials, increasing the sales markets and the sphere of capital investment; the tariff policy makes it possible to suppress foreign competition, to obtain surplus profit, and to put into operation the battering ram of dumping; the 'system' as a whole facilitates the increase of the rate of profit for the monopoly organizations. This policy of finance capital is imperialism.

Such a policy implies violent methods, for the expansion of the state territory means war. The reverse, however, is not true; not every war or every increase in the state territory implies an imperialist policy. The determining factor is whether the war expresses the policy of finance capital, the latter term being taken in accordance with the above definition.

10. Hilferding (1910), p. 412.

## References

BAUER, O. (1907), *Die Nationalitätenfrage und die Sozialdemokratie*, Vienna.
HILFERDING, R. (1910), *Das Finanzkapital*, Vienna.
LIEFMANN, R. (1913), *Beteiligungs- und Finanzierungsgesellschaften*, Jena.
MARX, K. (1867), *Capital*, vol. I, Foreign Languages Publishing House, Moscow (1970 edition).
MARX, K. (1894), *Capital*, vol. III, Foreign Languages Publishing House, Moscow (1966 edition).

SZABO, E., 'Krieg und Wirtschaftsverfassung', in *Archiv für Sozialwissenschaft und Sozialpolitik*, vol. 39, section 3.

VON WALTERSHAUSEN, S. (1907), *Das Volkswirtschaftliche System der Kapitalanlage im Auslande*, Berlin.

# Part One
## Perspectives on International Firms

This section is concerned with the general features of capital in the world economy today. Stephen Hymer (Reading 2) analyses the evolution of the international firm in terms of the increasing size and changing structure of enterprises and their relation to the market, and argues that the international firm perpetuates a world economy in its own image, distorting the international division of labour into a hierarchy of wealth and power. He emphasizes too the latent possibilities in many of the developments embodied in international firms.

Christian Palloix (Reading 3) argues that the contradictory nature of international firms can only be understood in terms of the internationalization of capital as a social relation, and using the analysis of the cycles of reproduction of capital developed in Vol. II of Marx's *Capital*. In this extract from the concluding essay in his recent book, he looks at the circuit of total social capital and its component circuits of money-capital, productive capital and commodity-capital, and thereby opens the way to a much clearer understanding of the interrelations of different elements in the internationalization process.

György Ádám's paper (Reading 4) is on the most recent phase in the development of international firms, world-wide sourcing. Whereas much of their earlier activities *could* be studied as movement outwards from a national production base, the logic of world-wide sourcing is globally optimal location of production, in terms of the firm's own private interests, for the supply of its world-wide markets. This has considerable implications for both home advanced countries and host less developed countries, and for the international division of labour.

# 2 Stephen Hymer

## The Multinational Corporation and the Law of Uneven Development

Stephen Hymer, 'The Multinational Corporation and the Law of Uneven Development', in J. Bhagwati (ed.), *Economics and World Order from the 1970s to the 1990s*, Collier-Macmillan, 1972, pp. 113–40.

The settler's town is a strongly-built town, all made of stone and steel. It is a brightly-lit town; the streets are covered with asphalt, and the garbage-cans swallow all the leavings, unseen, unknown and hardly thought about. The settler's feet are never visible, except perhaps in the sea; but there you're never close enough to see them. His feet are protected by strong shoes although the streets of his town are clean and even, with no holes or stones. The settler's town is a well-fed town, an easy-going town; its belly is always full of good things. The settler's town is a town of white people, of foreigners.

The town belonging to the colonized people, or at least the native town, the Negro village, the medina, the reservation, is a place of ill fame peopled by men of evil repute. They are born there, it matters little where or how; they die there, it matters not where nor how. It is a world without spaciousness: men live there on top of each other, and their huts are built one on top of the other. The native town is a hungry town, starved of bread, of meat, of shoes, of coal, of light. The native town is a crouching village, a town on its knees, a town wallowing in the mire. It is a town of niggers and dirty arabs. The look that the native turns on the settler's town is a look of lust, a look of envy ...
Fanon,<br>*The Wretched of the Earth.*

We have been asked to look into the future towards the year 2000. This essay attempts to do so in terms of two laws of economic development: the Law of Increasing Firm Size and the Law of Uneven Development.[1]

Since the beginning of the Industrial Revolution there has been a tendency for the representative firm to increase in size from the *workshop* to the *factory* to the *national corporation* to the *multi-divisional corporation* and now to the *multinational corporation*. This growth has been qualitative as well as quantitative. With each step, business enterprises acquired a more complex administrative structure to coordinate its activities and a larger brain to plan for its

1. See Marx (1867), chapter XXV, 'On the General Law of Capitalist Accumulation', chapter XII, 'Cooperation' and chapter XIV, part 4, 'Division of Labour in Manufacturing and Division of Labour in Society'; and (1894), chapter XXIII.

survival and growth. The first part of this essay traces the evolution of the corporation stressing the development of a hierarchical system of authority and control.

The remainder of the essay is concerned with extrapolating the trends in business enterprise (the microcosm) and relating them to the evolution of the international economy (the macrocosm). Until recently, most multinational corporations have come from the United States, where private business enterprise has reached its largest size and most highly developed forms. Now European corporations, as a by-product of increased size, and as a reaction to the American invasion of Europe, are also shifting attention from national to global production and beginning to 'see the world as their oyster'.[2] If present trends continue, multinationalization is likely to increase greatly in the next decade as giants from both sides of the Atlantic (though still mainly from the US) strive to penetrate each other's markets and to establish bases in underdeveloped countries, where there are few indigenous concentrations of capital sufficiently large to operate on a world scale. This rivalry may be intense at first but will probably abate through time and turn into collusion as firms approach some kind of oligopolistic equilibrium. A new structure of international industrial organization and a new international division of labour will have been born.[3]

What will be the effect of this latest stage in the evolution of business enterprise on the Law of Uneven Development, i.e. the tendency of the system to produce poverty as well as wealth, underdevelopment as well as development? The second part of this essay suggests that a regime of North Atlantic Multinational Corporations would tend to produce a hierarchical division of labour between geographical regions corresponding to the vertical division of labour within the firm. It would tend to centralize high-level decision-making occupations in a few key cities in the advanced countries, surrounded by a number of regional sub-capitals, and confine the rest of the world to lower levels of activity and income, i.e. to the status of towns and villages in a new Imperial system. Income, status, authority, and consumption patterns would radiate out from these centres along a declining curve, and the existing pattern of inequality and dependency would be perpetuated. The pattern would be complex, just as the structure of the corporation is complex, but the basic relationship between different countries would be one of superior and subordinate, head office and branch plant.

How far will this tendency of corporations to create a world in their own image proceed? The situation is a dynamic one, moving dialectically. Right now, we seem to be in the midst of a major revolution in international relationships as modern science establishes the technological basis for a

2. Phrase used by Anthony M. Salomon (1966), p. 49.
3. These trends are discussed in Hymer and Rowthorn (1970).

major advance in the conquest of the material world and the beginnings of truly cosmopolitan production.[4] Multinational corporations are in the vanguard of this revolution, because of their great financial and administrative strength and their close contact with the new technology. Governments (outside the military) are far behind, because of their narrower horizons and perspectives, as are labour organizations and most non-business institutions and associations. (As John Powers, President of Charles Pfizer Corporation,

4. Substituting the word *multinational corporation* for *bourgeois* in the following quote from *The Communist Manifesto* provides a more dynamic picture of the multinational corporation than any of its present day supporters have dared to put forth:

'The need of a constantly expanding market for its products chases the multinational corporation over the whole surface of the globe. It must nestle everywhere, settle everywhere, establish connections everywhere. The bourgeoisie has through its exploitation of the world-market given a cosmopolitan character to production and consumption in every country. To the great chagrin of Reactionists, it has drawn from under the feet of industry the national ground on which it stood. All old-established national industries have been destroyed or are daily being destroyed. They are dislodged by new industries, whose introduction becomes a life and death question for all civilized nations, by industries that no longer work up indigenous raw material, but raw material drawn from the remotest zones; industries whose products are consumed, not only at home, but in every quarter of the globe. In place of the old wants, satisfied by the production of the country, we find new wants, requiring for their satisfaction the products of distant lands and climes. In place of the old local and national seclusion and self-sufficiency, we have intercourse in every direction, universal interdependence of nations. And as in material, so also in intellectual production. The intellectual creations of individual nations become common property. National one-sidedness and narrow-mindedness become more and more impossible, and from the numerous national and local literatures there arises a world literature.

'The multinational corporation, by the rapid improvement of all instruments of production, by the immensely facilitated means of communication, draws all, even the most barbarian, nations into civilization. The cheap prices of all its commodities are the heavy artillery with which it batters down all Chinese walls, with which it forces the barbarians' intensely obstinate hatred of foreigners to capitulate. It compels all nations, on pain of extinction, to adopt the bourgeois mode of production, it compels them to introduce what it calls civilization into their midst, i.e. to become bourgeois themselves. In a word, it creates a world after its own image.

'The multinational corporation has subjected the country to the rule of the towns. It has created enormous cities, has greatly increased the urban population as compared with the rural, and has thus rescued a considerable part of the population from the idiocy of rural life. Just as it has made the country dependent on the towns, so it has barbarian and semi-barbarian countries dependent on the civilized ones, nations of peasants on nations of bourgeois, the East on the West.

'The multinational corporation keeps more and more doing away with the scattered state of the population, of the means of production, and of property. It has agglomerated population, centralized means of production, and has concentrated property in a few hands. The necessary consequence of this was political centralization. Independent, or but loosely connected provinces, with separate interests, laws, systems of taxation, and governments, became lumped together in one nation, with one government, one code of laws, one national class-interest, one frontier, and one customs tariff.'

has put it, 'Practise is ahead of theory and policy'.) Therefore, in the first round, multinational corporations are likely to have a certain degree of success in organizing markets, decision making, and the spread of information in their own interest. However, their very success will create tensions and conflicts which will lead to further development. Part III discusses some of the contradictions that are likely to emerge as the multinational corporate system overextends itself. These contradictions provide certain openings for action. Whether or not they can or will be used in the next round to move towards superior forms of international organization requires an analysis of a wide range of political factors outside the scope of this essay.

## Part I The evolution of the multinational corporation

### The Marshallian Firm and the Market Economy

What is the nature of the 'beast'? It is called many names: Direct Investment, International Business, the International Firm, the International Corporate Group, the Multinational Firm, the Multinational Enterprise, the Multinational Corporation, the Multinational Family Group, World Wide Enterprise, La Grande Entreprise Plurinationale, La Grande Unité Interterritoriale, La Grande Entreprise Multinationale, La Grand Unité Pluriterritoriale; or, as the French Foreign Minister called them, 'The US corporate monsters' (Michel Debré quoted in *Fortune*, August 1965, p. 126).

Giant organizations are nothing new in international trade. They were a characteristic form of the mercantilist period when large joint-stock companies, e.g. The Hudson's Bay Company, The Royal African Company, The East India Company, to name the major English merchant firms, organized long-distance trade with America, Africa and Asia. But neither these firms, nor the large mining and plantation enterprises in the production sector, were the forerunners of the multinational corporation. They were like dinosaurs, large in bulk, but small in brain, feeding on the lush vegetation of the new worlds (the planters and miners in America were literally *Tyrannosaurus rex*).

The activities of these international merchants, planters and miners laid the groundwork for the Industrial Revolution by concentrating capital in the metropolitan centre, but the driving force came from the small-scale capitalist enterprises in manufacturing, operating at first in the interstices of the feudalist economic structure, but gradually emerging into the open and finally gaining predominance. It is in the small workshops, organized by the newly emerging capitalist class, that the forerunners of the modern corporation are to be found.

The strength of this new form of business enterprise lay in its power and ability to reap the benefits of cooperation and division of labour. Without the capitalist, economic activity was individualistic, small-scale, scattered and unproductive. But a man with capital, i.e. with sufficient funds to buy raw materials and advance wages, could gather a number of people into a single shop and obtain as his reward the increased productivity that resulted from social production. The reinvestment of these profits led to a steady increase in the size of capitals, making further division of labour possible and creating an opportunity for using machinery in production. A phenomenal increase in productivity and production resulted from this process, and entirely new dimensions of human existence were opened. The growth of capital revolutionized the entire world and, figuratively speaking, even battered down the Great Wall of China.

The hallmarks of the new system were *the market* and *the factory* representing the two different methods of coordinating the division of labour. In the factory, entrepreneurs consciously plan and organize cooperation, and the relationships are hierarchical and authoritarian; in the market, coordination is achieved through a decentralized, unconscious, competitive process.[5]

To understand the significance of this distinction, the new system should be compared to the structure it replaced. In the pre-capitalist system of production, the division of labour was hierarchically structured at the *macro* level, i.e. for society as a whole, but unconsciously structured at the *micro* level, i.e. the actual process of production. Society as a whole was partitioned into various castes, classes, and guilds, on a rigid and authoritarian basis so that political and social stability could be maintained and adequate numbers assured for each industry and occupation. Within each sphere of production, however, individuals by and large were independent and their activities only loosely coordinated, if at all. In essence, a guild was composed of a large number of similar individuals, each performing the same task in roughly the same way with little cooperation or division of labour. This type of organization could produce high standards of quality and workmanship but was limited quantitatively to low levels of output per head.

The capitalist system of production turned this structure on its head. The macro system became unconsciously structured, while the micro system became hierarchically structured. The market emerged as a self-regulating coordinator of business units as restrictions on capital markets and labour mobility were removed. (Of course the State remained above the market as a conscious coordinator to maintain the system and ensure the growth of

5. See R. H. Coase (1952) for an analysis of the boundary between the firm and the market: 'outside the firm, price movements direct production which is coordinated through a series of exchange transactions on the market. Within the firm these market transactions are eliminated and in place of the complicated market structure with exchange transactions, is substituted the entrepreneur coordinator who directs production.'

capital.) At the micro level, that is the level of production, labour was gathered under the authority of the entrepreneur capitalist.

Marshall, like Marx, stressed that the internal division of labour within the factory, between those who planned and those who worked (between 'undertakers' and labourers), was the 'chief fact in the form of modern civilization, the "kernel" of the modern economic problem'.[6] Marx, however, stressed the authoritarian and unequal nature of this relationship based on the coercive power of property and its anti-social characteristics. He focused on the irony that concentration of wealth in the hands of a few and its ruthless use were necessary historically to demonstrate the value of cooperation and the social nature of production.[7]

Marshall, in trying to answer Marx, argued for the voluntary cooperative nature of the relationship between capital and labour. In his view, the market reconciled individual freedom and collective production. He argued that those on top achieved their position because of their superior organizational ability, and that their relation to the workers below them was essentially harmonious and not exploitative. 'Undertakers' were not captains of industry because they had capital; they could obtain capital because they had the ability to be captains of industry. They retained their authority by merit, not by coercion; for according to Marshall, natural selection, operating through the market, constantly destroyed inferior organizers and gave everyone who had the ability – including workers – a chance to rise to managerial positions. Capitalists earned more than workers because they contributed more, while the system as a whole provided all its members, and especially the workers,

6. 'Even in the very backward countries we find highly specialized trades; but we do not find the work within each trade so divided up that the planning and arrangement of the business, its management and its risks, are borne by one set of people, while the manual work required for it is done by higher labour. This form of division of labour is at once characteristic of the modern world generally and of the English race in particular. It may be swept away by the further growth of that free enterprise which has called it into existence. But for the present it expands out for good and for evil as the chief fact in the form of modern civilization, the "kernel" of the modern economic problem.' Marshall (1962), pp. 74–5. Note that Marshall preferred to call businessmen Undertakers rather than Capitalists (p. 74).

7. 'Division of labour within the workshop implies the undisputed authority of the capitalist over men that are but parts of a mechanism that belongs to him . . . The same bourgeois mind which praises division of labour in the workshop, life-long annexation of the labourer to a partial operation, and his complete subjection to capital, as being an organization of labour that increases its productiveness – that same bourgeois mind denounces with equal vigour every conscious attempt to socially control and regulate the process of production, as an inroad upon such sacred things as the rights of property, freedom and unrestricted play for the bent of the individual capitalist. It is very characteristic that the enthusiastic apologists of the factory system have nothing more damning to urge against a general organization of the labour of society, than that it would turn all society into one immense factory.' Marx (1867), p. 356.

with improved standards of living and an ever-expanding field of choice of consumption.[8]

## The Corporate Economy

The evolution of business enterprise from the small workshop (Adam Smith's pin factory) to the Marshallian family firm represented only the first step in the development of business organization. As total capital accumulated, the size of the individual concentrations composing it increased continuously, and the vertical division of labour grew accordingly.

It is best to study the evolution of the corporate firm in the United States environment, where it has reached its highest stage.[9] In the 1870s, the United States industrial structure consisted largely of Marshallian type, single-function firms, scattered over the country. Business firms were typically tightly controlled by a single entrepreneur or small family group who, as it were, saw everything, knew everything and decided everything. By the early twentieth century, the rapid growth of the economy and the great merger movement had consolidated many small enterprises into large national corporations engaged in many functions over many regions. To meet this new strategy of continent-wide, vertically integrated production and marketing, a new administrative structure evolved. The family firm, tightly controlled by a few men in close touch with all its aspects, gave way

8. The following analysis by E. S. Mason (1958). of current attempts to justify hierarchy and inequality by emphasizing the skill and knowledge of managers and the technostructure is interesting and of great significance on this connection:

'As everyone now recognizes, classical economics provided not only a system of analysis, or analytical 'model', intended to be useful to the explanation of economic behaviour but also a defence – and a carefully reasoned defence – of the proposition that the economic behaviour promoted and constrained by the institutions of a free-enterprise system is, in the main, in the public interest.

'It cannot be too strongly emphasized that the growth of the nineteenth-century capitalism depended largely on the general acceptance of a reasoned justification of the system on moral as well as on political and economic grounds.

'It seems doubtful whether, to date, the managerial literature has provided an equally satisfying apologetic for big business.

'The attack on the capitalist apologetic of the nineteenth century has been successful, but a satisfactory contemporary apologetic is still to be created. I suspect that, when and if an effective new ideology is devised, economics will be found to have little to contribute. Economists are still so mesmerized with the fact of choice and so little with its explanations, and the concept of the market is still so central to their thought, that they would appear to be professionally debarred from their important task. I suspect that to the formulation of an up-to-date twentieth-century apologetic the psychologists, and possibly, the political scientists will be the main contributors. It is high time they were called to their job.

9. This analysis of the modern corporation is almost entirely based on the work of Chandler (1961), and Barnard (1938).

to the administrative pyramid of the corporation. Capital acquired new powers and new horizons. The domain of conscious coordination widened and that of market-directed division of labour contracted.

According to Chandler (1961), the railroad, which played so important a role in creating the national market, also offered a model for new forms of business organization. The need to administer geographically dispersed operations led railway companies to create an administrative structure which distinguished field offices from head offices. The field offices managed local operations; the head office supervised the field offices. According to Chandler and Redlich (1961), this distinction is important because 'it implies that the executive responsible for a firm's affairs had for the first time, to supervise the work of other executives'.[10]

This first step towards increased vertical division of labour within the management function was quickly copied by the recently-formed national corporations which faced the same problems of coordinating widely scattered plants. Business developed an organ system of administration, and the modern corporation was born. The functions of business administration were sub-divided into *departments* (organs) – finance, personnel, purchasing engineering and sales – to deal with capital, labour, purchasing, manufacturing, etc. This horizontal division of labour opened up new possibilities for rationalizing production and for incorporating the advances of physical and social sciences into economic activity on a systematic basis. At the same time a 'brain and nervous' system, i.e. a vertical system of control, had to be devised to connect and coordinate departments. This was a major advance in decision-making capabilities. It meant that a special group, the Head Office, was created whose particular function was to coordinate, appraise, and plan for the survival and growth of the organism as a whole. The organization became conscious of itself as organization and gained a certain measure of control over its own evolution and development.

The corporation soon underwent further evolution. To understand this next step we must briefly discuss the development of the United States market. At the risk of great oversimplification, we might say that by the first decade of the twentieth century, the problem of production had essentially been solved. By the end of the nineteenth century, scientists and engineers had developed most of the inventions needed for mass producing at a low cost nearly all the main items of basic consumption. In the language of systems analysis, the problem became one of putting together the available components in an organized fashion. The national corporation provided *one* organizational solution, and by the 1920s it had demonstrated its great power to increase material production.

The question was which direction growth would take. One possibility was

10. Chandler and Redlich (1961), pp. 103–28.

to expand mass production systems very widely and to make basic consumer goods available on a broad basis throughout the world. The other possibility was to concentrate on continuous innovation for a small number of people and on the introduction of new consumption goods even before the old ones had been fully spread. The latter course was in fact chosen, and we now have the paradox that 500 million people can receive a live TV broadcast from the moon while there is still a shortage of telephones in many advanced countries, to say nothing of the fact that so many people suffer from inadequate food and lack of simple medical help.

This path was associated with a choice of capital-deepening instead of capital-widening in the productive sector of the economy. As capital accumulated, business had to choose the degree to which it would expand labour proportionately to the growth of capital or, conversely, the degree to which they would substitute capital for labour. At one extreme, business could have kept the capital–labour ratio constant and accumulated labour at the same rate they accumulated capital. This horizontal accumulation would soon have exhausted the labour force of any particular country and then either capital would have had to migrate to foreign countries or labour would have had to move into the industrial centres. Under this system, earnings per employed worker would have remained steady and the composition of output would have tended to remain constant as similar basic goods were produced on a wider and wider basis.

However, this path was not chosen, and instead capital per worker was raised, the rate of expansion of the industrial labour force was slowed down, and a dualism was created between a small, high-wage, high-productivity sector in advanced countries, and a large, low-wage, low-productivity sector in the less advanced.[11]

The uneven growth of per capita income implied unbalanced growth and the need on the part of business to adapt to a constantly changing composition of output. Firms in the producers' goods sectors had continuously to innovate labour-saving machinery because the capital output ratio was increasing steadily. In the consumption goods sector, firms had continuously to introduce new products since, according to Engel's Law, people do not generally consume proportionately more of the same things as they get richer, but rather reallocate their consumption away from old goods and towards new goods. This non-proportional growth of demand implied that goods would tend to go through a life-cycle, growing rapidly when they were first introduced and more slowly later. If a particular firm were tied to only

11. Neoclassical models suggest that this choice was due to the exogenously determined nature of technological change. A Marxist economic model would argue that it was due in part to the increased tensions in the labour market accompanying the accumulation of capital and the growth of large firms. This is discussed further in Hymer and Resnick (1970).

one product, its growth rate would follow this same life-cycle pattern and would eventually slow down and perhaps even come to a halt. If the corporation was to grow steadily at a rapid rate, it had continuously to introduce new products.

Thus, product development and marketing replaced production as a dominant problem of business enterprise. To meet the challenge of a constantly changing market, business enterprise evolved the multidivisional structure. The new form was originated by General Motors and DuPont shortly after World War I, followed by a few others during the 1920s and 1930s, and was widely adopted by most of the giant US corporations in the great boom following World War II. As with the previous stages, evolution involved a process of both differentiation and integration. Corporations were decentralized into several *divisions*, each concerned with one product line and organized with its own head office. At a higher level, a *general office* was created to coordinate the division and to plan for the enterprise as a whole.

The new corporate form has great flexibility. Because of its decentralized structure, a multidivisional corporation can enter a new market by adding a new division, while leaving the old divisions undisturbed. (And to a lesser extent it can leave the market by dropping a division without disturbing the rest of its structure.) It can also create competing product-lines in the same industry, thus increasing its market share while maintaining the illusion of competition. Most important of all, because it has a cortex specializing in strategy, it can plan on a much wider scale than before and allocate capital with more precision.

The modern corporation is a far cry from the small workshop or even from the Marshallian firm. The Marshallian capitalist ruled his factory from an office on the second floor. At the turn of the century , the president of a large national corporation was lodged in a higher building, perhaps on the seventh floor, with greater perspective and power. In today's giant corporation, managers rule from the top of skyscrapers; on a clear day, they can almost see the world.

US corporations began to move to foreign countries almost as soon as they had completed their continent-wide integration. For one thing, their new administrative structure and great financial strength gave them the power to go abroad. In becoming national firms, US corporations learned how to become international. Also, their large size and oligopolistic position gave then an incentive. Direct investment became a new weapon in their arsenal of oligopolistic rivalry. Instead of joining a cartel (prohibited under US law), they invested in foreign customers, suppliers and competitors. For example, some firms found they were oligopolistic buyers of raw materials produced in foreign countries and feared a monopolization of the sources of supply. By investing directly in foreign producing enterprises, they could gain the security implicit in control over their raw material requirements. Other firms invested abroad to control marketing outlets and thus maximize quasi-rents on their technological discoveries and differentiated products. Some went abroad simply to forestall competition.[12]

The first wave of US direct foreign capital investment occurred around the turn of the century followed by a second wave during the 1920s. The outward migration slowed down during the depression but resumed after World War II and soon accelerated rapidly. Between 1950 and 1969, direct foreign investment by US firms expanded at a rate of about 10 per cent per annum. At this rate it would double in less than ten years, and even at a much slower rate of growth, foreign operations will reach enormous proportions over the next 30 years.[13]

Several important factors account for this rush of foreign investment in the 1950s and the 1960s. First, the large size of the US corporations and their new multidivisional structure gave them wider horizons and a global outlook. Secondly, technological developments in communications created a new awareness of the global challenge and threatened established institutions by opening up new sources of competition. For reasons noted above, business enterprises were among the first to recognize the potentialities and dangers of the new environment and to take active steps to cope with it.

A third factor in the outward migration of US capital was the rapid growth of Europe and Japan. This, combined with the slow growth of the United States economy in the 1950s, altered world market shares as firms confined to the US market found themselves falling behind in the competitive race and losing ground to European and Japanese firms, which were growing rapidly because of the expansion of their markets. Thus, in the late 1950s, United States corporations faced a serious 'non-American' challenge. Their answer was an outward thrust to establish sales production and bases in foreign territories. This strategy was possible in Europe, since government there provided an open door for United States investment, but was blocked in Japan, where the government adopted a highly restrictive policy. To a large extent, United States business was thus able to redress the imbalances

12. The reasons for foreign investment discussed here are examined in more detail in Hymer (1968), pp. 949–73, and in Hymer and Rowthorn (1970).

13. At present, US corporations have about 60 billion dollars invested in foreign branch plants and subsidiaries. The total assets of these foreign operations are much larger than the capital invested and probably equal 100 billion dollars at book value. (American corporations, on the average, were able to borrow 40 per cent of their subsidiaries' capital requirements locally in the country of operation.) The total assets of the 200 largest non-US firms are slightly less than 200 billion dollars. See US Department of Commerce (1969), and *Fortune* list of the 500 largest US corporations and 200 largest non-American.

caused by the Common Market, but Japan remained a source of tension to oligopoly equilibrium.

What about the future? The present trend indicates further multinationalization of all giant firms, European as well as American. In the first place, European firms, partly as a reaction to the United States penetration of their markets, and partly as a natural result of their own growth, have begun to invest abroad on an expanded scale and will probably continue to do so in the future, and even enter into the United States market. This process is already well under way and may be expected to accelerate as time goes on. The reaction of United States business will most likely be to meet foreign investment at home with more foreign investment abroad. They, too, will scramble for market positions in underdeveloped countries and attempt to get an even larger share of the European market, as a reaction to European investment in the United States. Since they are large and powerful, they will on balance succeed in maintaining their relative standing in the world as a whole – as their losses in some markets are offset by gains in others.

A period of rivalry will prevail until a new equilibrium between giant US firms and giant European and Japanese firms is reached, based on a strategy of multinational operations and cross-penetration.[14] We turn now to the implications of this pattern of industrial organization for international trade and the law of uneven development.

## Part II Uneven development

Suppose giant multinational corporations (say 300 from the US and 200 from Europe and Japan) succeed in establishing themselves as the dominant form of international enterprise and come to control a significant share of industry (especially modern industry) in each country. The world economy will resemble more and more the United States economy, where each of the large corporations tends to spread over the entire continent, and to penetrate almost every nook and cranny. What would be the effect of a world industrial organization of this type on international specialization, exchange and income distribution? The purpose of this section is to analyse the spatial dimension of the corporate hierarchy.

A useful starting point is Chandler and Redlich's scheme for analysing the

14. At present unequal growth of different parts of the world economy upsets the oligopolistic equilibrium because the leading firms have different geographical distributions of production and sales. Thus, if Europe grows faster than the United States, European firms tend to grow faster than American firms, unless American firms engage in heavy foreign investment. Similarly, if the United States grows faster than Europe, US firms will grow faster than European firms because Europeans have a lesser stake in the American market. When firms are distributed evenly in all markets, they share equally in the good and bad fortunes of the various submarkets, and oligopolistic equilibrium is not upset by the unequal growth of different countries.

evolution of corporate structure. They distinguish 'three levels of business administration, three horizons, three levels of task, and three levels of decision making . . . and three levels of policies'. Level III, the lowest level, is concerned with managing the day-to-day operations of the enterprise, that is with keeping it going within the established framework. Level II, which first made its appearance with the separation of head office from field office, is responsible for coordinating the managers at Level III. The functions of Level I – top management – are goal-determination and planning. This level sets the framework in which the lower levels operate. In the Marshallian firm, all three levels are embodied in the single entrepreneur or undertaker. In the national corporation, a partial differentiation is made in which the top two levels are separated from the bottom one. In the multidivisional corporation, the differentiation is far more complete. Level I is completely split off from Level II and concentrated in a general office whose specific function is to plan strategy rather than tactics.

The development of business enterprise can therefore be viewed as a process of centralizing and perfecting the process of capital accumulation. The Marshallian entrepreneur was a jack-of-all-trades. In the modern multidivisional corporation, a powerful general office consciously plans and organizes the growth of corporate capital. It is here that the key men who actually allocate the corporation's available resources (rather than act within the means allocated to them, as is true for the managers at lower levels) are located. Their power comes from their ultimate control over *men* and *money* and although one should not overestimate the ability to control a far-flung empire, neither should one underestimate it.

The senior men could take action because they controlled the selection of executive personnel and because, through budgeting, they allocated the funds to the operating divisions. In the way they allocated their resources – capital and personnel – and in the promotion, transferral and retirement of operating executives, they determined the framework in which the operating units worked and thus put into effect their concept of the long term goals and objectives of the enterprise . . . Ultimate authority in business enterprise, as we see it, rests with those who hold the purse strings, and in modern large-scale enterprises, those persons hold the purse strings who perform the functions of goal setting and planning.[15]

What is the relationship between the structure of the microcosm and the structure of the macrocosm? The application of location theory to the Chandler-Redlich scheme suggests a *correspondence principle* relating centralization of control within the corporation to centralization of control within the international economy.

Location theory suggests that Level III activities would spread themselves

15. Chandler and Redlich (1961), p. 120.

over the globe according to the pull of manpower, markets, and raw materials. The multinational corporation, because of its power to command capital and technology and its ability to rationalize their use on a global scale, will probably spread production more evenly over the world's surface than is now the case. Thus, in the first instance, it may well be a force for diffusing industrialization to the less developed countries and creating new centres of production. (We postpone for a moment a discussion of the fact that location depends upon transportation, which in turn depends upon the government which in turn is influenced by the structure of business enterprise.)

Level II activities, because of their need for white-collar workers, communications systems, and information, tend to concentrate in large cities. Since their demands are similar, corporations from different industries tend to place their coordinating offices in the same city, and Level II activities are consequently far more geographically concentrated than Level III activities.

Level I activities, the general offices, tend to be even more concentrated than Level II activities, for they must be located close to the capital market, the media, and the government. Nearly every major corporation in the United States, for example, must have its general office (or a large proportion of its high-level personnel) in or near the city of New York, because of the need for face-to-face contact at higher levels of decision making.

Applying this scheme to the world economy, one would expect to find the highest offices of the multinational corporations concentrated in the world's major cities – New York, London, Paris, Bonn, Tokyo. These along with Moscow and perhaps Peking, will be the major centres of high-level strategic planning. Lesser cities throughout the world will deal with the day-to-day operations of specific local problems. These in turn will be arranged in a hierarchical fashion: the larger and more important ones will contain regional corporate headquarters, while the smaller ones will be confined to lower level activities. Since business is usually the core of the city, geographical specialization will come to reflect the hierarchy of corporate decision making, and the occupational distribution of labour in a city or region will depend upon its function in the international economic system. The 'best' and most highly paid administrators, doctors, lawyers, scientists, educators, government officials, actors, servants and hairdressers, will tend to concentrate in or near the major centres.

The structure of income and consumption will tend to parallel the structure of status and authority. The citizens of capital cities will have the best jobs – allocating men and money at the highest level and planning growth and development – and will receive the highest rates of remuneration. (Executives' salaries tend to be a function of the wage bill of people under them. The larger the empire of the multinational corporation, the greater the earnings of top executives, to a large extent independent of their performance.[16] Thus, growth in the hinterland subsidiaries implies growth in the income of capital cities, but not vice versa.)

The citizens of capital cities will also be the first to innovate new products in the cycle which is known in the marketing literature as trickle-down or two-stage marketing. A new product is usually first introduced to a select group of people who have 'discretionary' income and are willing to experiment in their consumption patterns.[17] Once it is accepted by this group, it spreads, or trickles down to other groups via the demonstration effect. In this process, the rich and the powerful get more votes than everyone else; first because they have more money to spend, second, because they have more ability to experiment, and third, because they have high status and are likely to be copied. This special group may have something approaching a choice in consumption patterns; the rest have only the choice between conforming or being isolated.

The trickle-down system also has the advantage – from the centre's point of view – of reinforcing patterns of authority and control. According to Fallers (1963),[18] it helps keep workers on the treadmill by creating an illusion of upward mobility even though relative status remains unchanged. In each period subordinates achieve (in part) the consumption standards of their superiors in a previous period and are thus torn in two directions: if they look backward and compare their standards of living through time, things seem to be getting better; if they look upward they see that their relative position has not changed. They receive a consolation prize, as it were, which may serve to keep them going by softening the reality that in a competitive system, few succeed and many fail. It is little wonder, then, that those at the top stress growth rather than equality as the welfare criterion for human relations.

In the international economy trickle-down marketing takes the form of an international demonstration effect spreading outward from the metropolis to the hinterland.[19] Multinational corporations help speed up this process, often the key motive for direct investment, through their control of marketing channels and communications media.

The development of a new product is a fixed cost; once the expenditure needed for invention or innovation has been made, it is forever a bygone. The actual cost of production is thus typically well below selling price and the limit on output is not rising costs but falling demand due to saturated markets. The marginal profit on new foreign markets is thus high, and cor-

16. See Simon (1957).
17. Gervasi (1964).
18. Fallers (1963), pp. 208–216.
19. See Vernon (1966).

porations have a strong interest in maintaining a system which spreads their products widely. Thus, the interest of multinational corporations in underdeveloped countries is larger than the size of the market would suggest.

It must be stressed that the dependency relationship between major and minor cities should not be attributed to technology. The new technology, because it increases interaction, implies greater interdependence but not necessarily a hierarchical structure. Communications linkages could be arranged in the form of a grid in which each point was directly connected to many other points, permitting lateral as well as vertical communication. This system would be polycentric since messages from one point to another would go directly rather than through the centre; each point would become a centre on its own; and the distinction between centre and periphery would disappear.

Such a grid is made *more* feasible by aeronautical and electronic revolutions which greatly reduce costs of communications. It is not technology which creates inequality; rather, it is *organization* that imposes a ritual judicial asymmetry on the use of intrinsically symmetrical means of communications and arbitrarily creates unequal capacities to initiate and terminate exchange, to store and retrieve information, and to determine the extent of the exchange and terms of the discussion. Just as colonial powers in the past linked each point in the hinterland to the metropolis and inhibited lateral communications, preventing the growth of independent centres of decision making and creativity, multinational corporations (backed by state powers) centralize control by imposing a hierarchical system.

This suggests the possibility of an alternative system of organization in the form of national planning. Multinational corporations are private institutions which organize one or a few industries across many countries. Their polar opposite (the antimultinational corporation, perhaps) is a public institution which organizes many industries across one region. This would permit the centralization of capital, i.e. the coordination of many enterprises by one decision-making centre, but would substitute regionalization for internationalization. The span of control would be confined to the boundaries of a single polity and society and not spread over many countries. The advantage of national planning is its ability to remove the wastes of oligopolistic anarchy, i.e. meaningless product differentiation and an imbalance between different industries within a geographical area. It concentrates *all* levels of decision-making in one locale and thus provides each region with a full complement of skills and occupations. This opens up new horizons for local development by making possible the social and political control of economic decision-making. Multinational corporations, in contrast, weaken political control because they span many countries and can escape national regulation.

A few examples might help to illustrate how multinational corporations reduce options for development. Consider an underdeveloped country wishing to invest heavily in education in order to increase its stock of human capital and raise standards of living. In a market system it would be able to find gainful employment for its citizens within its *national boundaries* by specializing in education-intensive activities and selling its surplus production to foreigners. In the multinational corporate system, however, the demand for high-level education in low-ranking areas is limited, and a country does not become a world centre simply by having a better educational system. An outward shift in the supply of educated people in a country, therefore, will not create its own demand but will create an excess supply and lead to emigration. Even then, the employment opportunities for citizens of low-ranking countries are restricted by discriminatory practices in the centre. It is well-known that ethnic homogeneity increases as one goes up the corporate hierarchy; the lower levels contain a wide variety of nationalities, the higher levels become successively purer and purer. In part this stems from the skill differences of different nationalities, but more important is the fact that the higher up one goes in the decision-making process, the more important mutual understanding and ease of communications become; a common background becomes all-important.

A similar type of specialization by nationality can be expected within the multinational corporation hierarchy. Multinational corporations are torn in two directions. On the one hand, they must adapt to local circumstances in each country. This calls for decentralized decision making. On the other hand, they must coordinate their activities in various parts of the world and stimulate the flow of ideas from one part of their empire to another. This calls for centralized control. They must, therefore, develop an organizational structure to balance the need for coordination with the need for adaptation to a patch-work quilt of languages, laws and customs. One solution to this problem is a division of labour based on nationality. Day-to-day management in each country is left to the nationals of that country who, because they are intimately familiar with local conditions and practices, are able to deal with local problems and local government. These nationals remain rooted in one spot, while above them is a layer of people who move around from country to country, as bees among flowers, transmitting information from one subsidiary to another and from the lower levels to the general office at the apex of the corporate structure. In the nature of things, these people (reticulators) for the most part will be citizens of the country of the parent corporation (and will be drawn from a small, culturally homogeneous group within the advanced world), since they will need to have the confidence of their superiors and be able to move easily in the higher management circles. Latin Americans, Asians and Africans will at best be able to aspire to a management position in the intermediate coordinating centres at the continental level. Very few will be able to get much higher than this, for the closer one gets to the top, the more important is 'a common cultural heritage'.

Another way in which the multinational corporations inhibit economic development in the hinterland is through their effect on tax capacity. An important government instrument for promoting growth is expenditure on infrastructure and support services. By providing transportation and communications, education and health, a government can create a productive labour force and increase the growth potential of its economy. The extent to which it can afford to finance these intermediate outlays depends upon its tax revenue.

However, a government's ability to tax multinational corporations is limited by the ability of these corporations to manipulate transfer prices and to move their productive facilities to another country. This means that they will only be attracted to countries where superior infrastructure offsets higher taxes. The government of an underdeveloped country will find it difficult to extract a surplus (revenue from the multinational corporations, less cost of services provided to them) from multinational corporations to use for long-run development programmes and for stimulating growth in other industries. In contrast, governments of the advanced countries, where the home office and financial centre of the multinational corporation are located, can tax the profits of the corporation as a whole as well as the high incomes of its management. Government in the metropolis can, therefore, capture some of the surplus generated by the multinational corporations and use it to further improve their infrastructure and growth.

In other words, the relationship between multinational corporations and underdeveloped countries will be somewhat like the relationship between the national corporations in the United States and state and municipal governments. These lower-level governments tend always to be short of funds compared to the federal government which can tax a corporation as a whole. Their competition to attract corporate investment eats up their surplus, and they find it difficult to finance extensive investments in human and physical capital even where such investment would be productive. This has a crucial effect on the pattern of government expenditure. For example, suppose taxes were first paid to state government and then passed on to the federal government. What chance is there that these lower level legislatures would approve the phenomenal expenditures on space research that now go on? A similar discrepancy can be expected in the international economy with overspending and waste by metropolitan governments and a shortage of public funds in the less advanced countries.

The tendency of the multinational corporations to erode the power of the nation state works in a variety of ways, in addition to its effect on taxation powers. In general, most governmental policy instruments (monetary policy, fiscal policy, wage policy, etc.) diminish in effectivness the more open the economy and the greater the extent of foreign investments. This tendency applies to political instruments as well as economic, for the multi-national corporation is a medium by which laws, politics, foreign policy and culture of one country intrude into another. This acts to reduce the sovereignty of all nation states, but again the relationship is asymmetrical, for the flow tends to be from the parent to the subsidiary, not vice versa. The United States can apply its anti-trust laws to foreign subsidiaries or stop them from 'trading with the enemy' even though such trade is not against the laws of the country in which the branch plant is located. However, it would be illegal for an underdeveloped country which disagreed with American foreign policy to hold a US firm hostage for acts of the parent. This is because legal rights are defined in terms of property-ownership, and the various subsidiaries of a multinational corporation are not 'partners in a multinational endeavour' but the property of the general office.

In conclusion, it seems that a regime of multinational corporations would offer underdeveloped countries neither national independence nor equality. It would tend instead to inhibit the attainment of these goals. It would turn the underdeveloped countries into branch-plant countries, not only with reference to their economic functions but throughout the whole gamut of social, political and cultural roles. The subsidiaries of multinational corporations are typically amongst the largest corporations in the country of operations, and their top executives play an influential role in the political, social and cultural life of the host country. Yet these people whatever their title, occupy at best a medium position in the corporate structure and are restricted in authority and horizons to a lower level of decision making. The governments with whom they deal tend to take on the same middle management outlook, since this is the only range of information and ideas to which they are exposed.[20] In this sense, one can hardly expect such a country to

20. An interesting illustration of the asymmetry in horizons and prospectives of the big company and the small country is found in these quotations from *Fortune*. Which countries of the world are making a comparable analysis of the Multinational Corporation?

'A Ford economist regularly scans the international financial statistics to determine which countries have the highest rates of inflation; these are obviously prime candidates for devaluation. He then examines patterns of trade. If a country is running more of an inflation than its chief trading partners and competitors and its reserves are limited it is more than a candidate; it is a shoo-in. His most difficult problem is to determine exactly when the devaluation will take place. Economics determines whether and how much, but politicians control the timing. So the analyst maintains a complete library of information on leading national officials. He tries to get 'into the skin of the

bring forth the creative imagination needed to apply science and technology to the problems of degrading poverty. Even so great a champion of liberalism as Marshall recognized the crucial relationship between occupation and development.

For the business by which a person earns his livelihood generally fills his thoughts during the far greater part of those hours in which his mind is at its best; during them his character is being formed by the way in which he uses his facilities in his work, by the thoughts and feelings which it suggests, and by his relationship to his associates in work, his employers to his employees.[21]

## Part III  The political economy of the multinational corporation

The viability of the multinational corporate system depends upon the degree to which people will tolerate the unevenness it creates. It is well to remember that the 'New Imperialism' which began after 1870 in a spirit of Capitalism Triumphant, soon became seriously troubled and after 1914 was characterized by war, depression, breakdown of the international economic system and war again, rather than Free Trade, Pax Britannica and Material Improvement.

A major, if not the major, reason was Great Britain's inability to cope

---

man' who is going to make the decision. The economist's forecasts have been correct in sixty-nine of the last seventy-five crisis situations.

'DuPont is one company that is making a stab in the direction of formally measuring environmental incertainty, basically as a tool for capital budgeting decisions. The project is still in the research stage, but essentially the idea is to try to derive estimates of the potential of a foreign market, which is, of course, affected by economic conditions. The state of the economy in turn is partly a function of the fiscal and monetary policies the foreign government adopts. Policy decisions depend on real economic forces, on the attitudes of various interest groups in the country, and on the degree to which the government listens to these groups.

'In the fiscal and monetary part of their broad economic model, the Dupont researchers have identified fifteen to twenty interest groups per country, from small landowners to private bankers. Each interest group has a 'latent influence', which depends on its size and educational level and the group's power to make its feelings felt. This influence, subjectively measured, is multiplied by an estimate of 'group cohesiveness': i.e. how likely the group is to mobilize its full resources on any particular issue. The product is a measure of 'potential influence'. This in turn must be multiplied by a factor representing the governments' receptivity to each influence group.'

Rose (1968), p. 105.

21. This quote is taken from the first page of Marshall's *Principles of Economics.* In the rest of the book, he attempted to show that the economic system of laissez-faire capitalism had an overall positive effect in forming character. As we noted above, his argument rested upon the existence of competitive markets (and the absence of coercion). Because multinational corporations substitute for the international market they call into question the liberal ideology which rationalized it. (See footnote 8 above, quoting Mason.)

with the byproducts of its own rapid accumulation of capital; i.e. a class-conscious labour force at home; a middle class in the hinterland; and rival centres of capital on the Continent and in America. Britain's policy tended to be atavistic and defensive rather than progressive, more concerned with warding off new threats than creating new areas of expansion. Ironically, Edwardian England revived the paraphernalia of the landed aristocracy it had just destroyed. Instead of embarking on a 'big push' to develop the vast hinterland of the Empire, colonial administrators often adopted policies to slow down rates of growth and arrest the development of either a native capitalist class or a native proletariat which could overthrow them.

As time went on, the centre had to devote an increasing share of government activity to military and other unproductive expenditures; they had to rely on alliances with an inefficient class of landlords, officials and soldiers in the hinterland to maintain stability at the cost of development. A great part of the surplus extracted from the population was thus wasted locally.

The new Mercantilism (as the Multinational Corporate System of special alliances and privileges, aid and tariff concessions is sometimes called) faces similar problems of internal and external division. The centre is troubled: excluded groups revolt and even some of the affluent are dissatisfied with the roles. (The much talked about 'generation gap' may indicate the failure of the system to reproduce itself.) Nationalistic rivalry between major capitalist countries (especially the challenge of Japan and Germany) remains an important divisive factor, while the economic challenge from the socialist bloc may prove to be of the utmost significance in the next thirty years. Russia has its own form of large-scale economic organizations, also in command of modern technology, and its own conception of how the world should develop. So does China to an increasing degree.[22] Finally, there is the threat presented by the middle classes and the excluded groups of the underdeveloped countries.

The national middle classes in the underdeveloped countries came to power when the centre weakened but could not, through their policy of import substitution manufacturing, establish a viable basis for sustained growth. They now face a foreign exchange crisis and an unemployment (or population) crisis – the first indicating their inability to function in the international economy, and the second indicating their alienation from the people they are supposed to lead. In the immediate future, these national middle

22. A. A. Berle, Jr, (1967), has put the problem most succinctly:
'The Industrial Revolution, as it spread over twentieth-century life, required collective organization of men and things . . . As the twentieth century moves into the afternoon, two systems – and (thus far) two only – have emerged as vehicles of modern industrial economics. One is the socialist commissariat, its highest organization at present in the Soviet Union; the other is the modern corporation, most highly developed in the United States' (p. ix).

classes will gain a new lease on life as they take advantage of the spaces created by the rivalry between American and non-American oligopolists striving to establish global market positions. The native capitalists will again become the champions of national independence as they bargain with multinational corporations. But the conflict at this level is more apparent than real, for in the end the fervent nationalism of the middle class asks only for promotion within the corporate structure and not for a break with that structure. In the last analysis their power derives from the metropolis and they cannot easily afford to challenge the international system. They do not command the loyalty of their own population and cannot really compete with the large, powerful, aggregate capitals from the centre. They are prisoners of the taste patterns and consumption standards set at the centre, and depend on outsiders for technical advice, capital, and when necessary, for military support of their position.

The main threat comes from the excluded groups. It is not unusual in underdeveloped countries for the top 5 per cent to obtain between 30 and 40 per cent of the total national income, and for the top one-third to obtain anywhere from 60 to 70 per cent.[23] At most, one-third of the population can be said to benefit in some sense from the dualistic growth that characterizes development in the hinterland. The remaining two-thirds, who together get only one-third of the income, are outsiders, not because they do not contribute to the economy, but because they do not share in the benefits. They provide a source of cheap labour which helps keep exports to the developed world at a low price and which has financed the urban-biased growth of recent years. Because their wages are low, they spend a moderate amount of time in menial services and are sometimes referred to as underemployed as if to imply they were not needed. In fact, it is difficult to see how the system in most underdeveloped countries could survive without cheap labour since removing it (e.g. diverting it to public works projects as is done in socialist countries) would raise consumption costs to capitalists and professional elites. Economic development under the Multinational Corporation does not offer much promise for this large segment of society and their antagonism continuously threatens the system.

The survival of the multinational corporate system depends on how fast it can grow and how much trickles down. Plans now being formulated in government offices, corporate headquarters and international organizations, sometimes suggest that a growth rate of about 6 per cent per year in national income (3 per cent per capita) is needed. (Such a target is, of course, far below what would be possible if a serious effort were made to solve basic problems of health, education and clothing.) To what extent is it possible?

The multinational corporation must solve four critical problems for the

23. Kuznets (1966), pp. 423–4.

underdeveloped countries, if it is to foster the continued growth and survival of a 'modern' sector. First, it must break the foreign-exchange constraint and provide the underdeveloped countries with imported goods for capital formation and modernization. Second, it must finance an expanded programme of government expenditure to train labour and provide support services for urbanization and industrialization. Third, it must solve the urban food problem created by growth. Finally, it must keep the excluded two-thirds of the population under control.

The solution now being suggested for the first is to restructure the world economy allowing the periphery to export certain manufactured goods to the centre. Part of this programme involves regional common markets to rationalize the existing structure of industry. These plans typically do not involve the rationalization and restructuring of the entire economy of the underdeveloped countries but mainly serve the small manufacturing sector which caters to higher income groups and which, therefore, faces a very limited market in any particular country. The solution suggested for the second problem is an expanded aid programme and a reformed government bureaucracy (perhaps along the lines of the Alliance for Progress). The solution for the third is agri-business and the green revolution, a programme with only limited benefits to the rural poor. Finally, the solution offered for the fourth problem is population control, either through family planning or counter-insurgency.

It is doubtful whether the centre has sufficient political stability to finance and organize the programme outlined above. It is not clear, for example, that the West has the technology to rationalize manufacturing abroad or modernize agriculture, or the willingness to open up marketing channels for the underdeveloped world. Nor is it evident that the centre has the political power to embark on a large aid programme or to readjust its own structure of production and allow for the importation of manufactured goods from the periphery. It is difficult to imagine labour accepting such a re-allocation (a new repeal of the Corn Laws as it were[24]), and it is equally hard to see how the advanced countries could create a system of planning to make these extra hardships unnecessary.

The present crisis may well be more profound than most of us imagine, and the West may find it impossible to restructure the international economy on a workable basis. One could easily argue that the age of the Multinational Corporation is at its end rather than at its beginning. For all we know, books on the global partnership may be the epitaph of the American attempt to take over the old international economy, and not the herald of a new era of international cooperation.

24. See Polanyi (1944) on the consequences after 1870 of the repeal of the Corn Laws in England.

### Conclusion

The multinational corporation, because of its great power to plan economic activity, represents an important step forward over previous methods of organizing international exchange. It demonstrates the social nature of production on a global scale. As it eliminates the anarchy of international markets and brings about a more extensive and productive international division of labour, it releases great sources of latent energy.

However, as it crosses international boundaries, it pulls and tears at the social and political fabric and erodes the cohesiveness of national states.[25] Whether one likes this or not, it is probably a tendency that cannot be stopped.

Through its propensity to nestle everywhere, settle everywhere, and establish connections everywhere, the multinational corporation destroys the possibility of national seclusion and self sufficiency and creates a universal interdependence. But the multinational corporation is still a private institution with a partial outlook and represents only an imperfect solution to the problem of international cooperation. It creates hierarchy rather than equality, and it spreads its benefits unequally.

In proportion to its success, it creates tensions and difficulties. It will lead other institutions, particularly labour organizations and government, to take an international outlook and thus unwittingly create an environment less favourable to its own survival. It will demonstrate the possibilities of material progress at a faster rate than it can realize them, and will create a worldwide demand for change that it cannot satisfy.

The next round may be marked by great crises due to the conflict between national planning by governments and international planning by corporations. For example, if each country loses its power over fiscal and monetary policy due to the growth of multinational corporations (as some observers believe Canada has), how will aggregate demand be stabilized? Will it be possible to construct super-states? Or does multinationalism do away with Keynesian problems? Similarly, will it be possible to fulfill a host of other government functions at the supranational level in the near future? During the past twenty five years many political problems were put aside as the West recovered from the depression and the war. By the late sixties the bloom of this long upswing had begun to fade. In the seventies, power conflicts are likely to come to the fore.

Whether underdeveloped countries will use the opportunities arising from this crisis to build viable local decision-making institutions is difficult to predict. The national middle class failed when it had the opportunity and instead merely reproduced internally the economic dualism of the international economy as it squeezed agriculture to finance urban industry. What

25. See Levitt (1970) and Girvan and Jefferson (1968).

is needed is a complete change of direction. The starting point must be the needs of the bottom two-thirds, and not the demands of the top third. The primary goal of such a strategy would be to provide minimum standards of health, education, food and clothing to the entire population, removing the more obvious forms of human suffering. This requires a system which can mobilize the entire population and which can search the local environment for information, resources and needs. It must be able to absorb modern technology, but it cannot be mesmerized by the form it takes in the advanced countries; it must go to the roots. This is not the path the upper one-third chooses when it has control.

The wealth of a nation, wrote Adam Smith two hundred years ago, is determined by 'first, the skill, dexterity and judgement with which labour is generally applied; and, secondly by the proportion between the number of those who are employed in useful labour, and that of those who are not so employed'.[26] Capitalist enterprise has come a long way from this day, but it has never been able to bring more than a small fraction of the world's population into useful or highly productive employment. The latest stage reveals once more the power of social cooperation and division of labour which so fascinated Adam Smith in his description of pin-manufacturing. It also shows the shortcomings of concentrating this power in private hands.

26. See Smith (1937 edition), p. 1.

*References*

BARNARD, C. (1938), *The Functions of Executives*, Harvard University Press.
BERLE, A. A. Jr (1967), Foreword to E. S. Mason (ed.), *The Corporation in Modern Society*, Atheneum, New York.
CHANDLER, A. D. (1961), *Strategy and Structure*, Doubleday.
CHANDLER, A. D., and REDLICH, F. (1961), 'Recent Developments in American Business Administration and their Conceptualization', *Business History Review*, Spring.
COASE, R. H. (1952), 'The Nature of the Firm', reprinted in G. J. Stigler and K. E. Boulding (eds.), *Readings in Price Theory*, Richard D. Irwin.
FALLERS, L. A. (1963), 'A Note on the Trickle Effect', in P. Bliss (ed.), *Marketing and the Behavioural Sciences*, Allyn & Bacon.
GERVASI, S. (1964), 'Publicité et Croissance Économique', *Économie et Humanisme*, November–December.
GIRVAN, N., and JEFFERSON, O. (1968), 'Corporate vs Caribbean Integration', *New World Quarterly*, vol. IV, no. 2.
HYMER, S. (1968), 'La Grande Corporation Multinationale', *Revue Économique*, vol. XIX, no. 6, November.
HYMER, S., and RESNICK, S. (1970), 'International Trade and Uneven Development', in J. N. Bhagwati, R. W. Jones, R. A. Mundell and J. Vanek (eds.), *Kindleberger Festschrift*, MIT Press.
HYMER, S., and ROWTHORN, R. (1970), 'Multinational Corporations and International Oligopoly: The Non-American Challenge', in C. P. Kindleberger (ed.), *The International Corporation*, MIT Press.

KUZNETS, S. (1966), *Modern Economic Growth*, Yale University Press.

LEVITT, K. (1970), *Silent Surrender: The Multinational Corporation in Canada*, Macmillan Company of Canada.

MARSHALL, A. (1962), *Principles of Economics*, Macmillan, 8th edition.

MARX, K. (1867), *Capital*, vol. I, Foreign Languages Publishing House, Moscow (1961).

MARX, K. (1894), *Capital*, vol. III, Foreign Languages Publishing House, Moscow (1966).

MASON, E. S. (1958), 'The Apologetics of Managerialism', *The Journal of Business of the University of Chicago*, vol. XXXI, no. 1, January.

POLANYI, K. (1944), *The Great Transformation*, Farrar & Rinehart.

ROSE, S. (1968), 'The Rewarding Strategies of Multinationalism', *Fortune*, 15 September.

SALOMON, A. M. (1966), in *International Aspects of Antitrust*, 'Part I: Hearings before the Sub-Committee on Antitrust and Monopoly of the Senate Committee on the Judiciary', April.

SIMON, H. A. (1957), 'The Compensation of Executives', *Sociometry*, March.

SMITH, A., *The Wealth of Nations*, The Modern Library, New York (1937 edition).

US DEPARTMENT OF COMMERCE (1969), *Survey of Current Business*, September.

VERNON, R. (1966), 'International Investment and International Trade in the Product Cycle', *Quarterly Journal of Economics*, Vol. LXXX, May.

# 3 Christian Palloix

## The Internationalization of Capital and the Circuit of Social Capital*

Extract from Christian Palloix, *Les firmes multinationales et le procès d'internationalisation*, Maspero, 1973, pp. 137–63. Translated by Judith White.

> The actual circuit of industrial capital in its continuity is not alone the unity of the processes of circulation and production but also the unity of all its three circuits.
>
> Karl Marx
> *Capital* vol. II, ch. IV, p. 103

### The multinational firm

Finance capital, appearing with the capitalist mode of production itself, is not confined to the twentieth century; and multinational firms too entered their first phase of development in the nineteenth century. Firms like Singer, International Harvester and Westinghouse Electric were operating in Tsarist Russia,[1] and Gillette, Otis, Parke Davis and Ford by this time all had plants elsewhere than their countries of origin. There have nonetheless been changes in the way multinational firms develop. Whereas in the nineteenth and early twentieth century it was the rising value of raw materials and agricultural products that provided the basis for such firms as Unilever, Penarroya, Shell and Standard Oil, today's firms rely essentially on so-called 'mass' commodity production.

There is for example a very good account by L. G. Franko of why the French car industry only penetrated the world market, in the way Ford did with the Model-T, in the early sixties, despite the fact that at the beginning of the century, with cars like the Panhard and Bugatti, it was technologically very up to date. The fact is that the French car industry produced for an elite, and this was why it did not expand. Ford, by contrast, produced for the mass market from the beginning.[2] Ford, with a thorough understanding that what matters is not technology,[3] but the 'marketable' quality of the product,

* This extract forms the first section of part I of a chapter entitled 'The Internationalization of Capital'. The second section is on 'Internationalization and the Parts of Capital', while Part II of the chapter is on 'The Internationalization of Capital and the Strategy of Multinational Firms'.

1. Cf. Palloix (1972), ch. 2; and Wilkins (1970).
2. Cf. Franko (1972).
3. I cannot agree with L. Karpik's conception of the 'great technological enterprise'. Cf. Karpik (1972a, 1972b).

has now been able to launch a new project in the underdeveloped countries, carrying on there with lines which become obsolete in the advanced capitalist countries. Fiat have also learned that their cars would not recover their 'marketable' quality on the US market, but would on the socialist market or in less developed economies (e.g. Yugoslavia, Spain).

The way in which multinational firms develop raises as a central problem the question of whether their products will recover their 'marketable' quality,[4] their character of commodities for mass consumption. Subsidiaries can be used to conquer markets offering similar conditions for renewing the 'marketable' quality of a product, and transforming it into a commodity, but it is not easy to get into markets where this transformation takes place in a different way.[5]

But through the commodity, capital is being expanded. The strategy of the multinational firms, in this instance their marketing strategy, represents a strategy for the self-expansion of capital and the particular side of this involved in the internationalization of capital.

## The internationalization of capital

The internationalization of the various branches of industry, notably steel and machinery, underlines the importance of the 'push' factors in the formation of multinational firms. Multinational firms seem to emerge only as a result of the process by which the branch becomes internationalized. Looked at in this way, it is possible to single out some elements of the strategy of multinational firms – marketing or commercial strategy – but not to grasp it completely. What has to be taken into account in discussing the internationalization of capital is the strategy of the 'capital' invested in the particular branch of industry.

The internationalization of capital lies not in the fact that shares in the firms' capital are held by different nationalities, which is only the effect of internationalization; nor in international movements of capital, either for international investment in the narrow sense[6] or in the broader definition given by Stephen Hymer.[7]

4. In a sense this is the same thing as R. Vernon's 'international life cycle' of the new product.

5. Cf. Franko (1971).

6. Cf. Bertin (1972a, 1972b).

7. Cf. Hymer (1972), p. 1:

'International capital movements: By this I refer not only to the direct investment of corporations in their overseas branches and subsidiaries (which at present amounts to about $80 billion for American multinationals and about $50 billion for non-American multinationals) but also the associated flows of short-term, long-term and equity capital stimulated by the multinational corporation and in turn stimulating the further growth of international banking. ... The point I wish to make is that direct foreign investment by corporation is only the base of a vast superstructure of credit drawing capital from all over the world.'

There are two levels at which the strategy of multinational firms expresses the strategy of internationalization of capital:

– the strategy of capital expansion within the circuit of social capital, which is no longer national but international in scope; though the fact that the circuit moves more and more on an international plane is not itself the decisive criterion for the internationalization of capital;

– the strategy of capital expansion within the different portions of capital, the lines of division among these portions now running across national boundaries. Here again, the fact that the lines extend internationally is not sufficient to define the internationalization of capital.

## The circuit of social capital and the internationalization of capital

The development of international investments and short- and medium-term capital transfers, together with the appearance of the Euro-dollar market and the expansion of the international reserves of commercial and deposit banks, is evidence enough that the circuit of social capital operates increasingly at world level, in the case of money-capital, productive capital and commodity-capital alike.

But the internationalization of the extent of the circuit of social capital should not be confused with the internationalization of capital in the movement of the circuit itself.

*A: Internationalization of the extent of the circuit of social capital*

In the extended formula for the circuit of social capital[8]:

$$M - C\left(^{L}_{MP}\right....P....C'\left|^{C}_{+}_{c}\right| - \left|^{M}_{+}_{m}\right| - \left|^{C}_{+}_{c}\right| C\left(^{L}_{MP}\right......P.....C' - M'$$

I is the circuit of money-capital $(M ... M')$,
II is the circuit of productive capital $(P ...P)$, and
III is the circuit of commodity-capital $(C' ... C')$,
while the total circulation process $(Tc)$ is expressed by $C' - M' - C'$ the starting point of the circuit of commodity-capital.

8. Cf. Marx (1970), vol. 2, part 1.

$M$ = money-capital; $C$ = commodity; $P$ = productive process; $c$ = surplus-value in commodity form; $m$ = surplus-value in money form; $L$ = labour-power; $MP$ = means of production. $M' > M$; $C' > C$; $P' > P$.

The first point to note is the international extension of these circuits, which is a new phenomenon, especially for the money-capital circuit and the productive capital circuit, previously reliant basically on a rather limited area, generally within national boundaries. Only the circuit of commodity-capital has to a large extent operated internationally from the very beginnings of capitalism.

(a) *The circuit of money-capital.* The circuit of money-capital ($M-C \ldots P \ldots C'-M'$), the circuit of the self-expansion of capital, immediately gives an idea of the international self-expansion of money-capital in the form of international investment.

In 1960 the accountable real value of the world-wide direct investments controlled by American companies amounted to $30 billion. In 1972 the value of US investments was estimated at over $80 billion, still a serious underestimate according to G.Y. Bertin (1972a).[9] The value of total direct investments of non-American firms rose for the same year to $50 billion, again an under-estimate. The movement of US investments is directed centrally towards the advanced capitalist countries, as Table 1 shows:

Table 1 Accumulated American foreign investments (billions of dollars)[10]

|  | 1960 | 1965 | 1970 |
|---|---|---|---|
| *Advanced capitalist socio-economic formations* | | | |
| Canada | 11·2 | 15·2 | 22·8 |
| Europe | 6·7 | 14·0 | 24·5 |
| Japan | 0·3 | 0·7 | 1·5 |
| New Zealand–South Africa | 1·2 | 2·3 | 4·3 |
| total | 19·4 | 32·2 | 53·1 |
| *Dominated, exploited socio-economic formations* | | | |
| Latin America | 8·4 | 10·9 | 14·7 |
| Africa | | 1·4 | 2·6 |
| Middle East | | 1·5 | 1·6 |
| Asia and the Pacific | 4·2 | 1·4 | 2·5 |
| total | 12·6 | 15·2 | 21·4 |
| other | | 2·0 | 3·6 |
| total overall | 32·0 | 49·4 | 78·1 |

This expansion of US money-capital requires international financing. Brooke and Remmers' study (1970) of 115 branches of foreign companies in Great Britain clearly shows the importance of local financing (Table 2

9. Bertin (1972a), p. 5.
10. Source: *Survey of Current Business* (October 1971).

below), but since the cash-flow itself operates on the international plane, the term local finance begins to lose its meaning. J. N. Behrman (1970) for his part has estimated that only 25 per cent of American foreign investments are carried out by the actual export of American currency.

Studies by C. Coux and J.-F. Landeau show that the share of US investments in Europe financed by currency exports is falling; though this is not to gainsay the increasingly international character of the circuit of money-capital and finance, as the financing of US investments in Europe is done through the Euro-dollar market,[11] on the basis of an international cash-flow.

Table 2 Sources of finance for branches of foreign companies in Great Britain (%)[12]

|  | 90 American firms | 25 European firms | 115 firms |
| --- | --- | --- | --- |
| *Foreign finance* |  |  |  |
| capital | 4 | 9 | 6 |
| loans | 6 | 20 | 12 |
| total | 10 | 29 | 18 |
| *Local finance* |  |  |  |
| liquid assets | 2 | 2 | 2 |
| long term loans | 8 | 6 | 7 |
| bank credits | 12 | 10 | 12 |
| reserves and shares | 68 | 53 | 61 |
| total | 90 | 71 | 82 |
| total overall | 100 | 100 | 100 |

Table 3 Financing of American companies in Europe (%)[13]

|  | 1959 | 1967 |
| --- | --- | --- |
| reinvested profits | 15·9 | 8·9 |
| shares | 28·7 | 28·6 |
| funds coming from the USA | 25·5 | 16·1 |
| funds raised outside the USA | 29·0 | 46·6 |

The international self-expansion of the starting capital requires increasing recourse to long-term credit in the course of the circulation of capital, and this credit is also used internationally. It should at once be noted that there

11. Michallet (1972b).
12. Source: Brooke and Remmers (1970).
13. Taken from C. Coux and J.-F. Landeau, quoted by Moch (1972), p. 53.

is a necessary pre-condition for the international extension of the area of capital expansion in the form of money-capital, and that is the internationalization of capital as a social relation. The act $M$-$C$ at the beginning of the money-capital circuit in reality breaks down into $M$-$L$ (buying of labour-power) and $M$-$MP$ (buying of the means of production), as the basic relation of production in the capitalist mode of production. The internationalization of the area of the capital circuit, in this case the money-capital circuit, far from being at the centre of the internationalization of capital, is at most only the expression of the internationalization of the act $M$-$C$ in the form of $M$-$L$ and $M$-$MP$.

(b) *The circuit of productive capital.* The money-capital circuit $M$-$C \ldots P \ldots C'$-$M'$ expresses the operation of the self-expansion of capital through the productive process $P$:

In so far as they represent self-expanded value, capital acting as capital, they only express the result of the functioning of productive capital, the only function in which capital-value generates value.[14]

There is also an internationalization of the area of the productive capital circuit, in the general form:

$$P \ldots C'\text{-}M'\text{-}C' \ldots P'.$$

The process of the production and reproduction of capital is itself carried out over an increasingly internationalized area. The expression 'internationalization of production'[15] indicates the features of such a process.

But the phrase has a certain ambiguity: the production process defines and encompasses the circulation process. Is it the area of circulation – encompassed in the production process as $C'$-$M'$-$C'$ – that is internationalized, or the act of $P$ itself?

The internationalization of $C'$-$M'$-$C'$ relates to the internationalization of the circuit of commodity-capital. The internationalization of production indicates in effect the internationalization of the act of $P$ itself, outside of the internationalization of circulation. The multinational industrial firm, with an internal circulation of products among its subsidiaries[16] in place of a circulation of commodities, in a way expresses this internationalization of production. The figure for American invisible earnings, \$250 billion, is a concrete indication of the internationalization of the area of reproduction of US productive capital. J. N. Behrman estimates the internationalization of production on a world scale at \$500 billion.[17]

14. Marx (1970), vol. 2, chapter 1, p. 46.
15. Cf. Delilez (1972).
16. Michallet (1972c). International circulation inside multinational firms accounts for approximately 30% of world trade.
17. Behrman (1972), p. 3.

It was through the export of capital that Lenin identified the process of internationalization of production as a new phenomenon in the evolution of the capitalist mode of production. Yet an ambiguity still remains, for the form of the circuit of productive capital $-P \ldots Tc \ldots P-$ leads to a definition not of $P$ itself but of the area of $P \ldots P$ through $Tc$, here seen in the exchanges within the multinational firm. The expression internationalization of production is equivocal as it refers not to $P$ itself, but to the area in which productive capital is reproduced[18]: Behrman's figure of \$500 billion refers to the reproduction of productive capital in the act $P \ldots P$ through a $Tc$ of \$500 billion.

In relation to the money-capital circuit it has been stressed here that the internationalization of the area of the circuit effectively depends on the internationalization of capital as a social relation in the act $M$-$L$ and $M$-$MP$. The term internationalization of production is often used as an intuitive way of indicating the internationalization of capital as a social relation in the productive process. But the difficulty is precisely that it is impossible to uncover the relations of production in the process of production *itself*, as we shall see below.[19]

(c) *The circuit of commodity-capital.* The circuit of commodity-capital, which has the general form:

$$C'\text{-}M'\text{-}C' \ldots P \ldots C'$$

has its starting point in the overall act of circulation $Tc$. The extended formula for this is:

$$\begin{vmatrix} C \\ + \\ c \end{vmatrix} - \begin{vmatrix} M \\ + \\ m \end{vmatrix} - \begin{vmatrix} C\begin{smallmatrix} L \\ MP \end{smallmatrix} \ldots P \ldots C' \\ \\ c \end{vmatrix}$$

Contrary to the case of the productive capital circuit, the act of circulation is not 'embedded' in the productive process, but opens it up, is the condition for it:

In $C' \ldots C'$ capital in the form of commodities is the premise of production. It re-appears as a premise within this circuit in the second $C$. If this $C$ has not yet been produced or reproduced the circuit is obstructed. This $C$ must be reproduced, for the greater part as $C'$ of some other industrial capital. In this circuit $C'$ exists as the point of departure, of transition, and of the conclusion of the movement.[20]

18. Cf. Marx (1970), vol. 2, chapter 2, pp. 63 *seq.*
19. See below, section B.
20. Marx (1970), vol. 2, chapter 3, p. 94.

The circuit of commodity-capital, in contrast to that of the other two forms, presupposes the external existence of commodities and the world market. It is therefore not surprising that it was the first to be extended internationally, through international relationships of exchange. The theory of foreign trade applies very strictly to this circuit, and expecially to the act of circulation $Tc$. There has been an extraordinary expansion of world trade, and foreign trade plays a growing part in the formation of GNP, but here again the internationalization of the area of circulation is not enough to define the internationalization of commodity-capital.

## B: Internationalization of capital as a social relation

It must be borne in mind that the process of capitalist production in itself is an abstraction from the capitalist form itself. The form $P \ldots P'$, the ideological formula of all growth theories, takes production to be the object and ultimate goal of the system:

The general form of the movement $P \ldots P$ is the form of reproduction and, unlike $M \ldots M'$, does not indicate the self-expansion of value as the object of the process. This form makes it therefore so much easier for classical Political Economy to ignore the definite capitalistic form of the process of production and to depict production as such as the purpose of this process; namely that as much as possible must be produced . . . and that the produce must be exchanged for the greatest variety of other products . . . It is then possible to overlook the peculiarities of money and money-capital . . . In the same way profit is occasionally forgotten in commodity-capital . . .[21]

Innumerable economists, particularly when they discuss the internationalization of production, fall into the trap of growth for growth's sake. The circuit of productive capital is of course the central form for classical political economy, and this is what separates the classical school completely from the neo-classical.

Taking the circuit of commodity-capital in isolation from both the money-capital and productive capital circuits in turn leads to the neo-classical illusion that everything begins and ends with the market – as Marx himself points out.

Hence, if attention is fixed exclusively on this formula all elements of the process of production seem to originate in commodity circulation and to consist only of commodities. This one-sided conception overlooks these elements of the process of production which are independent of the commodity-elements.[22]

At first sight it appears that Marx only brought together, deepened and formalized the differing approaches of his predecessors: the mercantilist money-capital formula $M \ldots M'$, Quesnay's commodity-capital formula

21. ibid., p. 92.
22. ibid., pp. 98–9.

$C' \ldots C'$ and the classical formula for productive capital, $P \ldots P'$.[23] But it would be a mistake to see Marx as no more than a prodigious master of synthesis, for in the unity of the circuits, of the process of production and the process of circulation, he brought to light the movement of social relations, the class relations within the self-expansion of capital.

Marx clearly shows capital to be a social relation, a social relation which can absolutely not be conjured up in the course of the productive capital circuit alone, as Nicos Poulantzas attempts to argue[24] (and this is where every classical and neo-classical illusion arises), for the antagonistic relations of the process of production are only apparent in the continuity of these relations in terms of the process of circulation, and vice versa:

The capital-relation during the process of production arises only because it is inherent in the act of circulation, in the different fundamental economic conditions in which buyer and seller confront each other, in their class relation.[25]

The process of production in itself is an abstraction from the capitalist form: looking at the multinational firm only in terms of the internationalization of production gives rise to the same illusion – that class relations are dissolved. This is why, in relation to the process of production, share-holding and participation are ideological gambits which capital holds out to the working class.

The revelation of capitalist relations, and therefore the question of the internationalization of relations of production and hence of capital, comes in the circuits $M \ldots M'$ and $C' \ldots C'$.

The circuit $M \ldots M'$ raises the question of the basic capitalist relation, that is, the purchase of labour power by capital where this same capital has appropriated the means of production, so that labour power and capital (turned into means of production) confront each other antagonistically.

The circuit $C' \ldots C'$ expresses the capitalist relation in the form of the circulation of surplus-value or profit: it is no longer a question of the process of self-expansion of capital *within* the capitalist relationship as in $M \ldots M'$, but the *expression* of this relationship following on the self-expansion of capital. $C' \ldots C'$ is here the movement of capital, again as a social relation, in the form of capital movements and the movement of capitalist profit: surplus value. If relations of production are discussed outside of the process of self-expansion of capital in $M \ldots M'$ and $C' \ldots C'$, it is impossible to

23. Cf. ibid., p. 99: '$C' \ldots C'$ is the groundwork for Quesnay's *Tableau Economique*, and it shows great and true discretion on his part that in contrast to $M \ldots M'$ (the isolated and rigidly retained form of the mercantile system) he selected this form and not $P \ldots P$.'

24. Poulantzas (1972).

25. Marx (1970), vol. 2, chapter 1, p. 30.

analyse them [26], or even to pose the problem of the internationalization of capital.

As for the circuit $M \ldots M'$ it should be remembered that the relations of production *burst* forth in the act $M-C$ as the expression of $M-L$ and $M-MP$, where the conversion of money-capital into productive capital is carried out:

What lies back of $M-C \left\{ \begin{matrix} L \\ MP \end{matrix} \right.$ is distribution; not distribution in the ordinary meaning of a distribution of articles of consumption, but the distribution of the elements of production itself, the material factors of which are concentrated on one side, and labour-power, isolated, on the other.

The means of production, the material part of productive capital, must therefore face the labourer as such, as capital, before the act $M-L$ can become a universal social one.[27]

$M-MP$ therefore develops to the same extent as $M-L$ does, that is to say the production of the means of production is divorced to that extent from the production of commodities whose means of production they are. And the latter then stand opposed to every producer of commodities as commodities.[28]

In the course of the circuit of commodity-capital, the initial relationship $(M-L$ and $M-MP)$, the process of the self-expansion of capital in the form of the conversion of money-capital into productive capital, appears in its extended form as *the circulation of surplus value:*

The third form $(C' \ldots C')$ is distinguished from the first two by the fact that it is only in this circuit that the self-expanded capital-value – and not the original one, the capital-value that must still produce surplus-value – appears as the starting-point of its self-expansion. $C'$ as a capital-relation is here the starting-point and as such relation has a determining influence on the entire circuit because it includes the circuit of capital-value as well as that of the surplus-value already in its first phase, and because the surplus-value must at least in the average, if not in every single circuit, be expended partly as revenue, go through the circulation $c-m-c$, and must partly perform the function of an element of capital accumulation.[29]

Capital emerges as a class relation in the circuit of commodity-capital, as the opposition of $m$ (capitalized surplus-value) to $M$ (capital-value advanced):

The representation of $M'$ as a relation of $m$ to $M$, as a capital-relation, is not directly a function of money-capital but of commodity-capital $C'$, which in its

26. Cf. Rey (1973): 'The final secret of the capitalist relation of production, is that it is incorporated as a simple element of a sub-division of the production process.'
27. Marx (1970), vol. 2 chapter 1, p. 31.
28. ibid., p. 34.
29. ibid., chapter 3, pp. 92–3.

turn, as a relation of $c$ and $C$, expresses but the result of the process of production, of the self-expansion of capital-value which took place in it.[30]

What I earlier called 'the dominance of the circulation of commodities' becomes much clearer in examining the actual relations of production, as well as the process of production strictly speaking, as Marx himself notes:

Here it appears that the process of circulation sets in motion new forces independent of the capital's magnitude of value and determining its degree of efficiency, its expansion and contraction.[31]

The Marxist is not surprised by anything in the circulation process which *ensures its unity* with the process of production. As P.-P. Rey (1973) writes:

It is only in the capitalist mode of production that 'circulation is dependent on production' and if the concomitant of this is that circulation loses its autonomy, to the Marxist this does not mean a falling-off of circulation, but on the contrary a boost to it.

In the total circuit of social capital we can then methodologically locate the points at which capital is internationalized as a social relation, as follows:

$$M\text{-}C\left(\begin{matrix}L\\MP\end{matrix}\right)\ldots P\ldots \left|\begin{matrix}C\\+\\c\end{matrix}\right.\begin{matrix}-\\-\\-\end{matrix}\left|\begin{matrix}M\\+\\m\end{matrix}\right.\begin{matrix}-\\-\\-\end{matrix}\left|C\left(\begin{matrix}L\\MP\\c\end{matrix}\right)\right.\ldots P\ldots C'$$

$$\quad\quad\quad 1 \quad\quad\quad\quad\quad\quad\quad\quad\quad\quad\quad 2$$

Point 1 indicates the internationalization of capital in its process of self-expansion, while point 2, which can in turn be split up, gives the internationalization of the self-expanded capital, through the overall circulation $Tc$.

What is still unresolved is how the internationalization of capital in these various relationships 'passes through' the process of production, as much as being the expression of it.

*(a) The internationalization of capital in the process of its self-expansion: M-L/M-MP.*

1. – The main feature of the internationalization of capital in the process of its self-expansion today is that the act $M\text{-}L$ is an international act on the part of the capital of the firm, and this is what makes the firm multinational. The capital of the 500 biggest US firms buys the labour power of some 15 million workers in the USA, as against the labour power of the 12–13 million workers which it purchases internationally. The $M\text{-}L$ of the 500 biggest US firms is about 30–50 per cent of the world's total. The internationalization of capital as a social relation is tied up with a process of capital expansion

30. ibid., chapter 2, p. 77.
31. ibid., chapter 1, pp. 38–9.

which increasingly takes place on a world scale, through the act $M$-$L$. A French firm like Saint-Gobain-Pont-à-Mousson employs approximately 300,000 people in all, only 180,000 of them in France itself. The examples are endless: $M$-$L$, the basic capitalist relation, is increasingly being internationalized.

The question of immigrant workers represents the self-same internationalization of capital in the form $M$-$C$ ($L/MP$), internalized within national boundaries. If immigrant workers are excluded from the 'national' $M$-$L$ Saint-Gobain-Pont-à-Mousson, the internationalization of the capital of the firm in the form $M$-$L$, in the process of its self-expansion, goes up to 50 per cent. We have here the means to measure the internationalization of capital concretely, in the process of its self-expansion.

The internationalization of $M$-$L$ indicates, in part, the internationalization of class relations, relations of production,[32] in the sense that Marx in part defines class relations through this social act:

The class relation between capitalist and wage-labourer therefore exists, is presupposed from the moment that the two face each other in the act $M$-$L$ ($L$-$M$ on the part of the labourer). It is a purchase and a sale, a money-relation, but a purchase and a sale in which the buyer is assumed to be a capitalist and the seller a wage-labourer. And this relation arises out of the fact that the conditions required for the realization of labour-power, viz. means of subsistence and means of production, are separated from the owner of labour-power, being the property of another.[33]

The reasons behind this internationalization of the process of self-expansion lie in the need to produce, reproduce, and constantly expand the basic capitalist relation, the class relation:

We have seen on previous occasions that in its further development capitalist production, once it is established, not only reproduces this separation but extends its scope further and further until it becomes the prevailing social condition.[34]

At the same time the existence of a free labour force internationally is the condition of the act $M$-$C$, of the conversion of money-capital into productive capital, that is of the process of self-expansion of capital:

... the existence of the latter [the free wage labourer] on a social scale is a *sine qua non* for $M$-$C$, the conversion of money into commodities, to be able to represent the transformation of money-capital into productive capital.[35]

32. Cf. Palloix (1971). The main defect of this work is that it fails to bring out the international relations of production concretely, understanding them only in abstraction.
33. Marx (1970), vol. 2, chapter 1, p. 29.
34. ibid., p. 31.
35. ibid., p. 32.

We saw earlier, in examining the internationalization of the area of the circulation of commodities, of the area of $C' \ldots C'$, how the act of circulation created a free labour force on a world scale.

If it is added that the circuit of money-capital is the most advanced form of the movement of capital in the capitalist mode of production, it becomes easy to see the internationalization of capital in the form $M\text{-}L$ and $M\text{-}MP$ as representing the last stage of imperialism which Lenin defined in terms of the export of capital. The internationalization of capital via the operation of the multinational firms, represents the most advanced stage in the development of the capitalist mode of production.

Marx points out, for example, that the circuit of money-capital, based on the act $M\text{-}L$, can only appear as the last phase of the development of the circuit of social capital in the international arena.

It is therefore quite clear that the formula for the circuit of money-capital, $M\text{-}C \ldots P \ldots C'\text{-}M'$, is the matter-of-course form of the circuit of capital only on the basis of already developed capitalist production, because it presupposes the existence of a class of wage-labourers on a social scale.[36]

If therefore the act $M\text{-}L$ is to be internationalized, and the circuit of money-capital internationalized also as the expression of the previous act, the elements of the circuit of commodity-capital in the total circulation $Tc$, and of the circuit of productive capital, must first have become sufficiently extended into the international arena for labour power to have become a free commodity at every point of the world economy, so that capital may be able to expand.

Imperialism, with its specific features such as the export of capital and the partitioning of the world, involved the internationalization of capital, in the particular role played by the circuit of money-capital. This is the reason for the dominance of finance capital today and the importance of the banks and the finance market. An investigation of the internationalization of capital, through the interplay of money-capital, productive capital, and commodity-capital, opens up new ways of approaching the discussion of imperialism, which has too generally been confined to Lenin's theories and to the Lenin–Luxemburg debate. The most advanced stage of the capitalist mode of production is imperialism as in a sense the expression of the role of the circuit of money-capital in relation to the total reproduction of social capital:

. . . as the scale of each individual process of production and with it the minimum size of the capital to be advanced increases in the process of capitalist production, we have here another circumstance to be added to those others which transform the function of the industrial capitalists more and more into a monopoly of big money-capitalists, who may operate singly or in association.[37]

36. *loc cit.*
37. ibid., chapter 4, p. 107.

2. – Parallel to the internationalization of $M$-$L$, the internationalization of capital in the process of its self-expansion also takes place in the act $M$-$MP$. Here, through the self-expansion of capital in the combination of labour power and means of production,[38] or the conversion of money-capital into productive capital, a second phase of capital self-expansion can be discerned, the expansion of the dominant capital securing its own reproduction by being crossed with other capitals.

$MP$ is in reality the commodity-product resulting from the process of expansion of another capital and needing to secure its conversion from $C'$ into $M'$, so that the process of capitals crossing with each other in their process of self-expansion can in part be shown as follows:

$$M_1 - C_1 \left\{ \begin{array}{c} M'_2 \\ | \\ L \underline{\qquad\quad} MP \ldots P_1 \ldots C'_1 - M'_1 \\ \underbrace{\quad}_{|} \\ C'_2 \\ | \\ P_2 \\ | \\ C_2 \\ | \\ M_2 \end{array} \right.$$

In this formula, $C'_2$ (in the form of $MP$) becomes the input of the process of the capital $M_1$ through the productive process $P_1$, while a fraction of $M_1$ (the part of $M_1$ given over to the purchase of $MP$) is transformed into $M'_2$ and therefore becomes the condition for the expansion of $M_2$. The self-expansion of any capital constantly 'passes through' the reproduction of other capitals, through their own self-expansion, the more so because other points at which the reproduction of capitals crosses constantly appear in the formula, *once commodities appear*, at $C_2$ and $C'_1$. In this respect the process of capital expansion involves the self-expansion of other capitals within the branch, in line with other branches.

The internationalization of capital along the line of $M$-$MP$, parallel to $M$-$L$, therefore indicates an internationalization of the self-expansion of capital as it is crossed with other capitals which are also expanding. $M_1$ and $M_2$ can be taken to be capitals of differing national origin, let us say US capital and European capital. The internationalization of capital itself means that the reproduction of the capital of any nation is constantly crossed with the reproduction of other capitals on an international scale.

38. Cf. ibid., chapter 1, p. 35.

Internationalization here suppresses the autonomy of national processes of capital expansion, but it is never more than the reflection of the internationalization of the act $M$-$L$.

If $M_1$ indicates the dominant expansion of US capital, $M_2$ the dependent expansion of French capital, and the capital $M_3$ (capital which has been expanded in Africa) dependent on $M_2$ passes in its expansion through $C_2$, $M_2$ will, it must be noted, serve as a relay-capital between $M_1$ and $M_3$: the reproduction of $M_1$ takes place on the basis of $M_3$, passing via another capital. Various chains of dependence in the self-expansion of capital become apparent, the process of internationalization pushing different antennae into different regions – Brazil, the Ivory Coast, Turkey, etc. – on behalf of US capital.

Nicos Poulantzas (1973)[39] rightly stresses the international unity of the reproduction of capital: he is therefore able to polemicize with Mandel and others who 'oppose' the various processes of reproduction of capital to each other, US capital to European or French capital. But he then forgets to 'locate' the point at which they cross.

Firstly, we must agree with Nicos Poulantzas that this international 'unity' of the various processes of capital self-expansion is always a 'unity' of the unevenness of these processes: a given capital constantly tends to have the objective of coming into line with the other capitals. US capital 'passes through' the reproduction of other capitals, [40] just as the process of the self-expansion of the various European capitals is linked with the process of self-expansion of US capital. We might then ask what grounds there are for speaking of the 'American challenge'.

But on the basis of the process of internationalizing the branch, the various processes of self-expansion, in the crossing of the dominant capital with the subjected capitals, operate in a contradictory way. In the expansion of the capital of firms such as Creusot-Loire, Jeumont-Schneider and Merlin-Gerin, various solutions have been possible:

39. Cf. Poulantzas (1973), p. 1487:
'There are of course important contradictions at a whole number of points between the domestic bourgeoisies of the imperialist metropoles and American capital, contradictions assumed by each national State, most often giving its support to its native bourgeoisie (this is *one* of the features of the EEC). But it must also be said that these contradictions are not the main ones within the imperialist ruling classes today. The form of "inter-imperialist contradictions" which is dominant today is not that between "national capital" and "international capital", where the imperialist bourgeoisies appear as "entities" one after the other. To understand this point we have to see that the dependence of native capital on US capital *cuts across the different parts* of native capital: this is what creates its lack of internal articulation, the contradictions between American and native capital being mainly a complex form in which the contradictions of American capital itself are reproduced within native capital.'

40. For example Westinghouse and General Electric in relation to firms like Creusot-Loire, CGE, Jeumont-Schneider and Merlin-Gerin.

– capital expansion primarily through the nuclear project, which made it necessary to keep close to the reproduction of the US capital (Westinghouse in this case) dominant in the international branch of electrical engineering;
– capital expansion in a process in which the capital can move with relative autonomy from US capital, namely in the transport branch (Creusot-Loire is extremely active in this field, and real possibilities are opened up for Merlin-Gerin with the linear motor).

These firms have so far chosen Westinghouse because the state has no transport policy guaranteeing the promotion of capital expansion to firms in this field. There are then alternative ways in which the self-expansion of a firm's capital can take place: there will of course be conflicts between departments engaged in different processes of expansion, and this is what gives rise to the changes in the management of firms and to struggles within the board of directors in which finance capital has a stake, coming down for one solution or the other. From the point of view of capital, and especially of the process of internationalization, the firm is never a totally homogeneous, unified whole.

It now becomes evident how much the autonomy of national capital from international capital – reflected in repeated attempts to turn national capital into relatively dominant international capital – depends on state policy and state intervention – in energy policy, housing and transport policy, etc. The problem is whether within a capitalist framework state intervention in the process of internationalization can:

– only 'maintain' on a national and European scale the self-expansion of the capital of apparently national firms, on which nonetheless international and notably US capital rests (as in the case of nuclear power, where the reproduction of French capital, guaranteed by a 'certain' level of state intervention, is strictly subject to the self-expansion of US capital);

– ensure the promotion of a capital self-expansion as the *dominant* capital internationally, subjecting other processes to it; or

– secure the subjection of dependent capitals in given geographical areas (Africa) on behalf of US capital *or* European and French capital.

There in fact seems to be a contradictory 'interplay' at the level of the state itself between these three types of state policy. The State is still less homogeneous and unified than the capital of the firm.

(b) – *The internationalization of self-expanded capital: c-m-c/C-M-C*[41]
The whole of this act breaks down into $C'-M'$ and $M'-C'$, and the second stage contains developments already noted before: following on the process of self-expansion of capital there comes a capital beginning its self-expansion. I shall not dwell here on the internationalization of capital as the internationalization of the relationship $M-C$ $(L/MP)$ – in other words of the class

relation. I am concerned at this point only with the concretization of capitalist relations in the act of total circulation in the form of surplus-value and profit, and the internationalization of these relations in this form.

$C'$ appears as the functional form of the separation of capital-value from surplus-value ($c$ from $C$). In the same way, $M'$ is the act of separation of profit from capital-value ($m$ separated from $M$). Marx is very strict about this:

It is only in the circuit described by $C'$ itself that $C$ equal to $P$ and equal to the capital-value can and must separate from that part of $C'$ in which surplus-value exists, from the surplus-product in which the surplus-value is lodged. It does not matter whether the two things can be actually separated, as in the case of yarn, or whether they cannot, as in the case of a machine. They always become separable as soon as $C'$ is transformed into $M'$.[42]

The whole of the act is as follows:

$$\begin{vmatrix} C \\ + \\ c \end{vmatrix} - \begin{vmatrix} M \\ + \\ m \end{vmatrix} - \begin{vmatrix} C \\ \\ c \end{vmatrix} C \begin{matrix} L \\ MP \end{matrix}$$

This points to the internationalization of the relationship separating $c$ from $C$, $m$ from $M$, on the basis of the internationalization of $c$-$m$-$c$, the internationalization of the circulation of profit, and the internationalization of $C$-$M$-$C$ as its opposite form.

1. – This internationalization of capital as a social relation, through the opposition of the relations $c/C$ and $m/M$, is to be seen in both fact and theory.

The internationalization of capital income or profit is evident in the profit on US capital in Latin America, Europe and Asia; and the same goes for the profits of Japanese and European capital in international operations.

In the realm of theory the internationalization of capital as a social relation is the theme of Arghiri Emmanuel's theory (1972) of 'unequal exchange'.[43] But Emmanuel's theory betrays all the defects of a restricted

41. The act of circulation $Tc$ should never be taken to be autonomous, and is always linked to the production process in both directions – $C'$–$M'$, the transformation of productive capital into money-capital, and $M'$–$C'$, the transformation of money-capital into productive capital.

Note Marx's own warning, when he stresses that $C'$-$M'$ is not purely a formal conversion in the circulation process, but belongs also to the process of production: 'The transformation is not the result of a merely formal change of position pertaining to the circulation process, but of a real transformation experienced by the use-form and value of the commodity constituents of the productive capital in the process of production.' (Marx (1970), vol. 2, chapter 3, p. 94).

42. ibid., p. 88.

43. Cf. Palloix (1971), vol. 1.

theoretical position in relation to the total circuit of social capital: he generalizes about internationalization from the act $c$-$m$-$c$ alone. His whole theory of unequal exchange, of the unequal distribution of the world's surplus-value, rests on this act alone, though it is only the reverse side of the basic act $M$-$C$ $(L/MP)$. Inasmuch as his theory touches on only a part of the whole question of the internationalization of capital and of the relations of production, its bearing is limited. Emmanuel evades the heart of the question of the internationalization of the relations of production, and in particular *reduces* the existence of capitalist relations to the international circulation of surplus-value: in his theory the class conflicts $c/C$ and $m/M$ cannot arise, as it is not based on $M$-$L$ and $M$-$MP$. It is not surprising that he arrives at a conception of international relations of production along the lines of poor countries struggling against rich ones: this is in fact quite a likely conclusion to reach if one looks only at the circulation of surplus-value in abstraction from the processes of production, taking $c$-$m$-$c$ in itself and for itself.

The internationalization of capitalist profit is so obvious that it is scarcely worth dwelling on it. The profits of the foreign subsidiaries of US firms are well known to be higher than the profits of the same firms within the US, and the same holds for Japanese and European firms. The rate of profit on American foreign investments (annual net profits in relation to the accountable value of the sums invested by the parent company) rose from 12·1 per cent in 1960–69 to 13·1 per cent in 1970.[44] For manufacturing industry alone the rate was 12 per cent in the advanced countries and 12·3 per cent in the underdeveloped countries. Despite the fact that all such figures must be treated with caution, it is interesting to note that these rates are higher than the rate of profit on investments within the USA.

2. – It is important to understand that the internationalization of self-expanded capital in terms of the internationalization of the relationship $c/C$ and $m/M$ goes hand-in-hand with the internationalization of self-expanding capital, of the relationship $M$-$L/M$-$MP$. With the internationalization of $c/C$ and $m/M$, *the process of self-expansion of the dominant capital is extended*, on the one hand because it takes its share of the profit produced by other capitals in their self-expansion process (unequal exchange by the equalization of rates of profit)[45] and on the other because it finds the condi-

44. Cf. *Survey of Current Business* (October 1971).

45. The main problem with the current Byzantine discussions about the transformation problem and prices of production is that they place the problem only within the circuit of productive capital $P \ldots P'$, 'forgetting' to relate the transformation problem to the totality of the circuit of social capital, and especially of the self-expansion of capital. The result is a purely 'technical' discussion as dictated by the features of the circuit of $P \ldots P'$, which evades the question of the relations of production and class relations.

tions for the realization of value in exchange with commodities produced by dependent capitals, by other modes of production at the level of $C$-$M$-$C$, the first line in the total circulation $Tc$.

The circuits of money-capital $(M \ldots M')$ and productive capital $(P \ldots P')$ are, it will be recalled, closed in on themselves, and presuppose nothing lying outside themselves.[46] With the circuit $C' \ldots C'$, on the other hand, and therefore with its first act of circulation $Tc$, the commodity is twice presupposed outside of the circuit:

That $C$ appears as the premise of $C$ only in this Form III, within the circuit itself, is due to capital in commodity-form being its starting-point.[47]

$C' \ldots C'$ on the contrary presupposes the existence of $C$ (equal to $L$ plus $MP$) as commodities of others in the hands of others – commodities drawn into the circuit by the introductory process of circulation and transformed into productive capital, as a result of whose functioning $C'$ once more becomes the concluding form of the circuit.[48]

A recent GATT study confirms that 30 per cent of international trade takes the form of exchanges within multinational firms;[49] but it should not be concluded that the tendency is strong enough to encompass the whole of $C'$-$M'$-$C'$ as exchanges within multinational firms. Monopoly does not suppress competition, but raises it to a new level, institutionalizing it and renewing its content. And in the same way, the multinational firm does not suppress $C'$-$M'$-$C'$ at the international level or among multinational firms and firms related at the level of reproduction of capital even where no formal crossing is apparent, for example in share-holding. It is true that international trade is becoming more and more an internal activity of multinational firms, and this does make a difference to the classical analysis of world trade:

On this subject see some observations of Marx about the 'revolving' movement of value, which offer the only real way of approaching the 'transformation' problem in studying the circuit of social capital (Marx (1970), vol. 2, chapter 4). The 'revolving' movement of value leads to a differentiation between the circuit of money-capital $M \ldots M'$ and the other circuits productive capital $(P \ldots P')$ and commodity-capital $(C' \ldots C')$. Delilez and writers like him who stress the money-capital circuit end up with the theory that there is not an equalization of the rate of profit, while R. Borrelly defends the theory that there is equalization in the sphere of productive capital.

46. Cf. Marx (1970), vol. 2, chapter 3, p. 95: '... apart from the last extreme, the circuit of individual money-capital does not presuppose the existence of money-capital in general nor does the circuit of individual productive capital presuppose the existence of circuits of productive capital. In I, $M$ may be the first money-capital; in II, $P$ may be the first productive capital appearing on the historical scene.'

47. op. cit., p. 96.

48. loc cit.

49. The measure of the importance of this percentage for the internationalization of profit, is that $c$-$m$-$c$ is 30 per cent controlled by multinational firms.

– according to G. Ádám (1972), '50 per cent of what is supposed to be American foreign trade is made up of the foreign operations of multi-national companies for their greater profit'.[50]

– in 1970 the nine biggest commercial companies in Japan, most of them subsidiaries of the big multinational firms such as Mitsui, Mitsubishi and Sumitomo, accounted for 46·4 per cent of exports and 59·7 per cent of imports,[51] whereas these figures were only 41·4 per cent and 52·6 per cent respectively in 1961.

Insofar as the self-expansion of the dominant US – or in this case Japanese – capital 'passes through' the self-expansion of distinct capitals which it dominates through the existence of its subsidiaries (this being their role), the subsidiaries 'fasten onto' the products of other capitals or of other modes of production to turn them into 'commodities' in the circuit $C'-M'-C'$ of the dominant capital. The product of the productive process of dependent capitals only becomes a 'commodity' within the commodity-bundle[52] controlled by the multinational firm. The basic product of other dependent capitals is taken over by the multinational firm to transform it into commodities within the economic chains it controls, passing down the line of the commodity-bundle of housing, energy, transport, packaging or whatever.

Through the control it exercises over $C'-M'-C'$ (in this case $C-M-C$), the multinational firm includes the products of other capitals within its orbit of circulation in the same way as previously the national and international circulation of commodities 'fastened onto' the products of other modes of production than the capitalist mode of production, in order to turn them into commodities at the level of the act $Tc$, as Karl Marx emphasized:

Within its process of circulation, in which industrial capital functions either as money or as commodities, the circuit of industrial capital, whether as money-capital or as commodity-capital, crosses the commodity circulation of the most diverse modes of social production, so far as they produce commodities. No matter whether commodities are the output of production based on slavery, of peasants (Chinese, Indian ryots), of communes (Dutch East Indies), of state enterprise (such as existed in former epochs of Russian history on the basis of serfdom) or of half-savage hunting tribes, etc. – as commodities and money they come face to face with the money and commodities in which the industrial capital presents itself and enter as much into its circuit as into that of the surplus-value borne in the commodity-capital, provided the surplus-value is spent as revenue; hence they enter into both branches of circulation of commodity-capital. The character of the process of production from which they originate is immaterial. They function as commodities in the market, and as commodities they enter into

50. Cf. Ádám (1972), p. 596.
51. *Japon économie* no. 44, 5 October 1972.
52. Cf. C. Palloix (1972).

the circuit of industrial capital as well as into the circulation of the surplus-value incorporated in it. It is therefore the universal character of the origin of commodities, the existence of the market as world market, which distinguishes the process of circulation of industrial capital. What is true of the commodities of others is also true of the money of others.[53]

We can then say that there are two main ways in which $C'$-$M'$-$C'$ is articulated at the international level, depending on the periodization of the capitalist mode of production:

– *industrial capital*, the form of social capital, is *articulated with the products of other modes of production to transform these products into commodities in* $C'$-$M'$-$C'$, at the level of $C$-$M$-$C$ or $c$-$m$-$c$, depending on whether the products enter the productive process under $L$ or $MP$ (subsistence products for the labour force or raw materials), or enter into capitalist consumption as luxury products. This type of articulation belongs basically to the phase usually known as 'competitive capitalism', though the term is a questionable one;

– *money-capital* of the leading multinational firms is *articulated with products* not basically from other modes of production, but *from the dependent capitals it dominates in its* $C'$-$M'$-$C'$, at the various levels of this act of circulation, to transform these products into commodities in an increasingly favoured area, that of the commodity bundles directed towards $C$-$M$-$C$.

This new type of articulation characterizes the different chains of dependence in the self-expansion of capital, in particular the new type of articulation with the underdeveloped countries, which is no longer an articulation of the capitalist mode of production at the centre with other modes of production, but an articulation within the world CMP itself, among differing processes of self-expansion of capital and increasingly accentuated differentiation of this expansion as between the centre and the periphery.[54] The first type of articulation between the CMP and other modes of production is pushed back into the independent circulation of underdeveloped economic and social formations; it tends to become 'marginalized' in international circulation, and hence the appearance of export industries and business transfers in the underdeveloped countries [55] as a new characteristic of exchange relations between periphery and centre.

53. Marx (1970), vol. 2, chapter 4, pp. 109–10.
54. As Nicos Poulantzas observes (1972, p. 12): ' The CMP now dominates these formations not just from the outside with the reproduction of the relation of dependence, but establishes direct domination within them: the mode of production of the metropolis is reproduced in a particular form within these subjected, dependent formations.'
55. Cf. Azouvi, Kleimann and Paquier (1972).

Edith Penrose (1972)[56] is aware of what this new practice of multinational firms means in the underdeveloped countries, and recommends the practice of joint ventures between international capital and local capital, since in any case international capital has to expand on the basis of dependent capitals through $C'-M'-C'$. It should be noted that multinational firms are all ready to ensure the promotion of the capital of under developed countries – for their own benefit, of course. They leave these countries an important share in the production of the products, which then increase their value only in the 'commodity bundles' controlled by the multinational firms; but in this latter case there is no joint venture with dependent capital.

Once the expansion of the dominant capital rests on differentiated processes of self-expansion of subjected capitals, incorporating the 'products' of these capitals into the commodity bundles expanding in value at the centre, the following statement by G. Ádám (1972) becomes acceptable:

The optimal international redistribution of the resources of the firm has to be seen not as a goal for some time in the future, but as an actual concentration of production in the lowest-cost regions and of sales on the most profitable markets. In this light, production series which had previously justified their costs on a national scale can no longer do so on a world scale once international moves take place in production. This indicates that multinational firms are establishing growing numbers of foreign subsidiaries with the avowed intent not of supplying the market of the host country, or scarcely doing so at all, but mainly or exclusively exporting to third countries and back to the country of origin of the firm.

The Ford project to set up a 90 per cent export-oriented plant in Spain is a clear example of this process.[57] The development of export industries,[58] which are replacing policies of import substitution in the underdeveloped countries, is further evidence, together with a host of similar changes.

Such a phenomenon may seem to be in contradiction to the centralization of US investment in Europe, and the policy of multinational firms to keep plants in the central area, close to the market, as C. A. Michallet (1972a) points out, following R. Vernon's theory of the international life cycle of the new product. The result of an inquiry into 72 French firms showed that 87 per cent of the foreign plants of these firms are located on the market.[59]

Ádám and Michallet, however, are not discussing the same thing: the former refers to the articulation of the self-expansion of the dominant capital with the subjected capitals, through a 'taking up' of their products into

56. This new practice on the part of multinational firms is also documented by Ádám (1971).

57. *Le Monde*, 28 November 1972, p. 19.

58. Little, Scitovsky and Scott (1970).

59. Michallet (1972a), p. 648 seq.

its own circulation of commodities, though he does not really define this point. The latter refers to the self-expansion process of a dominant capital not along technical lines (the product) but economic lines, resulting in a commodity which is realized on the central market. In fact the two theories are complementary and are certainly not counter-posed to one another in the strategy of multinational firms.

The polemic between Lenin and Rosa Luxemburg over the internationalization of capital[60] is seen in a clearer light on the problem of realization, which tended to defeat them both.

Rosa Luxemburg at least based herself on the commodity-capital circuit $C' \ldots C'$, stressing the 'competitive capitalist' type of act of circulation of industrial capital with other modes of production. But she had very little understanding of how this in fact worked, insisting that surplus-value must be 'realized' in other modes of production than the CMP, though $C'-M'-C'$ clearly shows quite a different type of mechanism at work – the 'taking up' of the products of other modes of production to transform them into commodity $C$, so that the surplus-value contained in $C'(C + c)$ in the light of the act of exchange, could be realized.

It must be said for Lenin that he located the problem of $C'-M'-C'$ in relation to the self-expansion of capital, but for one thing he simply enclosed $Tc$ in the circuit of productive capital (which by definition does away with the 'realization' problem) and for another, he, like Rosa Luxemburg, failed to understand $C'-M'-C'$ as the starting-point of the circuit of commodity-capital.

There are, then, very close links between the multinational firm and the internationalization of capital – meaning by this the internationalization of the *relationships* contained in capital, in its expansion process and when it is expanded:
– in the relationship $M-L/M-MP$, and
– in the relationship $c-m-c/C-M-C$.

Only an examination of the internationalization of the circuit of social capital can give us the means to define the internationalization of capital as a social relation, and to understand the place of the multinational firm within the total circuit.

(c) – *The internationalization of the process of production and the labour process.*

We have so far left out of account the problem of the relations of production within the production process itself, or in other words, how capital as a social relation ($M-L/m-MP$ and $c-m-c/C-M-C$) 'passes through' the produc-

60. For a fuller account of this debate see Palloix (1971).

tion process, defining the system of relations of production *within and outside it* as

a system of positions assigned to the agents of production by relation to the chief means of production: this system determines the position of the immediate producers and eventually of the non-producers, these positions being themselves only the points at which certain functions are carried out (the process of appropriation from nature, the co-ordination of these processes, the distribution of the product, etc.).[61]

It is obvious that, on the one hand, the question of the relations of production *in* the process of production is dialectically linked to capital as a social relation (these relations being the basis of capital as a 'relation' and vice versa). On the other hand I have already observed that the question of these relations in the production process cannot be raised as such in isolation from the act of circulation (by which we mean the conversion of productive capital into money-capital through the mediation of commodity-capital). It is none the less the case that capital is determinant – and is determined – in relation to a production process and above all to a work process in which the class relations contained in capital are concretized in a system of positions among the agents which is the concrete expression of the relations of production. I refer to the division of labour between manual labour (in which there is in turn a process of division among various operations) and intellectual labour (itself specialized), involving executive and organizing functions, etc.

The internationalization of capital as a social relation spreads out the labour process on an international scale, fragmenting social labour not just at a local, regional or national level, but on a world scale. The various components of the chain come from the most far-flung parts of the globe: Taiwan, South Korea, USA, France, Britain, Latin America and Africa, pushing division of labour to its limits, with atomization as a general characteristic.[62] The car industry is a case in point.

When this atomization of social labour takes place within a branch which is becoming internationalized, a technical division of labour begins to operate on a world scale, as the new expression of the international social division of labour expressed generally in the opposition of manual labour to intellectual labour. Fiat's most productive lines are reproduced in Spain, Yugoslavia, etc.

But at the same time it is not only on the periphery that internationalization makes itself felt. It takes the atomization of social labour at the centre still further, driving the division between manual and intellectual labour deeper even in the advanced capitalist countries, and accentuating the repeti-

61. Bettelheim (1970) p. 57.
62. Cf. Furjot and Janco (1972).

tive nature of work movements, affecting line-speeds, reducing the skills of workers, etc.

These relations involved in the process of production and the work process can however only be elucidated by examining the strategy of the multinational firms in relation to the internationalization of capital.

*References*

ÁDÁM, G. (1971), 'New Trends in International Business: Worldwide Sourcing and Domiciling', *Acta Oeconomica*, Budapest, vol. 7, no. 304, pp. 349–67.

ÁDÁM, G. (1972), 'Les firmes multinationales dans les années 70', *Revue économique*, vol. 23, nos. 3–4, July.

AZOUVI, PAQUIER and KLEIMANN (1972), *Industries d'exportations et transferts d'activité*, SEDES, Paris (draft document for CORDES), November.

BEHRMAN, J. N. (1970), *National Interests and the Multinational Enterprise*, Prentice Hall, New York.

BEHRMAN, J. N. (1972), *Industrial Development through the Multinational Enterprise*, Rennes International Symposium, CNRS, September.

BERTIN, G. Y. (1972a), 'L'Expansion internationale des grandes entreprises americaines', *La Documentation française*, no. 25.

BERTIN, G. Y. (1972b), 'Les causes de la croissance des entreprises à l'étranger', *Revue économique*, vol. 23, nos. 3–4, July.

BETTELHEIM, C. (1970), *Calcul économique et formes de propriété*, Maspero.

BROOKE, M. Z., and REMMERS, H. L. (1970), *The Strategy of Multinational Enterprise*, Longman.

DELILEZ, J.-P. (1972), 'L'Internationalisation de la production', *Économie et politique*, ISEA.

EMMANUEL, A. (1972), *Unequal Exchange*, New Left Books.

FRANKO, L. G. (1971), 'European Business Strategies in the United States', *Business International: Research Report*, September.

FRANKO, L. G. (1972), *Strategic Planning for Internationalization: The European Dilemma and Some Possible Solutions*, The European Society of Corporate and Strategic Planners, Brussels.

FURJOT, D., and JANCO, M. (1972), *Informatique et capitalisme*, Maspero.

HYMER, S. (1972), *The Internationalization of Capital*, Rennes International Symposium, CNRS, mimeo, September.

KARPIK, L. (1972a), 'Multinationales et grandes entreprises technologiques', *Revue économique*, vol. 23, no. 4.

KARPIK, L. (1972b), 'Le capitalisme technologique', *Sociologie du travail*, no. 512, anuary–March.

LITTLE, I., SCITOVSKY, T., and SCOTT, M. (1970), *Industry and Trade in Some Less Developed Countries*, Oxford University Press, OECD.

MARX, K. (1970), *Capital*, Foreign Languages Publishing House, Moscow.

MICHALLET, C.A. (1972a), 'La Multinationalisation des enterprises françaises', *Revue économique*, vol. 23, nos. 3–4.

MICHALLET, C. A. (1972b), *Le marché des euro-obligations: un marché financier transnational*, mimeo.

MICHALLET, C. A. (1972c), 'La politique de financement des firmes multinationales', *Économies et Sociétés*, ISEA.

MOCH, P. (1972), *Les Entreprises Multinationales*, report to the Economic and Social Council, Paris, 15 November.

PALLOIX, C. (1971), *L'Économie mondiale capitaliste*, Maspero, 2 vol.

PALLOIX, C. (1972), *Note de recherche sur le procès d'internationalisation*, IREP, Grenoble, mimeo.

PENROSE, E. (1972), *The Growth of International Corporations and their Changing Role in Less Developed Countries (with special reference to East Africa)*, Rennes International Symposium, CNRS, mimeo, September.

POULANTZAS, N. (1972), 'Les Classes sociales', *L'Homme et la société*.

POULANTZAS, N. (1973), 'L'Internationalisation des rapports capitalistes et l'État-Nation', *Les temps modernes*, April.

REY, P.-P. (1973), *Les Alliances de classes*, Maspero.

WILKINS, M. (1970), *The Emergence of Multinational Enterprise*, Harvard University Press.

# 4  György Ádám

## Multinational Corporations and Worldwide Sourcing

First published in this volume.

In the late 60s and early 70s, a certain number of multinational corporations could be distinguished more and more clearly from the general run of the 7,000–8,000 US-based European and Japanese firms with more or less substantial foreign interests, having become what Professor Vernon (1971) in a US context called 'a class by themselves . . . an extraordinary group quite distinct in many respects from the rest of US corporate economy'. According to him, 187 of the entire group of *Fortune*'s 500 seemed in the US presumptively entitled to the '"multinational enterprise" label'.[1]

These 'real MNEs' had an edge in profitability, tended to concentrate their activities in oligopolistic industries, with heavy emphasis on skilled manpower and advertising, and their operations were greatly diversified. They had a dominant role in US exports and were also the main exporters of technology; as American FDPI (Foreign Direct Private Investment) is extremely concentrated,[2] the 'real MNEs' accounted for the bulk of net inbound flows of royalties and fees which reached nearly $2·3 billion in 1971 (an estimated 90 per cent was remitted to MNEs).[3] They were also overwhelmingly the most important spenders of research and development funds in the US.[4] The enumerations could be continued almost indefinitely.

I shall not list here similar data relating to the non-US-based 'real MNEs'. Their number is estimated at about 100 and they are dispersed

1. Vernon (1971), p. 11.
2. In 1957 45 corporations each with investments of more than $100 million, accounted for 57 per cent of all American foreign direct investment. 1957 Census: *US Business Investments in Foreign Countries*, Table 55, p. 144.
3. US Tariff Commission (1973), p. 10.
4. ibid., p. 555–7: 'Non-MNC firms hardly count. For the industries shown [in Table 1, p. 556], the MNC's share of total outlays for R&D averages 52 per cent. However, this average actually is pulled down by a few exceptionally low numbers in a few industries. Excluding these, it would be higher – about 80 per cent, or high enough to preclude any doubt that the amounts and patterns of R&D spending in the US in general are governed primarily by the amounts and patterns of R&D spending by the MNCs.'

between the main industrialized countries.[5] It is sufficient to note that they play an identical or similar role in the economies of their home countries with the difference that it is only recently that some of them (particularly the West German and Japanese giants) 'went global'.

What I am mainly concerned with here is that an increasing number of 'real MNEs' are:

– establishing subsidiaries abroad with the explicit purpose of supplying the markets of the host country to only a limited extent, if at all, but exporting mainly or exclusively to third countries *and* to the country which the parent companies used to call their home;[6]

– organizing veritable business empires with complex logistical networks among their affiliates;

– implementing in a worldwide context a centrally planned business strategy based on a 'global outlook' and availing themselves of their 'global scanning capacity'.

We have a number of definitions and pronouncements by leading executives of MNEs on what is meant by 'globalism'. To summarize some of them:[7]

The [global] company views the world as a single entity. Its perspectives transcend all national boundaries. Decisions are made not in terms of what is best for the home country or any particular product group, but in terms of what is best for the corporation as a whole on an international basis.

The basic principle on which these corporations operate is this: taking the entire world as their market, they tend to organize production, distribution and selling activities with as little regard for national [political] boundaries as the realities of time and space permit.

As this is already being put into practice by the most sophisticated of the 'real MNEs' in the form of worldwide sourcing (WWS), I wish to examine some of the consequences of one of the guiding principles of the latter, i.e. that lines of production that previously made cost sense in a national setting, lose their justification in a global setting, being followed by the international shifting of production.

## I

Worldwide sourcing suggests some facts which may be of great importance for the industrialization of the Third World as well as for the international division of labour:

5. Their list may be found in *Fortune*'s annual directory of the *Top 200 Industrials Outside the US*.
6. Ádám (1972a), p. 594.
7. Based upon Business International (1967), p. 90.

(a) At those low-cost sites of runaway plants where there is a lag in labour productivity in relation to DMECs (Developed Market Economy Countries), this is no impediment to WWS, as it is more than offset by a substantial difference in wage rates. Indeed, some of the recent experience in this field is stated in the following terms:

Not all 'low-wage' countries are primitive in the sense that they are unable to absorb and profit from techniques and disciplines of modern production. Furthermore, modern technology in some industries is such that *relatively unskilled labour can be combined with fairly sophisticated equipment*. This contradicts the stereotyped notion of 'high technology' as a process in which highly skilled labour always must be available to operate advanced, complex kinds of capital equipment. Usually this is so, but in some industries the stereotype never has described reality. The possibilities for using unskilled labour abroad open up for some firms the opportunity *to migrate to 'low-wage' countries* which have reached a level of development at which they are ready to accept them, *without significant divergence from productivity experience in the United States*.[8] (My italics).

(b) It is alleged that in some cases the introduction of modern plants and technology makes it possible to raise the productivity of Asian workers *to the same level* as that of American workers.[9]

(c) More than that, according to Chenery and Hughes (1972a), the marginal productivity of labour and capital is *higher* in some developing countries than in many DMECs![10]

The attractions offered by 'low-wage' countries are demonstrated *inter alia* by the subsequent phases of worldwide sourcing, i.e.:

(a) the migration of traditional, declining labour-intensive industries;

(b) the migration of industries with longer product-life cycles;

(c) the transfer of labour intensive portions of technology-based industries (electronics, engineering, etc.);

(d) the shifting of capital intensive mass consumption industries with many labour intensive operations (automobile industry);

(e) environmental controls in advanced countries are about to lead to the migration of a number of other capital intensive industries (some branches of chemical industry, metallurgy, paper industry etc. – the Japanese being in the vanguard of this movement);

(f) the means of preserving important foreign markets or penetrating them increasingly often requires the establishment of subsidiaries in the closest low-wage area in order to offset protectionist tariffs or other barriers (the rush of Japanese and European corporations to Mexico);

8. US Tariff Commission (1973), p. 118.
9. Mecklin (1970), p. 77.
10. Chenery and Hughes (1972a), p. 10.

(g) export points or bases to supply certain regional areas (Australia, Israel, Spain, etc.);

(h) some new growth products may now not be manufactured in the country where they were developed originally, but in lower-wage countries (e.g. home video tape recorders in Japan). This precedent may be repeated in the case of a number of other products.

This development was stressed in a significant comment by Professor Vernon (1971):

By 1970, the product cycle model was beginning in some respects to be inadequate as a way of looking at the US-controlled multinational enterprise. *The assumption of the product cycle model ... was beginning to be challenged by illustrations that did not fit the pattern.* The new pattern that these illustrations suggested was one in which *stimulation to the system could come from the exposure of any element in the system to its local environment, and response could come from any part of the system that was appropriate for the purpose.*[11] (My italics.)

Sizing up the scope of WWS, it should also be mentioned that it at first encompassed mainly small countries which could and were considered special cases (such as Taiwan, Hong Kong, South Korea in the Far East and Mexico in Latin America); now more and more small countries are getting involved (Singapore, Macao, Malaysia, Mauritius, etc.), and *they are being joined to an increasing extent by big countries with enormous cheap labour reserves, such as Indonesia, India and Brazil.*

This is a development of great significance, and therefore some details are warranted.

*Indonesia:* In order to learn how to attract firms that produce labour-intensive goods for exports to South East Asia and elsewhere, Indonesia's Investment Board is sending an expert to Malaysia and Singapore. The Investment Board cited PT Ness Industries Indonesia – a firm that exports its entire output of transistors and other components to the US and Latin America – as an example of the kind of investment it wishes to attract. In this context the Board stressed the following points: Indonesia's wage levels are competitive with those in Hong Kong, Malaysia, Singapore and Taiwan and will remain so for many years to come; Indonesia is geographically close to many Asia/Pacific markets; Indonesian workers have proved adaptable and trainable, particularly in the manual skills needed to produce many electrical and fine mechanical products; the country has industrial estates and bonded warehouses, which are already operating.[12]

*India:* The Indian Government has approved four proposals for the transfer of complete manufacturing units from Britain and the Netherlands.

11. Vernon (1971), p. 108.
12. *Business Asia*, 10 March 1972, p. 75–7; ibid., 1 September 1972, p. 273–4.

The three British companies involved will discontinue some of their operations in Britain and hand over their machinery and equipment to their Indian collaborators. Their products can be manufactured more cheaply here than in Britain because of low labour costs in India, and *will be exported back to Britain*. The shifting of complete industrial plants to India to take advantage of low labour costs is being encouraged by the Indian Government and was recently discussed by the Indo-British Technological Group.[13]

A leading Indian business man stated recently in West Germany: 'I am interested in every industrial plant that may be transferred to India . . .' It is reported that more and more industrial plants from the US, Britain and the Netherlands are migrating to India, induced to do so by the recent 'explosion of production costs'. At least one company from the FRG made this move.[14]

*Brazil:* US investments in electronics assembly and manufacturing are adding a new dimension to Brazil's industrial boom. Companies that by-passed Brazil in the first wave of offshore electronics investment in the 1960s are being lured by an increasingly attractive incentives package and guarantees for foreign investors.

Texas Instruments started up (in February 1973) Latin America's first integrated circuit plant. It will assemble components from the US, mostly for export to the US and Europe, but part of the output will be used in a new TI minicalculator plant. For more high-powered data processing, IBM is spending $13·5 million to start assembling its 370/145 computer in Brazil. Brazil hopes to attract other electronic plants, including *operations transferred from other countries*; one inducement is a new law that allows a functioning factory to be imported duty-free if most of its output will be exported.[15]

It is no secret that off-shore manufacturing for DMEC markets is meeting increased resistance, not exclusively, but first and foremost in the US. US-based MNEs were after all the most active in foreign sourcing and its American antagonists wish to put a brake on it *inter alia* by the Burke-Hartke Bill and/or by provisions attached to other bills with some chance of being passed by Congress.

Without wishing to evaluate here the positive and negative aspects of WWS both for DMECs and LDCs (Less Developed Countries), I shall attempt to set out some reasons why I believe that WWS is an irreversible process, an integral part of oligopolistic competition as well as – although perhaps in a distorting way – of the evolution of the international division of labour.

International subcontracting – as opposed to the shift of industries or

13. *Financial Times*, 7 March 1972.
14. *Handelsblatt*, Düsseldorf, 12 April 1972, p. 3.
15. *Business Week*, 3 March 1973, p. 32.

production plants – appears to be gaining ground. It may be implemented less spectacularly than the transfer of whole production units, for products which are inputs into final goods manufactured in the DMECs, whether they be parts of footwear or electronic components, particularly if and when MNEs are the producers of both components and final products, i.e. the operations may be carried out within the framework of their business empires. *Such imports are harder to identify* and they are often difficult to restrict as it is not easy to specify a variety of continually changing components.[16] There is some evidence that international subcontracting is expanding. According to the US Tariff Commission, combined US imports under tariff items Nos. 807.00 and 806.30 increased from $1 billion in 1966 to $2·8 billion in 1971.[17] The share of developing countries rose from 7 per cent in 1966 to 22 per cent in 1969, having become – probably temporarily – stabilized at 24 per cent in 1970 and 1971.[18]

It is quite possible that offshore manufacturing and sub-contracting may grow even when the volume of other sorts of direct investment in the developing countries slackens, although it is rather difficult – for lack of adequate data – to quantify this assertion.

Direct pressure from labour on MNEs in the US was probably not completely unsuccessful: some MNEs are believed to have reacted by modifying or even abandoning plans for further operation abroad. A case in point is the US car industry. It has invested in superior production facilities in the US; in so doing, it has held out the explicit promise that, *rather than going to its overseas subsidiaries for cars and parts to be sold in the US*, *it will rely on domestic production*, thus continuing to maintain a high level of employment here. Yet in the wake of recent debates over work conditions, General Motors (and doubtlessly other auto firms too) are becoming aware that the American labour market, thought to be much more reliable than its foreign counterparts, if more expensive, is acquiring what may be termed from their viewpoint a new kind of 'unpredictability'. And GM's difficulties are considered only the tip of the iceberg.[19]

The inference from this is that the decision 'to stay at home' may be subject to silent revision.

In a recent Congressional Hearing, one of the representatives of the AFL–CIO (Andrew J. Biemiller) referred to press reports, according to which in the first 7 weeks of 1972 there were quite a number of shutdowns or cutbacks in plants manufacturing a wide assortment of products (bicycle brakes, semiconductors, typewriters, resistors, vacuum cleaners, shoes, industrial

16. Chenery and Hughes (1972b), p. 23.
17. US Tariff Commission (1973), p. 130.
18. Sharpston (n.d.), p. 6.
19. *Financial Times*, 10 October 1972, p. 5.

machinery, etc.), the implicit inference being that this is at least partly due to foreign sourcing. He quoted also a directory of some of the larger US consumer electronics end-product ventures currently expanding their operations (or starting new ones) in Taiwan. And the list was quite impressive.[20]

The spread of the runaway phenomenon is attested also by information from Labour sources that Haiti too is becoming a site for offshore manufacturing. Some 15,000 jobs have been created in hundreds of light manufacturing and assembly plants in Haiti, mostly American owned. It is proposed to make Costa Rica another haven for runaway firms.[21]

Worldwide sourcing also falls very much in line with the traditions and habits of US industry:

In the US, the multidivisional firm is commonplace, with plants operating in many different regions and engaging in large amounts of cross-hauling of components and finished goods – some generated on the firm's own production lines, some purchased from far-flung independent suppliers and distributors. This is the phenomenon of 'multi-sourcing' in a domestic context. Internationally, the same development takes place . . .[22]

## II

I have drawn so far mainly on the data available on worldwide sourcing by US firms. However, my conviction that worldwide sourcing is an irreversible process, is based also on evidence derived from the operations of European and Japanese corporations.

The leaders of West German industry are going on record, one after another, stressing the necessity and inevitability of international sourcing.[23] This opinion is shared by the spokesmen of West German high finance, such as F. H. Ulrich (Deutsche Bank), who sees the future of his country (and of other industrialized countries too) in the following terms:

Many entrepreneurs believe that the present plummeting of their earnings is due to a downturn in the economic cycle. Putting their faith into a new upswing, they stick to products about which it has already been established that their continued manufacture in the F R G will not pay off. Thus they omit to search for new fields of activities with more assured prospects. This means, however, that, as far as the structure of West German industry is concerned, the big shakeout is still to come

20. US Government (1972), pp. 39 and 46–7.
21. AFL–CIO Executive Council (1972).
22. US Tariff Commission (1973), pp. 126–7.
23. See Ádám (1972c), referring to the statements of the general managers of AEG-Telefunken, Bayer and some top executives of the West German engineering industry (e.g. *Financial Times*, 15 December 1971; in *Wirtschaftswoche*, etc.).

[*Das grosse Sterben kommt noch*]. What is visible today is only the beginning of the imminent 'clearing of the ranks'.

As regards the level of production costs, West German industry will be among those countries at the top of the list in the industrialized world. Another trend which West German industry must take into consideration is the broadening international division of labour.

This means that it will be more and more difficult to manufacture labour intensive products or those with a low technology content (clothing, footwear, electrical and optical products of mass consumption) in West Germany.

The efforts of the developing countries to overcome their specialization on primary products *will make the productive potential of a number of industries in advanced countries redundant* (e.g. in the metal industry, food industry, rubber industry, etc.).

This structural transformation affects the big corporations too. For example, AEG is bound to revise its product planning ... domestic products in the lower and middle price ranges are no longer competitive. According to a recent forecast about the evolution of imports in consumer electronics, the share of imports in portable radios will increase by 1980 from 58 per cent to 75 per cent, of non-coloured sets from 29 per cent to 90 per cent, and of coloured sets from 6 per cent to 30 per cent.

The inference to be drawn is that *production plants must be transferred to lower-cost countries*. The goal should be an industrial structure like that of Switzerland, i.e. concentration on products requiring sophisticated know-how and engineering.

Some branches of the toy industry must migrate too; there are problems in certain branches of the paper industry; the same is true for the steel industry, the construction of containers and ships, not to speak of coal mining and a number of other basic industries [*Grundstoffindustrien*].[24]

West German manufacturers of heavy industrial equipment competing for 'turnkey' projects are threatening – in view of what they call 'the negative attitude of the government' – to go abroad.[25]

The spokesman of the West German chemical industry – in response to what they consider unjustified wage demands – recently announced similar intentions. President Rolf Sammet of Farbwerke Hoechst said bluntly that his corporation's domestic investments will aim in 1974 at the maintenance of the existing plant and equipment in order to assure its smooth operation and that they will put heavy emphasis on foreign investments. Similar references were made by Bayer's Kurt Hansen.[26]

West Germany's Institut für Weltwirtschaft (Institute for World Economy) has begun a research programme whose objectives include the identification of those industrial branches which are likely to come under strong competitive pressure from developing countries in order to contribute to

24. *Wirtschaftswoche*, 25 February 1972, pp. 16–18 and 21–3.
25. *Wirtschaftswoche*, 14 July 1972, pp. 68–72.
26. Müller-Haesler (1973), p. 9.

the adjustment of the prevailing economic structure to future market conditions.[27]

In Britain the TUC (Trades Union Congress) stated in March 1972 that a number of major companies have run down or closed investments, while simultaneously expanding production in Portugal, Spain, Barbados, South Korea or Hong Kong.[28] Earlier, at the annual conference of the Confederation of Shipbuilding and Engineering Unions it was revealed that Britain's electronic industry was suffering financial losses and redundancies because of imports from cheap-labour factories in Asia; semi-conductors were being imported at a price which was lower than that which British manufacturers had to pay for raw materials. Electronic products manufactured in Hong Kong never say: 'Made in Hong Kong'. Instead the labels of leading British and American companies in the Colony's workshop (and also the labels of Japanese firms) are slapped on electronic equipment made there, these products entering the British market 'in this special way'.[29]

The Dunlop-Pirelli union council claimed that the Sumitomo Rubber Company, which is 44 per cent owned by Dunlop, has worked out a production adjustment with Dunlop in certain areas of the world. According to this project, Dunlop subsidiaries in Asia, Africa, Australia and New Zealand will halt plant expansions and Sumitomo Rubber will pick up all increased tyre demand in these areas and supply them under Dunlop brand names.[30]

France is also beginning to feel the pinch. French imports in radios, television sets, and gramophones were substantially increased from Singapore, Hong Kong, Taiwan and South Korea. (Most spectacularly from the first: an estimated 62,700 units in 1970, 1,000,000 units in 1972.)[31] French enterprises are also engaged in subcontracting with the former colonies in North Africa.

A distinguishing feature of sourcing in Western Europe is that more and more companies are shifting labour intensive operations not only to the Far East (like West Germany's Rollei and Holland's Philips to Singapore, to mention only two of the best known ventures), but also to 'peripheral' European countries such as Spain, Greece, Turkey and sometimes to Italy. Particularly in West Germany – where the birth rate is rather low – the importation of foreign workers meets increased resistance and the concept that the machines should be brought to the workers instead of vice versa is gaining ground.

27. Fels (n.d.).
28. *Trades Union Congress Economic Review 1972*, p. 40.
29. *Financial Times*, 23 June 1971, p. 19; TUC (1970), p. 42.
30. *Financial Times*, 23 June 1972; *The Times*, 3 July 1972, p. 17.
31. *Usine Nouvelle*, no. 7 1973, pp. 96–8; see also *Le Nouvel Observateur*, 23 December 1972, p. 40.

Finally, as regards Japan, this country is restructuring its economy, proposing to change over as quickly as possible to 'knowledge and technology intensive industries' and to 'high grade commodities'. This implies a migration *en masse* of the labour intensive industries to the well known runaway sites such as Hong Kong, Taiwan, South Korea, Malaysia and also to Thailand, etc.

The progress of international sourcing is shown by the most recent survey of the Export-Import Bank of Japan, covering 234 investor firms in manufacturing industries. The survey shows that:

44 firms (19 per cent) went abroad in order to export finished goods to third countries;

28 firms (12 per cent) went abroad to export finished goods to Japan.

The survey reflects the situation as of the end of March 1970. Thus at this date no less than 31 per cent, i.e. nearly a third of the firms in the sample aimed at sales to third countries or Japan, the respective ratio of the previous survey being 16 per cent.[32] As 1970–72 were the years of a substantial expansion of Japanese industry abroad, it may be assumed that the aforementioned ratio is even higher today.

*III*

Thus internationally integrated industries; a global system of vertical integration in manufacturing is emerging, incorporating labour from many countries into a worldwide productive structure by bringing together, among other things, low-cost labour and high-cost manufacturing tasks. It appears that *almost anything can be produced in any country*[33] *so long as the necessary capital, technical, managerial and* – last but not least – *marketing know-how is available*, thanks to today's methods of communication and transportation and to the fact that technical achievements and skills are readily transferable from one country to another; with the addendum that the actors of this process are largely the global companies, the most dynamic of the 'real MNEs'.

The impression I want to convey is that restructuring on a large scale is going on in the world economy and that US-based MNEs are by no means the only ones participating in it. Indeed, scanning the world press provides new evidence nearly every day for the strength of the trend outlined here,

32. Export-Import Bank of Japan (1972) pp. 10–11.
33. 'The unschooled girls of Taiwan can do just as well assembling complex TV components as the high-school graduates of New Jersey. The untrained workers of African or Asian nations can be taught to produce complex products, ranging from tiny transistors to giant turbines, as readily as the skilled workers of Pennsylvania or the West Coast.' Quoted from the speech of Rep. Gaydos (D.Pa), Congressional Record, House (20 July 1971), H 6922; see Ádám (1972b), p. 311.

for the permanent spread of WWS as implemented by European and Japanese corporations in 1973. (Just a few random items from March 1973: Fiat plant in Brazil to build 190,000 cars a year; three affiliated companies of the Mitsubishi Group signed a $US32-million agreement to establish a major shipbuilding and repairing facility in Singapore – the joint venture is Mitsubishi's *first* such undertaking outside Japan; Sony, the Japanese electronics manufacturer is to start UK production of colour television sets, hoping to raise production of Trinitron colour receivers to 10,000 per month by the summer of the following year.[34]

These developments are reflected also in the statistical data referring to trade in manufactures of developing countries. According to the Report prepared by the UNCTAD Secretariat[35] covering the period of 1960–70:

(a) the value of exports of manufactures rose from $65·6 billion in 1960 to $165·1 billion in 1969, an average annual rate of growth of 10·8 per cent;

(b) exports of manufactures from the developing countries increased at a faster rate, at 14·3 per cent p.a., from $2·8 billion in 1960 to $9·3 billion in 1969 – as a result, the developing countries' share in world exports of manufactures rose from 4·3 per cent in 1960 to 5·6 per cent in 1969;

(c) during the same period the share of DMECs in the total exports of manufactures of the LDCs increased from 50 per cent to 59 per cent – an annual average growth of 16·4 per cent;

(d) the share of manufactures in the LDCs' total exports rose from approximately 10 per cent in 1960 to 18 per cent in 1969;

(e) the most impressive fact is, however, that *it is the category of machinery and transport equipment in which the highest rate of increase occurred.* The value of LDC exports of this group of products rose from less than $0·3 billion in 1960 to $1·4 billion, *an average rate of growth of almost 20 per cent,* i.e. much greater than the corresponding rate of 12 per cent for world exports of the same category. The UNCTAD Secretariat, however, calls attention to the very small base value in 1960 from which the LDCs' exports started, and that even in 1969 such exports accounted for only 1·8 per cent of total world exports of this category!

(f) it may be noted too that imports of 'other engineering and metal products' by DMECs from LDCs rose from about $95 million in 1962 to $721 million in 1969, an increase of almost 34 per cent a year on average. *This is the highest rate of growth achieved by any product group and more than two and a half times as fast as the increase in the imports into DMECs of this product group from the world.* Notwithstanding, the LDCs' share in the DMECs' total imports of such products was still less than 2 per cent in 1969.

34. *Financial Times*, 1 March 1973, p. 1.; ibid., 2 March 1973, p. 28.
35. UNCTAD Secretariat (1971), particularly pp. 3–11.

*IV*

In view of these data it may be asserted that worldwide sourcing is an 'un-qualified success', that the panacea to heal the 'development gap' has been found; all that is required is to build the LDCs' economies on the investment of global companies.

I argue that despite some appearances many caveats are in order.

I admit that 'the development of electronic and electrical components introduced a new phase of industrial exports in the mid-1960s, combining the international mobility of capital and its associated technology and management with the ready availability of relatively skilled low-cost labour and technicians', as well as that 'the movement of international corporations to LDC locations as a base of supply for DMECs introduced a new element in the international division of labour'.[36] This takes place, however, on a rather shaky basis for more than one reason:

(a) Veritable export enclaves for manufacturing goods (export processing zones) have been established whose operations are geared largely to the shifting requirements of the global strategy of the said international corporations;

(b) As the main outlets for manufactured goods are the DMECs (according to the study of UNCTAD cited above, during the period 1962-9, one-half of the LDCs' industrial exports was accounted for by the US, over one-fifth by the European Economic Community, just under one-seventh by the EFTA, a little over one-fifteenth by Japan),[37] the LDCs are exposed to the changes and shifts of the advanced countries' foreign trade policies, particularly those of the US. This means greater dependence than ever on DMEC markets, on import surcharges, 'voluntary' restrictions, quotas, all sorts of tariff and non-tariff barriers.

(c) Processing activities and component manufacturing midway within the production process may generate an output for which there is no outlet other than the parent firm or subcontractor which commissioned the activity in the first place.[38] To quote Professor G. K. Helleiner:

Export orientated labour-intensive industries selling to multinational firms, and totally unintegrated with the rest of the countries in which they are located, would seem to combine some of the most disagreeable features of outward orientation and foreign investment. Particularly where there are 'export processing zones', the manufactured sector constitutes an 'enclave', an 'outpost of the mother country' in as real a sense as a foreign-owned mine ever did. These disagreeable features, moreover, are combined in a manner which leaves the host country with a minimum of bargaining advantage.

36. Chenery and Hughes (1972), p. 9.
37. UNCTAD Secretariat (1971), p. 11.
38. Helleiner (1972), p. 3.

Not only is the export manufacturing activity extraordinarily 'footloose', dependent as it is on neither local resources nor local markets, but it is also likely to bind the host country both to sources of inputs and to market outlets *over which it has an absolute minimum of control. Bargaining strength is likely to be considerably less* for a country manufacturing components or undertaking middle-stage processing *than it is even for a raw material exporter*; for copper or cocoa beans can, after all, be sold on a world market or bartered with socialist states or even used domestically . . .[39]

(d) Apart from the 'dependence effect', there are rather significant 'cost effects' too. Incentives (the establishment of an infrastructure, tax holidays, immunity from import duties, cheap credits, etc.) may be excessive, channelling into the export sector resources which are not available for, and whose lack is preventing, the development of agriculture and industrial sectors that cater to the needs of the domestic market, implying large imports of consumer goods and foodgrains and all sorts of foreign inputs (raw materials, intermediary products, etc.). This has an impact upon foreign exchange earnings which may be less than substantial. This again means indebtedness, with the servicing of the loans becoming a heavy burden. In some such cases the only way to fill the gap seems to be to attract new investment which then increases still more the dependence upon external sources of financing.

(e) In the case of Mexico, the usual dependence and cost effects are complemented by the fact that Mexican workers spend a great part of their earnings in the towns on the US side of the border, or for imports of consumption goods manufactured in the US, so that at least a part of the area covered by the Border Industrialization programme *becomes to some extent economically integrated into the United States*. (Not to speak of a number of sociological problems such as increasing prostitution and delinquency as a result of heavier-than-normal migration to the border zone with unfulfilled job expectations; as the in-bond industries employ mainly women, changing traditional male–female family roles and male frustration lead in general to increased social tensions rather than their decrease through higher employment.)[40] The border area is also attracting, to a growing extent, skilled workers and technicians from other parts of the country.

(f) It should be mentioned too that the whole concept of worldwide sourcing is based on wage rates low enough to offset almost any other considerations. The easing of unemployment and marginality is a respectable goal anywhere and particularly so in areas with a 'population explosion'. The mobility of the global companies makes them able to migrate quickly to other low-wage areas. Also, they are supported by the authorities in some countries to keep down wages. In South Korea, for

39. ibid., pp. 13–14.
40. *Electronics*, 11 September 1972, pp. 65–8.

instance, several laws have been recently revised with the aim of making the country more attractive to foreign capital, one change being the introduction of tough regulations to curb labour disputes where the employer is a foreign corporation.[41] In Mexico, too many US firms are pushing their activities beyond the geographical limits laid down for them and transferring operations to areas where prevailing wage levels are even lower than in the border areas.[42]

Summing it up: instability, dependence, 'over-kill' of incentives, the lack of linkages, etc. makes worldwide sourcing a doubtful tool in the longer term for solving the problems of the Third World, despite some job creation and export earnings. Stressing the creation of too much labour intensive industry conjures up the danger of an over-supply of these goods – 'banana republics becoming pyjama republics'.[43] The issue appears to be diversification into higher productivity capital intensive goods. Hong Kong and Singapore have made a start but one may wonder how many LDCs may be able to tread this path. And even Hong Kong's and Singapore's success is largely conditional on whether protectionism can be kept in check in DMECs.

As to the effects of worldwide sourcing upon employment in DMECs, not even the very thorough recent study of the US Tariff Commission could reach definitive conclusions. All I wish to do is to refer to a study prepared within the framework of New York University's MNC project.[44] It seems to prove that the displacement effect falls predominantly on production workers, heavily weighted in the semi-skilled categories. The role of the international corporations ('real MNEs', 'global companies') as a vehicle for structural change in US production and employment is reflected in the fact that the new jobs associated with their foreign expansion are created primarily in the managerial, clerical and professional occupations, while the bulk of the membership of the unions is recruited from blue collar workers.

The situation – at least for the time being – is somewhat different in the two countries excelling beside the US in worldwide sourcing, i.e. in West Germany and Japan, both of which are characterized by a relative shortage of labour in many areas. Yet the employment situation in the West, owing partly to recent developments such as the oil shortage, is fraught with great uncertainties; the American experience might become far from irrelevant for the home countries of non-US based MNEs.

41. *Business Asia*, 11 December 1970, p. 56.
42. *Free Labour World*, November 1970, p. 18.
43. See comments of Helen Hughes in English and Hay (1972), p. 214.
44. Hawkins (n.d.).

## References

ÁDÁM, G. (1972a), 'Les Firmes multinationales dans les années 70', *Revue économique*, vol. 23, nos. 3–4, July.

ÁDÁM, G. (1972b), 'Some Implications and Concomitants of Worldwide Sourcing', *Acta Oeconomica*, vol. 8 (3–4).

ÁDÁM, G. (1972c), 'Reply to Comments and Criticisms', *Acta Oeconomica*, vol. 9.

AFL–CIO EXECUTIVE COUNCIL (1972), *Statement on the Export of US Jobs*, Chicago, mimeo.

BUSINESS INTERNATIONAL (1967), *1985 – Corporate Planning Today for Tomorrow's World Market*, July (Research Report).

CHENERY, H., and HUGHES, H. (1972a), *The International Division of Labor: The Case of Industry*, IBRD-IDA Economic Staff Working Paper No. 123, mimeo.

CHENERY, H., and HUGHES, H. (1972b), *Trade and Industrialization: Some Issues for the Seventies*, IBRD Seminar on Industrialization and Trade Policies in the 1970s, mimeo.

ENGLISH, H. E., and HAY, K. A. J. (eds.) (1972), *Obstacles to Trade in the Pacific Area: Proceedings of the Fourth Pacific Trade and Development Conference*, School of International Affairs, Carleton University, Ottawa.

EXPORT-IMPORT BANK OF JAPAN (1972), *Japanese Private Investments Abroad: The Summary of the Third Questionnaire Survey*.

FELS, G. (n.d.), *Research Activities of the Institut für Weltwirtschaft in the Field of the International Division of Labor and Employment Creation in Developing Countries*, mimeo.

HAWKINS, R. G. (n.d.), *Job Displacement and the Multinational Firm*, mimeo.

HELLEINER, G. K. (1972), *Manufactured Exports and Multinational Firms: Their Impact upon Economic Development*, mimeo.

MECKLIN, J. M. (1970), 'Asia's Great Leap in Textiles', *Fortune*, October.

MÜLLER-HAESLER, W. (1973), 'Exodus der deutschen Chemie?', *Frankfurter Allgemeine Zeitung*, 8 January.

SHARPSTON, M. (n.d.), *International Sub-Contracting*, mimeo.

TUC (1970), *Report of a Conference on International Companies*.

UNCTAD SECRETARIAT (1971), *Review of Trade in Manufactures of the Developing Countries 1960–1970*, Report, TD/111.

US GOVERNMENT (1972), *Hearings before the Subcommittee on Foreign Economic Policy on Trade Adjustment Assistance*, Washington.

US TARIFF COMMISSION (1973), *Implications of Multinational Firms for World Trade and Investment and for US Trade and Labor*, Report to the Committee on Finance of the US Senate, Washington, USGPO.

VERNON, R. (1971), *Sovereignty at Bay*, Longman.

# Part Two
# Capital and State in the World Economy

Robin Murray (Reading 5) starts from the 'territorial non-coincidence' between the firm and the nation state. Analysing the economic functions of the state required by capital, he considers the ways in which these functions can be maintained as the firm leaves its home territory. The implication of increasing internationalization is that national economies and states become increasingly interdependent, and the powers of control of individual nation states may be weakened. Bill Warren (Reading 6) argues that Murray's analysis of the economic functions of the state lacks historical perspective, that the power of the nation state *vis-à-vis* the large firm has if anything increased, and that interdependence due to internationalization pushes states into stronger intervention in their national economies.

   In terms of Bukharin's analysis (Reading 1), nationalization, which includes as a major component today the strength and scope of the state's economic interventions, and internationalization both remain fundamental trends. The argument between Murray and Warren is really about the articulation of these trends today: while Warren appears to argue that they are moving in step more or less automatically, Murray sees the two trends as conflicting, with major shifts in emphasis in different periods. What must be remembered is that the reproduction of capital in the world economy reproduces the division of its sphere of operations, and yet continually transcends the boundaries thus set up: the nation state in its very essence reflects this contradiction.

# 5  Robin Murray

## The Internationalization of Capital and the Nation State

R. Murray, 'The Internationalization of Capital and the Nation State', *New Left Review*, no. 67, May–June 1971, pp. 84–109.

Liberal models of the international economy, as of international relations in general, still spring predominantly from an early utilitarianism. The nation state is treated as the basic category in the world: the atom of the system. States are assumed to be rational, self-conscious, self-determining units, analogies of economic man. International relations, whether political or economic, are above all relations between these independent states whose conduct is assumed to be based on the principle of maximizing their own net benefit subject to internal and external constraints. Developments in the structure of economic organizations since 1945, especially the rapid growth of international firms, have brought into question the solitary concern of international relations with international state relations. International institutions have grown up, like the IMF, the World Bank or the largest of the international corporations themselves, which have a greater significance than many nation states, developed or underdeveloped. Raymond Vernon (1968), the head of the Harvard Business School Research Programme on the international firm, puts the point in this way: 'the advanced world, carried ebulliently on the crest of a technological revolution in transportation and communication, has absentmindedly set up a virile system of international institutions and relationships that sit alongside the system of nation-states'.[1] Moreover, together with the appearance of these international institutions comes a weakening of the nation states themselves: Kindleberger (1969) for example argues that 'the nation state is just about through as an economic unit'.[2]

### The Problem of Territorial Non-Coincidence

The rapid post-war expansion of international firms has therefore brought into question the analytical primacy of the basic elements of the liberal model of the international system, and in doing so, has raised to the forefront the question of the relationship between political and economic organization. For it now appears that, for certain countries at least, there is

1. Vernon (1968), pp. 119–20.
2. Kindleberger (1969), p. 207.

no longer a one-to-one correspondence between the two. An editorial in *Fortune* summed up this view: 'the real point is that business everywhere is outgrowing national boundaries and, in so doing, is creating new tensions between the way the world is organized politically and the way in which it will be increasingly organized economically'.[3] Now while this territorial non-coincidence is a common observation, there is little developed analysis by, let alone agreement between, liberal writers on the subject as to the consequences of such non-coincidence on political organization. In this they are reflecting a more general lack of attention in Anglo-Saxon economic theory to the structural relationship between private capital and public power.

In contrast to the atomistic liberal model, Marxist writers have tended to see the international economy, not as an aggregation of national economies, but as a total system in which nations are subordinate structures. Trotsky for example writes that the world economy should be seen 'not as the simple addition of its national units, but as a powerful independent reality created by the international division of labour and by the world market which dominates all the national markets'.[4] Marx himself emphasized that capitalist production was indissolubly linked with foreign trade[5] and that the capitalist division of labour was an international one. 'Thanks to the machine, the spinner can live in England while the weaver resides in the East Indies.'[6] The international division of labour represents an advanced stage of the socialization of production.

Within the world economy some national capitals are more powerful than others. Their territorial expansion is the subject matter of the Marxist theories of imperialism, yet it is an expansion into fundamentally pre-capitalist areas. The political organizations of the imperialist powers are in this case expanded alongside the territorial expansion of their economic organizations: the one-to-one relationship is preserved at the expense of the pre-capitalist public structures of the imperialized regions.

The post-Second World War developments of colonial liberation and the interpenetration of the advanced capitalist states themselves has now raised the question of what we called 'territorial non-coincidence' which liberal writers have registered but not answered. The issue is whether, with an

3. *Fortune*, 15 August 1969, p. 73.
4. Trotsky (1930), p. 146.
5. This point is well made by Kemp (1967) in his chapter on Marx. It is interesting that in Vol. 1 of *Capital* Marx purposely assumes away the international aspect of capitalist systems: 'In order to examine the object of our investigation in its integrity, free from all disturbing subsidiary circumstances, we must treat the whole world as one nation, and assume that capitalist production is everywhere established and has possessed itself of every branch of industry' (p. 581).
6. Marx (n.d.), p. 156 (see also p. 161).

increasingly interdependent international economic system, national capitalist states will continue to be the primary structures within the international economic system, or whether the expanded territorial range of capitalist production will require the parallel expansion of coordinated state functions, either through the *de facto* annexation of weaker nations by the stronger, or through some form of supranational state.

This does of course regenerate the Kautsky/Lenin controversy on ultra-imperialism. Kautsky suggested the possibility of 'a new ultra-imperialist policy, which will introduce the joint exploitation of the world by internationally united finance capital in place of the mutual rivalries of national finance capital'.[7] In his reply, Lenin argued that the international alliances which Kautsky observed were no more than truces between wars, for these alliances were based upon the economic, financial and military strength of the parties at the time of the formation of the alliance, and since these strengths develop unequally between nations, the alliances would inevitably become anachronistic. The necessary rivalry between capitalist states would remain.[8] Secondly, while Lenin regards as indubitable the 'growing international interweaving between the cliques of finance capital' which Kautsky saw as a basis for his forecast, he cites the armament industry to support the thesis that the internationalization of capital may increase rather than reduce national rivalry. 'Interlinked on a world-wide scale, capital is thriving on armaments and wars.'[9]

While we may agree with Lenin's castigation of Kautsky's position as 'lifeless abstractions' which mystify rather than reveal international antagonisms as they then existed, we should also note that Lenin does not discuss the consequences for the power and independence of nation states resulting from the interpenetration of national capitals. Certainly there is a tendency in twentieth-century Marxist writing on the world economy to infuse the nation state with an independence set apart from the range and power of its own national capital. Nation states become an entity without substance.[10]

This, in part at least, reflects the predominantly political treatment which the state has received in Marxist literature. Until recently it was primarily the repressive role of the state in capitalism which has been emphasized: a recent work, by Miliband, has brought out its ideological function.[11] What is remarkable is how little attention has been given to the economic role of

7. K. Kautsky, *Die Neue Zeit*, no. 5 (30 April 1915), p. 144, quoted in Lenin (1915), p. 19.

8. Lenin (1917), pp. 114–15.

9. Lenin (1915), p. 234–5.

10. A notable exception to this point is Ernest Mandel, particularly in his more recent writings.

11. See also the review by N. Poulantzas of Miliband's book in *New Left Review*, no. 58.

the state in capitalism, and it is this which seems to me to be central to any discussion on the robustness of the nation state in an era of interpenetration of national capitals, the subject raised without a satisfactory answer in the Lenin–Kautsky debate.

Thus I would argue that, in spite of its underlining of the trends of accumulation and centralization of capital, and in spite of its discussion of the political role of the state, Marxist theory has not brought these two aspects of analysis together to clarify the problem of the substance and the adequacy of nation states at a time of international centralization and concentration. There is as yet no adequate approach to the issue we first raised, that of territorial non-coincidence. As a result recent Marxist forecasts of the political implications of the internationalization of capital have been as uncertain, unsubstantiated, and in some cases as 'lifelessly abstract' as those made by liberal writers.

In what follows, I have tried to sketch out the factors which seem to me important in developing a more adequate approach. There are three main sections: (i) discusses the structural role of the state in capitalism; (ii) covers the relationship between state and capital at a time of capitalist territorial expansion; (iii) deals with this relationship as it pertains to the contemporary world economy.

## 1 The structural role of the state as an economic instrument of capitalism

I want to suggest in this section that the state is an objective structure in any capitalist system, that, contrary to liberal models, capitalism cannot be analysed as a system without taking account of the role of the state, and that, more particularly, in the process of capitalist production and reproduction the state has certain economic functions which it will always perform, though in different forms and to different extents. It is these economic functions with which we will be concerned, for, in tracing the territorial expansion of individual capitals, one of the central points at issue will be what bodies perform these structural economic functions for the expanded capitals. If the performance of certain economic functions by a state body is a *sine qua non* of any capitalist system, the territorial expansion of that system will imply the need for the performance of state economic functions in the expanded territory.

Two points should be made immediately clear. First, state economic functions for any given capital or coherent body of capitals need not be exercised by a single authority, though commonly there will be a dominant authority. Second, the body or bodies which perform these functions are not necessarily the governing authorities of nation states. For when we talk of 'state' economic functions we refer to what may most aptly be called 'economic *res publica*', those economic matters which are public, external to individual private capitals. These public economic matters may be dealt with by a grouping of private capitals, by national governments, or by international public bodies. For the moment we are more concerned with the character of these public matters than with the bodies that deal with them.

I will distinguish six economic '*res publica*', or state functions:[12]

1. *Guaranteeing of property rights.* For Engels this was the primary function of the state. This guarantee is backed by forces of law: the police and armed forces. In modern capitalist states, one interesting area of its active application is in the protection of the integrity of self-declared fishery limits. Or, to take another example, in Britain there is a demand by the private sector for the extension of the guarantee to the 'sanctity' of private information in the form of heavier sanctions against industrial spying.

2. *Economic liberalization.* This involves the establishment of the conditions for free, competitive exchange: the *abolition* of restrictions on the movement of goods, money or people within the territorial area and the *standardization* of currency, economic law, weights and measures and so on. The process characterizes the early stages in the establishment of an expanded territorially distinct system and is the substance of the neo-classical formulation of economic integration as the absence or progressive elimination of discriminations (see for example Balassa, 1962). Indeed one of the clearest current examples of such liberalization is the European Common Market. The double process of the abolition of restrictions and standardization is the principle characteristic of the decade which has followed the coming into force of the Treaty of Rome: though it is a process nowhere near complete. Within advanced capitalist countries, economic liberalization is primarily 'regressive' in character and takes the form of anti-monopoly legislation, action against restrictive practices, including resale price maintenance, and restrictions on trade unions and the use of labour's power.

3. *Economic orchestration*: a matter which includes the regulation of business cycles, and economic planning. The forthcoming role of public

12. I do not want to go into here the question of the 'overdetermination' of the economic functions by the political functions, a point which is emphasized by Poulantzas (1968) who sees the state as 'the factor of cohesion of a social formation and the factor of reproduction of the conditions of production of a system', with the state in its economic role being the factor of cohesion in this particular level of the social formation. The economic functions of the state are simultaneously political functions, corresponding to the political interests of the dominant class. See Poulantzas (1968), especially pp. 53–4. It seems to me that we can usefully examine the economic functions of the state in this paper as a preliminary step to understanding more fully its overall political significance.

bodies in this case contrasts with their retiring role in the case of economic liberalization, and it is this more active form of intervention which distinguishes the social democratic view of economic integration from the neoclassical one. The former sees economic integration as not simply the removal of discriminations but the pursuit of an economic policy aimed at productive harmony: 'to integrate is to increase for a given space the compatibility of the plans of a group of decision centres which together form a single economic system' (Byé, 1958).[13] The state is in this case most clearly the factor of cohesion of an economic formation, playing an increasingly strong ideological role *vis-à-vis* the productive system (see the British National Plan of 1965 where the propaganda function of the Plan is stated to be among the most important).

4. *Input provision.* Public bodies have been required to secure the availability of key inputs at low cost:

(a) Labour. States have acted to ensure (i) the existence of a proletariat, either directly or indirectly; see for example the statutory extension of the working day in England, the Stein-Herdenberg reforms of agrarian relations in early 19th-century Prussia, or the results of the French credit policy in Indo-China in the colonial period: (ii) the training of proletariat, visible both in public education systems or current industrial training schemes: (iii) the control of wages of a proletariat, for examples of which we need go no further than the contemporary incomes policies of advanced capitalist countries. It is particularly interesting in respect to the question of labour provision that Swedish social democratic governments have put the main emphasis of their post-war economic policy not on nationalization (of which there is probably less than in other advanced Western European countries) but on the control of the labour force – its size, its quality, and its redeployment.[14]

(b) Land. A market for land has been required not only for the development of commodity agriculture (see the state's role in the English enclosure movement) but also for the siting of public utilities, notably transport and housing (see the right of 'eminent domain' given to private corporations in the United States in the 19th century which enabled those developing public utilities to compulsorily acquire any land needed for their operations).[15]

13. A useful survey of concepts of economic integration can be found in Erbes (1966).

14. See Shonfield (1965), pp. 200–201. In relation to labour provision, Dobb (1963) suggests that 'there seems to be at least *prima facie* evidence for connecting periods when the policy of the state in a class society moves in the direction of economic regulation with periods of actual or apprehended labour-scarcity, and periods when State policy is inspired by a spirit of economic liberalism with an opposite situation'. He is speaking of regulations and controls by the state governing price or output or entry to a trade or change of employment, during peace-time; see pp. 23–4.

15. Shonfield (1965), p. 306.

(c) Capital. Governments have acted to ensure the supply of finance to its industry through (i) the establishment and backing of a national banking system and private money market, as exemplified in the post-war history of certain countries in the British Commonwealth as well as in the history of French banking; (ii) the establishment of Funds for particular industrial projects; (iii) the granting of credits, and subsidies in other ways, including tax allowances, investment grants, special interest rates and so on: in France for example in the early 1960s it was estimated that 80 per cent of business borrowers were servicing their loans at rates of interest below the market rate,[16] and one calculation for Britain suggests that about half of all private fixed capital formation in the country is effectively financed by the government.

(d) Technology. The role of advanced capitalist states in the development of technology is well documented: the Department of Defence is estimated to finance over half of all R&D done in the US, with figures up to 90 per cent for the aviation and spacecraft industries, and 85 per cent for electronics, for all government R&D financing. Governments have also been active importers of foreign technology: the French government introduced new industrial processes from abroad by the import of machines and skilled labour in the 17th century, as did the Japanese in the early period of their industrial revolution. The state's pronounced role in the development of new technology rests on four factors: (i) technological research and development involves high risk; (ii) it is subject to economies of scale; (iii) it is by its nature closely connected to academic institutions, which have been public and financed by the state; (iv) technology has always been closely bound to the military which in turn is almost always controlled and financed by the state; indeed it would be strange to find new military technology whose development was not considerably funded by a state.[17]

(e) Economic infrastructure, particularly energy and communications. These sectors are distinguished not only by their being 'natural monopolies' but by being inputs common to almost all productive activity: there is accordingly a particularly clear interest in the presence of cheap, secure supplies of these services. In Risorgimento Italy, the first years of the new state were characterized by a frantic burst of railway building by the government, and although the new system was sold to private capital in 1865 the financial vicissitudes of the latter caused the government to return and by 1905 control the bulk of the system. In Germany, too, the railways were increasingly a state system after 1871, with notably low rates, while in Japan

16. ibid., p. 86.
17. The relationship of the state to the development of technology in modern capitalism is extensively discussed in an unpublished work by Sergio Barrio and John Rickliffs.

in the decade after 1868 it was the state which built and operated railways and telegraph systems, opened coal mines and established agricultural experimental stations. The public control of these utilities in contemporary Western Europe, and the system of regulation in the United States is well known: what should be emphasized of course is their controlled rates to industry – controls which are in the process of being given their ideological rationale in the form of the theory of marginal cost pricing.[18]

(f) General manufactured inputs. These comprise those manufactured products with the strongest forward linkages for the economy in general, or for a key sector in the economy. They tend to be less general than the utilities discussed above, and are less directly controlled by the state though often regulated. Steel is a prime example, publicly owned in Britain, Austria, and to a lesser extent in Italy. Austria has nationalized a variety of electrical and engineering firms. In Italy I R I plays an important, though minority role in the cement industry. The Japanese government, in the same period as it set up public utilities, also established iron foundries, shipyards, machine shops and model factories to manufacture cement, paper and glass.

5. *Intervention for social consensus.* Here the public function is concerned to mollify the most manifest disruptive effects on and exploitation of non-capitalist classes. It covers:

(a) Prevention of public external diseconomies such as pollution, the degradation of land- and townscape, or wide regional disparities.

(b) Regulation of conditions of work, including the enforcement of industrial safety, the limitation of working hours, and some wage-setting such as minimum wages or equal pay for women.

(c) Regulation of conditions of sale, as in the Swedish state consumer protection system, trade description laws, or the nationalization of pubs in Carlisle by Lloyd George to control drinking by munitions workers at Gretna.

(d) Certain aspects of social security, notably unemployment provisions.

(e) Ideological functions *vis-à-vis* the productive system, carried out not only by the more general cultural institutions such as the education system and the communications media, but by specific institutions like the Prices and Incomes Board.

6. *Management of the external relations of a capitalist system.* No capitalist system is closed. The organization of the relations of this system with foreign systems, both within and outside the domestic territory of the system has been a prime function of states at all stages of capitalist development. One part of this function is aggressive: the support of the state's own capitalists in their expansion into foreign economic and territorial space. It involves the

18. A brief discussion of the Italian and German experiences is contained in Kemp (1969). For the use of I R I to hold down prices in Italy, see Shonfield (1965), p. 186.

attack on monopolistic walls which discriminate against domestic capitalists, such as tariff barriers, exchange controls, discriminatory taxation, unfavourable purchasing policies by foreign monopolists or states. It also involves the support of domestic capitalists in competitive foreign markets, and the attempt not merely to reduce foreign discrimination but build up monopolistic positions for domestic capitalists abroad.

A second part of the function is defensive, and consists in defending quasi-monopolistic positions established by domestic capitalists relative to foreign capital. It involves the maintenance of discriminations against foreign capital, tariffs, exchange control, purchasing tied to domestic capital: the maintenance of preferential trading areas and monetary zones favourable to the domestic capital: the restriction of the carriage of goods abroad to national ships or airlines: and the maintenance of the property rights of nationals overseas.

The instruments used in the performance of these functions are:

(i) Military power, whether defensively against a foreign force, or aggressively in terms of punitive expeditions or of more permanent annexations. The defensive use of force has usually been over the challenge to property rights, not only in domestic territory but the nationalization of property overseas: we have already mentioned fishing as a less publicized area where military power is common, and it is interesting to note that over and above the defence of fishery limits, the British government sent a gunboat to support British trawlers during the Icelandic fishing dispute from 1958–61, asserting in this case a right to what it as a state regarded as common property.

(ii) Aid, or foreign public assistance, which is used in two forms. First, it lends support to national firms engaged in foreign competition through lowering costs (either by direct subsidization as in the case of French fine linen exports in the 18th century, or through export credit and foreign investment guarantee programmes such as those provided by the FCIA, the Export-Import Bank and AID in the United States) and/or by tying markets (AID financing tied to US exports now accounts for 85–90 per cent of total AID financing, while a total of 4 per cent of all US exports are now financed by direct loans to the purchaser from the US government). Second, the threat of withdrawing an established aid flow or withholding a new aid flow acts as a protection to the property rights of domestic firms in the foreign country, as well as an inducement to the receiving country to lower discriminations against the donor's capital: the effect of the Hickenlooper amendment on recipients of US aid lies as much in the threat as in the execution.[19]

19. I have discussed the subject of aid as an overseas extension of state functions *vis-à-vis* its private capital in Murray (1969).

(iii) Commercial sanctions, in the form of trade boycotts (South Africa, Rhodesia, newly independent Guinea, the Middle East, Cuba, North Vietnam, China), quotas, or tariff changes.

(iv) Financial sanctions in terms of the blocking of funds (the post-war history of the US film industry in Britain presents an interesting example where, following the imposition of a 75 per cent customs duty by the UK and a subsequent 8 month boycott of Britain by the US cinema industry, an agreement was reached that no more than $17 million of US film earnings in the UK would be allowed to be repatriated: these controls lasted until 1961), or the establishment of exchange premiums.

(v) Government controls within domestic territory, such as the reserving of certain sectors for domestic industry, the prevention of particular take-overs, discriminatory buying policies and so on.[20]

Over and above the function of partiality to domestic capital *vis-à-vis* foreign competitors, whether this partiality is offensive or defensive, the state has the second function of coordinating or orchestrating domestic–foreign economic relations in the form of supervising the Balance of Payments. We will have cause to discuss the contradictions that exist between these two functions in dominated states in the third part of the paper.

These six functions seem to me the primary functions of a capitalist state: the guaranteeing of property rights; economic liberalization; economic orchestration; input provision; intervention for social consensus; and the management of the external relations of a capitalist system. Five further functions suggest themselves.

(i) The role of the state in securing demand in the form of mass purchases from the private sector on long-term contract: private capital is here acting as quasi-agent for the state, and this character is made explicit in the management contracts concluded by firms like Booker Brothers and ENI with the governments of underdeveloped countries;

(ii) The state as a taxation authority, a function whose importance is particularly evident in the development of capitalist economies;

(iii) The state as the enforcer and protector of particular monopolies *within* a capitalist system;

(iv) The state as a provider of first aid to ailing sectors and firms: we have mentioned above the relationship of the Italian state to its railways in the 19th century; the salvaging of four major banks by the Weimar Republic in 1931 and their return to private owners in 1937 when they were assured of good profits is a further instance;

(v) The state as an absorber of surplus: a point emphasized by Baran and Sweezy (1968).

20. The mechanics of neo-colonialism are more fully discussed in a number of places: see, for example, the *May Day Manifesto*, Penguin, 1968.

I have not included these among the primary functions since they all follow from those we have included. Thus to take the question of 'first aid', it is notable that such action has been principally directed either towards those sectors producing general inputs or to those sectors which are important in foreign relations, whether in the field of exports, invisible earnings or military power. If we look at those industries which have been nationalized in the advanced capitalist countries – a solution almost always accompanied by the ultimate in first aid, namely handsome compensation – these are most commonly in the sectors providing basic inputs; there are a few in the export sector (Ireland has a number of public manufacturing concerns in this category); and almost none in the sector producing manufactured goods for final consumption (the public interests were in Renault and Volkswagen an exception, born from particular circumstances). First aid, in the form of subsidies, restructuring, and credits to particular firms, follows this pattern. I have therefore treated it as a secondary function deriving from the provision of basic inputs and the management of external relations. I would argue that the other functions are secondary in a similar manner.

## Determinants of variation

The point about the primary functions is that they are found in some form at all stages of capitalist development, though the degree to which they are carried out by public bodies as well as the type of public bodies which carry them out will vary. Among the factors causing such variation we may distinguish five:

(i) The degree of international competition or, to put it more strongly, critical rivalry. This is perhaps strongest in wartime and the penumbra of preparation and recovery that surrounds war: such periods feature heavily in public activity in all of the functions. But similarly the developing industries in early periods of industrialization tend to face critical external competition, as List emphasized; Japan, Germany and Italy all exemplified the principle of strong government direction of the early days of their national systems of political economy. Currently it is notable how sharp an increase in public activity followed the return to convertibility of Western economies in 1958.[21]

(ii) The stage of capitalist development, for the increase in the division of labour within a system, the increase in mutual interdependence, heightens

21. This last point is emphasized in Kidron (1968). On the more general issue, List argued in the 1840s that Britain's argument for *laissez faire* and the relegation of the economic role of the state was itself merely the use of the state to support the already well-established British private interests. Robinson (1966) makes the point succinctly in her inaugural lecture when she says that 'It seems after all that the free-trade doctrine is just a more subtle form of mercantilism. It is believed in only by those who will gain an advantage from it.'

the vulnerability of the system to the failure of particular parts of the system.

(iii) The strength of the labour movement, since a strong movement will win concessions in the form of greater public activity in the field of measures aimed at social consensus; further, by raising the cost of labour, a strong labour movement may (a) weaken the capital's competitive position *vis-à-vis* foreign capital; (b) lower the rate of profit to critical levels in sectors producing general inputs.

(iv) The traditional ideology with respect to the role to be played by government.

(v) The degree of centralization of capital within the economy.

This last point is important, for it should be re-emphasized that the functions we have called public are not universally exercised by government or public bodies. They may be performed by the private firms themselves. For these functions arise from what can be described as external economies: whether they be Marshallian as in the case of fish conservation or specialized labour provision, i.e. where they are external to the firm but internal to the industry; or economies which are external to the firm and industry but internal to the productive system, such as the provision of basic inputs and the establishment of the necessary conditions for free exchange; or, finally, where they are external to the firm, the industry and the productive system, but internal to the society.

The fact that such external economies exist does not mean that single firms will not themselves undertake the function. Many firms have their own police force: the East India Company had its own army; US corporations are currently engaged in cutting down their own pollution of the atmosphere because of their fear that such external diseconomies will harm their company image. Firms build their own roads, railways, generating plants; they run their own training schemes, and welfare systems. The point is rather that these are all activities which it may be relatively costly for the firm itself to undertake. Where there are indivisibilities, as in the basic utilities, it will clearly cost less to spread fixed costs over many firms. Where it is difficult for a firm to privatize the output from its investment, as in the case of labour training and some kinds of research, the firm will clearly prefer the investment to be shared by those who benefit. Where there is high risk, a firm will clearly prefer a large body which is more indifferent to risk to finance the project. Private capital is also invariably reluctant to be seen to be the organizers of armed forces and police.

In underdeveloped countries, where a firm, or small group of firms, *are* the economy, these functions often are performed by the firms themselves, though they will always attempt to obtain contributions from others who benefit from their investment. But within the developed economies themselves, the size of the major firms means that some of the external economies are becoming internal, and that, in the field of communications in particular, firms are providing some of their own services. The British Steel Corporation owns the largest private air fleet in Britain. Fords Europe have the largest internal telephone system in Europe. AT&T have an internal communications system which gives them decisive competitive advantages.

Thus, though the public functions we have discussed are latently public by their nature, the degree to which they are exercised by public authorities will not be constant.

This section has been concerned with the role of the state in capitalism treated as an economic space. The next section will treat of the relationship of state and capital in territorial space.

## 2 State and capital in territorial space

The socialization of production under capitalism, the widening division of labour and interdependence between capitals, have a territorial as well as an economic dimension. As Mandel (1968) puts it, 'in place of the fragmentation of patriarchal, slave-owning or feudal society into thousands of tiny cells, each one independent of every other, with only rudimentary links (particularly exchange links) between them, there has come the worldwide relationship between men'.[22] Capitalist systems developed in territorially identifiable areas, often in areas which had already been made identifiable by pre-capitalist states. During the national period of capitalisms, the roots of both private capitals and the states which performed the public functions we have described above were territorially coincident and predominantly exclusive. Both capitals and states extended beyond their own boundaries; we have already noted that, from the first, capitalist systems have an international dimension. But the bulk of their activities covered the same geographical space.

When any capital extends beyond its national boundaries, the historical link that binds it to its particular domestic state no longer *necessarily* holds. A capital which has extended itself in this way will require the performance of the primary public functions for its extended operations. But the body which performs them need not be the same as the body that performs them within the area of the capital's early development. The domestic state may perform the public functions abroad for its own national capital. A national state body is not territorially limited in its range of activity, even though it may be territorially identified over an exclusive area. But the geographic coincidence of the economic ranges of an extended capital with its domestic state must be empirically established and cannot be assumed.

We can identify five possible executors of the state functions for the overseas operations of an extended capital:

22. Mandel (1968), p. 170.

(i) As we have already mentioned, the domestic state may perform these functions directly, which for the majority of the functions will involve the extension of the state's own boundaries through annexation. Since this involves an extension of the national *defendenda*, a considerable cost, and usually a problem, to say the least, in the performance of the function of ensuring social consensus in the foreign territory, the geographic expansion of the domestic state is a method less preferred from a capitalist point of view for fulfilling the state functions overseas. It will be supported when alternative systems are economically or politically impossible.

(ii) The arrangement that foreign state structures should perform them. Such an arrangement may be made by the capital itself or its domestic state, either through persuasion, pressure or intrigue. The foreign state becomes in effect a macro-political agent. It is an arrangement which forms the basis for any conception of economic neo-colonialism: though the existence and degree of neo-colonialism will depend on the extent of the concessions to the foreign state to induce it to perform the functions in question.

The guaranteeing of the property rights of the extended firm, and the prevention of major discriminations by the foreign state against it are backed by the type of negative sanctions outlined above in the section on the management of external relations. The provision of basic inputs, as well as the establishment of organizational structures to carry out the normal business of a capitalistic state (police forces, mass media, tax authorities, economic 'orchestrators') are on the other hand often directly funded. In underdeveloped countries, economic services for a particular area may be financed, planned and technically supervised by the public authorities and private contractors of the domestic state *after* an exploitable resource has been discovered by one of its capitalists abroad. If one looks at foreign extractive firms operating in Africa, for example, they have almost without exception got finance for necessary infrastructure from their domestic governments or international agencies – though this finance is channelled through the host government.[23] The establishment of organizational structures may again involve seconded nationals from the home country directly fulfilling the function or the training of host nationals in domestic or host country institutions. One of the early actions of the Americans in Vietnam after 1954 was the dispatch of a Michigan State University Group to advise President Diem's brother Nhu on police organization. By 1956, 600 policemen had been trained, 12,000 civil guard or militia, and a scheme instituted to fingerprint the whole South Vietnamese population. This, like the financing of other organizational structures, would come under the heading of technical aid – though technical aid of course covers a wider field.

The performance of public functions by foreign agent states is accom-

23. Murray (1969).

plished, therefore, by a mixture of positive supplies channelled through the agent states, and negative threats and sanctions. It is not limited to underdeveloped countries: Marshall aid is in many ways parallel as far as Europe is concerned. What I would argue, and this relates to the point I made at the end of the sub-section on geographical expansion, is that neo-colonialism in its various degrees is the more normal way for a home state to ensure the fulfilment of state functions for its capital in weaker areas abroad, and that direct annexation is a departure from this norm. Annexation may result from a foreign state refusing to act as agent, from the absence of a foreign state capable of carrying out the functions, or from the lack of concern by the expanding capital for a consensus in the area in which it is operating. The relationship of colonialism to neo-colonialism has many other facets, but in one sense we could see the colonial period as a necessary stage for the establishment of neo-colonialism in those regions.

(iii) The extended capital may itself perform the functions, either singly or in conjunction with other capitals. We noted above examples of this in the field of policing and input provisions.[24] It also extends to the threat of negative sanctions on foreign states discriminating or nationalizing the firms in question; the international oil majors have exercised oligopolistic solidarity against national governments on a number of occasions – notably against Iran after the nationalization of Anglo-Iranian.[25] Non-ferrous metal corporations have exercised similar threats in the form of withdrawing key inputs or closing international markets.

(iv) Foreign states may already be performing or be willing to perform the functions of their own accord. Most advanced capitalist countries would extend protection of property rights, freedom of exchange, input provision, macro-orchestration and consensual intervention to foreign investors in their country. The major function which they may be reluctant to perform is that of partiality *vis-à-vis* other foreign interests, and impartiality in terms of their own domestic capital. Of course, many of the instruments used by a state to favour its own national capital, will also apply to foreign capitals who have invested within the national boundaries. This is true of tariff and monetary agreements, export credits, services of commercial branches of the country's embassies abroad and so on. Indeed it is often this ability to enjoy the monopolistic discriminations of foreign countries that induces a firm to invest abroad; US firms invest in Britain to service more cheaply

24. An interesting example of private policing on an international level is provided by the companies who own submarine cables. They have their own patrol vessels operating particularly in fishing areas with a view to enforcing what would be an otherwise virtually unenforceable international public agreement regarding the damage of cables.

25. For a useful discussion on operations of international oil companies, see Tanzer (1970).

their export markets in the Sterling Area or EFTA. There are instances, too, as with ICI in Argentina, where a firm negotiates a favourable discrimination from a foreign government as a condition for investing in the country. Smaller countries, such as Ireland, go even further than this by making general offers of monopolistic advantages to foreign investors which exceed those offered to their national capital. The one notable exception to this picture of discriminations operating in favour of foreign investors comes in the field of government purchasing: the reason is clear in the case of military contracts, but the UK government, for example, operates the principle more generally. It openly favoured British firms in the allocation of North Sea drilling blocks, while in the computer field IBM claim that they supply only 2 out of the 72 computers used by the government.[26] Yet even this unfavourable discrimination is *a priori* limited to countries which have national producers of the contracted products, which in the field of advanced technology tends to be few. The overall picture, therefore, is one of remarkably little discrimination against foreign capitals which invest in a host country; extended capital has been able to rely on host governments to fulfill the public functions certainly as far as the advanced capitalist countries in Europe are concerned.

(v) The final group of executors of state functions are existing state bodies in cooperation with each other. Instances of such cooperation can be found in the following fields:

(a) property protection (mutual investment guarantees, international policing, extradition treaties, military alliances).

(b) implementation of free exchange and standardization between countries. (Free trade areas, customs unions, common markets – which attach greater importance to standardization, monetary unions.)

(c) mutual orchestration – a function performed to some extent in the IMF, the OECD, and in the BIS by central bankers.

(d) provision of inputs; the cooperation arising for reasons of scale as in technological cooperation, or in the provision of power supplies, or because the service is trans-national such as the Tan Zam railway.

(e) the exploitation of international resources, as is the case in river development schemes, or the numerous international fish conservation agreements.

(f) supervision of mutual economic interests *vis-à-vis* other economic powers: OPEC and the meetings of the four major copper producing countries in the underdeveloped world are examples of this form of cooperation; multilateral aid agencies could also be seen in this light.

In contrast to the intranational public functions which we noted were fulfilled by foreign states, these cooperative agreements are aimed at trans-

26. Turner (1969), p. 29.

national functions. But many of them have been far from successful in fulfilling their aim: this is notably so in the field of inter-governmental technological cooperation, and in fishery regulations. Even where the co-operation has been more successful, the success is in most cases temporary: those involving international external economies (economies which are external to the nation but international to the capitalist world economy) particularly in the fields of free exchange and mutual orchestration, may be thought unlikely to survive a major international depression. The conditions for the establishment of a more permanent form of integrated cooperation, a *de facto* international state body, we will discuss in a moment.

*Forms of extending capital*

The line of argument up to this point has been that a national capital extending abroad will require the primary public functions we outlined in Section 1 to be performed: but that the performance need not be undertaken by the capital's home government. There is no necessary link between the extended capital and its home government in the extended area. The body or bodies which do perform the functions may differ according to whether the functions are to be undertaken *within* areas with already constituted capitalist states, *between* areas with already constituted capitalist states, or *within* areas without already constituted capitalist states. In each case the home government could perform the functions, but in each case there are alternatives; and there is also the possibility – a very real one which we have underplayed until now – that the contradictions of the international system will be such as to prevent the fulfilment of the functions at all. The outcome for any one extending capital will depend on the power of its domestic government, both economic and political, to 'follow' its own capital, on the territory of extension, and on the particular form taken by the extension. It is this last point about the form of extension which I now want to take up.

Extending capital is not homogeneous, even though many discussions of overseas investment and its implications treat it as such. More particularly, the interest of the capital in the types of public function to be performed, and the bodies to perform them, will differ according to the following factors:

(i) *The degree of productive centralization*, that is to say the degree to which foreign markets are served by output whose production and inputs supplies are concentrated in one country. Those companies with a high export to foreign sales ratio stand at one pole; those serving foreign markets from production and input provision in the market concerned stand at the other. Steel and parts of the electrical industry would stand nearer the first pole; service industries nearer the second. Clearly those with centralized production, with a high proportion of trade to decentralized production, will be most concerned with the establishment and maintenance of conditions of free international exchange. Productive centralization with high trade to foreign sales ratios is a characteristic of the early period of capitalist international expansion, and is reflected in the frequent international disputes over tariffs that occurred prior to this century.

The conflicting pressures relating to the international centralization of production – economies of scale tending towards centralization on the one hand, transport costs, tariff barriers, spare part and market servicing requirements tending towards decentralization on the other – leads commonly to *regional centralization of production*. This is true of consumer durables in particular, as well as other branded goods (Colgate-Palmolive or Mars products for example). South-East Asia may be served from Australia or Malaysia, Central America from Mexico, EFTA from Britain, and the EEC from Holland. Such companies will again have a primary interest in regional free trade.

(ii) *Stage of overseas company development.* Many companies have expanded abroad by what might be called an ink-blot strategy. They expand outwards from existing operations both territorially, and structurally. In consumer durables, for instance, one notes an expansion path which involves exporting through overseas agents, exporting through company marketing organizations, local assembly, local full production, then regional centralization of production or regional division of labour in production, and in some cases the development of an international division of labour in production.[27] Such expansion paths have been followed by some US companies in Europe in the post-war period, with a number now reaching the stage of productive centralization or regional division of labour within the EEC. It is instructive that by the end of 1968 there were over 800 European headquarters groups in Brussels, though it is the productive rather than organizational division of labour with which we are primarily concerned.[28] Thus the stage of company development will be one of the factors determining the degree of productive centralization or, an equally important point, the degree of *international division of labour in production.*

(iii) *Forms of international flow.* Certain firms are principally concerned with the international flow of information and personnel rather than goods. Many service industries have this characteristic: with decentralized production served by a centralized information and management system. Advertising, management consultancy, data processing, film production, hotel management, and department stores all exemplify the point. They may either work on a management contract (like many of the Hilton hotels), or raise capital in the local market on the strength of their international name

27. For a discussion of the ink-blot form of foreign expansion, see Aharoni (1966).
28. See Parkes (1969).

in order to fund local operations. The size of the overseas interests in the general field of management services, licencing, leasing, and so on can be gauged by the receipts of US companies of royalties and fees. In 1968 these totalled $1·18 billion, comprising $0·54 billion in the form of royalties, licence fees and rentals, and $0·64 billion in the form of management fees and service charges. These figures compare with total earnings of US direct investment abroad in the same year of $7 billion. The important feature of this type of international operation is that in general the movement of people and information is not subject to the same restrictions as the movement of goods: though they are subject to restrictions on the movement of capital. Be that as it may, firms such as those we have discussed may in general be presumed to be less concerned with international exchange restrictions than firms depending on the international movement of goods.

(iv) *Degree of dependence on state partiality.* Some companies by the nature of their operations depend more heavily on their domestic state for preferential aid. This is true of the contracting industry, of exporters to and investors in underdeveloped countries, and of firms whose sales may be predominantly in the home market but whose inputs they produce or buy from abroad. These firms will be concerned to see the maintenance of the strength of their domestic states in international markets.

(v) *The strength of foreign competition.* Where domestic states are incapable of providing preferential protection and aid to firms highly dependent on them either in domestic or foreign markets, there will be an interest among firms in this position to either transfer to stronger state structures or to encourage its own state structure to cooperate with others. There are few examples of the former move – Mars changed nationalities principally because of the rationalizing of its international operations by its founder – but in respect to the latter, European firms have evidently favoured intergovernmental European cooperation because they regard their domestic governments as inadequate in the field of protection.

We are now in a position to make an important distinction. There are some firms whose main concern with respect to their extended capital is the *intranational* performance of public functions. The current system of nation states may be largely adequate for a system, say, of decentralized production. For some indeed the current system shows positive advantages. We have noted already how some capitals have expanded abroad precisely in order to take advantage of other nations' sets of discriminations. We may add to this the fact that companies which are financially centralized internationally may in effect play off rival states against each other, locating where incentives are greatest either for production or profit retrieval. Given that the performance of public functions has to be paid for, such firms may minimize the costs (in terms of taxation) of the services they receive. The system of tax havens has given rise to what might almost be called flagless capitals, firms registered in Curaçao, Malta or Luxembourg operating internationally under public 'umbrellas financed by rival capitals. Thus even where there is extensive territorial non-coincidence between domestic states and their extended capitals, this does not imply that the system of atomistic nation states is outdated. The remark by the editors of *Monthly Review* that 'multinational corporations and nations are therefore fundamentally and irrevocably opposed to each other'[29] is not necessarily true.

In contrast, there are other firms whose interests lie, not only in their intranational performance of public functions for its extended capital, but in the *inter-national* performance of them as well. We noted the following types of capital to whom this applied:

(a) those principally engaged in servicing foreign markets by trade.

(b) those with regionally centralized production.

(c) those operating with an international or regional division of labour in production.

(d) those concerned with an international exchange of goods rather than information or labour.

(e) those whose domestic government gave insufficient partial support in the face of foreign competition.

Again, the fact these interests in favour of the international performance of state functions exist does not mean that the system of nation states cannot contain them.

### The political framework

A dominant state may perform them. States in cooperation may perform them. Or the interests in the current national-based system, that is to say the national bourgeoisies and those international firms discussed in the previous paragraphs, may be powerful enough to cause a disintegration in the system. Finally, those firms pressing for international coordination for defensive reasons may sacrifice their identity by merging or being taken over by capital from the dominant country. This spirit of submission is characteristic of leading firms in the countries of Southern Europe; they opt for being second in Rome rather than first in a village, when it comes to a question of their identity in the face of foreign competition. Greek capital's position on their country's proposed association with the EEC provided an interesting instance of this.

At the same time we have noted the difficulty of inter-governmental cooperation on certain central public functions, and the fragility of such cooperation in times of depression. Whether those capital interests in favour of consolidated state power for the performance of the international public

29. *Monthly Review*, November 1969, p. 12.

functions are stronger than those defending existing state forms is a question which can be answered only by examining their relative positions at a particular historical juncture.

If the capital is dominant, its own state may be unable to impose international coordination either directly or indirectly. If the capital is threatened, it may nevertheless feel itself strong enough to resist within a wider coordinated territory. Finally, we have noted above the difficulties of achieving such coordination through mutual cooperation between nation states, though forms of cooperation may constitute a stage in which the forces in favour of a unified international coordinated power are strengthened.

If we look at the economic origins of the Second Reich, for example, we note that the establishment of the customs union by Prussia in 1818 and its later extension as the Zollverein in 1834 appear to be the result of the need to raise revenue from customs duties plus a certain administrative convenience, rather than the response to an expanding capital seeking a wider area of discriminated protection. Thus the tariff on transit goods stood much higher in 1818 than the relatively low import duty. Yet the liberalization within the area furthered industrialization, encouraged the development of a bloc system of transport (Prussian landowners who had opposed railways accepted them in the 1840s) and, in Kemp's words, 'established vested interests in the further consolidation of this preliminary unity'.[30] Protective tariffs were heightened particularly on British pig iron and cotton yarn, weights and measures, commercial and civil law were all standardized, and mining rights were changed to make them more accessible to capitalist exploitation. By the end of the Franco-Prussian war, again to quote Kemp, 'the business middle class did not mind so much how unification was to be achieved, or under whose auspices, as long as they could depend upon stable and orderly government at home and backing for their enterprise abroad'.[31] International liberalization brought about through cooperation led to an internationalization of capital which then required a unified coordination of state powers covering the expanded territory.[32]

What I have wanted to suggest in this section is a framework for analysing the consequences for political organization of a territorial expansion of capital. I have intentionally depicted capital as politically opportunist; Germany exemplified the point but one could look equally well at the support that foreign firms have given to liberation movements in Africa. I have tried to outline the alternative forms of state organization which present themselves to such an opportunist capital, and the distinctions

30. Kemp (1969), p. 96.
31. ibid., p. 103.
32. See Parker (1970), and also Engels (1968).

within the body of extending capital which may be thought to lead to differing interests among them. I have not devoted much attention to the strength and interests of what one might call the stranded nation states in a period of internationalization. This is clearly important for any discussion of the continued critical rivalry between nation states in an era of expanding capitals. The next section will therefore turn to this in the context of some suggestions on the contemporary international economy in the light of the previous discussion.

## 3 Capital and state in the contemporary world economy

1. *Internationalization.* The period since 1950 has been characterized by a major increase in the internationalization of capitalist economies, in the form of trade, investment and finance capital. In terms of direct investment alone the OECD calculated that by the end of 1966 for DAC countries foreign investment totalled $90 billion, of which US firms accounted for $54·5 billion, and UK firms $16 billion. US direct investment abroad has now risen over five times its total in 1950. International trade has been growing, too, at an astonishing speed, while more recently we have seen the development of truly international private capital markets. In five years since 1963 the international bond market has grown by 900 per cent; by the end of 1968 $11·4 billion worth of bonds has been issued on the international capital market, 75 per cent of them Eurobonds ($8·6 billion); while on the short-term market it is now estimated that there are in the region of $35 billion worth of Eurodollar deposits as against a figure of $5 billion for 1963.

This process has led to the increasing importance of foreign economic territory for sales, profits and finance for major capitalist firms. Of the 100 largest US firms in the 1967 *Fortune* list, 62 had production facilities in 6 or more nations; for European firms the figures are only slightly smaller. Even more significantly, in 1965 81 US firms operating internationally had over 25 per cent of their sales or earnings derived from overseas operations, with 11 of them over 50 per cent and International Packers deriving as much as 96 per cent of their sales revenue from abroad.[33] On the financial side, US firms have in recent years funded about 40 per cent of their overseas operations from cash flows generated abroad, 35 per cent from external sources abroad, and 25 per cent from capital transfers from the US. This last figure was heavily reduced after the Johnson measures in 1968, being largely replaced by borrowings on the Eurodollar market. The monetary restrictions in the US domestic market have caused a considerable inflow of Eurodollars into the US in the form of transfers from US branch banks abroad to their head offices, with their peculiar form of international liability.

33. See Bruck and Lees (1968).

The important point about these developments is that, being concentrated for the most part in the markets of developed capitalist countries overseas, where intranational state functions are extensively performed, there is a growing territorial non-coincidence between extending capital and its domestic state.

2. *The demand for international state functions.* As suggested in Section 2, we should distinguish between those extended capitals concerned primarily with the performance of intranational state functions and those concerned with trans-frontier operations. In the latter category, firms who have expanded primarily as trading concerns, either by the nature of their business or the stage of the overseas development, have dominated the French, German, Italian and Japanese international expansions, though many are now moving to the next stage of local assembly or more extensive local marketing companies. Such firms, primarily concerned with trade rather than foreign production, had, we suggested, a strong interest in international liberalization while being still firmly bound to their domestic state. In the case of the European countries we have discussed, however, the domestic states have been gradually less able to afford the protection, either in home or foreign markets, that dominant European capital has required. The resulting change in attitude towards the operation of economic state powers away from the nation state has been most marked in certain advanced sectors of French industry.[34] Thus we find 'threatened' capitals expanding abroad at the same time as finding inadequate support from their domestic state, both factors which strengthen an interest in the performance of international state functions.

The second group of firms most concerned with the coordinated execution of international state functions are those who have developed an international division of labour in production, either regionally, as in the Common Market, EFTA, the Sterling Area, or North America, or internationally. The operation of an international division of labour has of course characterized those international firms engaged in extraction for some years, particularly the Anglo-Saxon ones. A number are nevertheless engaged in setting up more integrated international production processes: Pechiney-Ugine's expansion into Africa since the mid-50s being an excellent example of a more general trend. In the manufacturing field IBM is strongly integrated, producing specialized parts from nine main plants, outside the US. Fords, Chrysler and General Motors are all developing integrated production facilities in Western Europe, and the same is true in a number of trading areas in less developed countries where consumer goods manufacturers distributed specialized plants country by country as the result of

34. An interesting discussion of the effects of the opening up of the French economy is given by Balassa (1965).

or as a guard against local nationalism. Finally the preliminary results from the Harvard Business School Research Project on their investigations into the validity of the product cycle theory of trade suggests that this particular phasing of an international division of labour is not uncommon.[35]

The development of a widespread international integration of production within a firm is still in its early stages; but it is a clear trend, and it is significant that in the recent survey into the trade relations of US parents with their overseas affiliates, it was found that 51·8 per cent of the exports from the parent companies surveyed were channelled through foreign affiliates.[36]

Yet even those extending capitals which do not come into the two categories we have already discussed have an interest in the performance of inter-national state functions inasmuch as the economy in which they operate is affected by changes in the world economy. The fact that national interdependence has also grown rapidly is therefore of the first importance in any assessment of the interests of extending capital.

3. *National economic interdependence.* Another face to the internationalization of capital is the decreasing independence of national economies, and their vulnerability to changes in external economic conditions. This has, of course, been true for some time, as the inter-war depression showed, but the increase of trade, investment and finance capital flows have furthered the trend. The Common Market, for example, has both opened up and made more vulnerable the economies involved. The Germans swung from a current surplus in 1964 to large deficit in 1965; Italy, which had had a current deficit in 1963, swung to a large surplus in 1965. These swings reflected both the easing of restrictions on capital movements as well as increased trade. France, too, was decisively opened up, exporting 9 per cent of the GNP value of traded goods to countries outside France and the associated territories, and importing 12·7 per cent in 1953. By 1963 these figures were 17·5 per cent and 19·2 per cent, and had already profoundly affected the nature of French foreign economic policy.[37]

In the capital market, Eurodollars have created a market which provides what is effectively an international interest rate. Eurodollars are denominated in dollars, which cuts down the exchange risk, and they have a cost of transfer as low as an eighth of a per cent. In Altman's words:

Interest rates on deposits of all currencies that command a forward premium over the dollar tend to be lower by the amount of this premium than interest rates on Eurodollar deposits, while interest rates on deposits of all currencies that stand at a forward discount relative to the dollar tend to be higher by the amount of this discount than interest rates on Eurodollar deposits.

35. Vernon (1966), see also Hirsch (1967).
36. Bradshaw (1969).
37. Balassa (1965), p. 540.

Forward exchange rates, which had previously provided an international form of interest structure have become subsidiary to Eurodollar rates. National monetary systems have grown increasingly exposed.[38]

4. *Decreasing national powers.* Economic internationalization has opened economies and increased instability. At the same time the process has weakened the existing national state powers in their ability to control this instability. In the case of Eurodollars, national monetary policies in Europe have undoubtedly been weakened. First, the market provides a source of credit outside the control of national authorities. Second, as we have just seen, their character as international vehicle assets acts as a transmitter of changes in rate structures abroad into the home money market. Thirdly, they have undoubtedly eased the process of international speculation, with all that that entails for domestic monetary and financial policy. The influence on the US economy is less clear. Certainly it seems that it affects US monetary policy much less than the policies of other capitalist countries.

In addition to the corrosive effects of the international money market, international firms have a flexibility and mode of operations which further blunts traditional instruments of domestic economic management. This has been clear for some time in terms of foreign investment in underdeveloped countries. In many cases, such as the copper investment by Charter Consolidated in Mauretania, Keynesian instruments are fixed by long-term contract: tax rates, sources of funds, exchange rates, and so on. There is still little hard evidence for developed economies, however. What we do know derives from discussions with individual firms and the following points emerge:

(a) Firms operating with an international division of labour will commonly not alter the flows of goods and amounts produced in the country following a change in exchange rate, since production depends on an international market with inputs in a fixed proportion. The change in price of one input is unlikely to substantially affect the overall demand. This has certainly been true of I B M after the U K devaluation.

(b) The financial flexibility of international firms allows them to circumvent to some degree both exchange controls and the capital value effects of exchange rate changes. One channel for the movement of funds is by now well-known, that of international intra-company transfer pricing. The extent to which this is used varies: but certainly in the drug industry it extensively operates (as the Eli Lilly case revealed), as in the oil industry, in consumer durables, for bank charges and so on. But equally important are other ways of shifting funds: intra-company loans, leads and lags in trading payments, payments of fees and royalties to parent companies. Companies have the choice as to which country is most profitable for raising finance:

38. Altman (1960, 1965).

Philips make a practice for example of borrowing in weak currency areas, which indirectly further weakens the currency. When most currency changes by developed capitalist economies are capable of being foreseen, the fact that extensive hedging takes place is not at all surprising. Nevertheless, it contributes substantially to the instability of international exchange rates, as the operations of certain international firms in the German exchange crisis showed.

(c) Financial independence. The access to the international capital markets (of which international firms are major users from the information that is extant) and to their own sources of funds both within any operation or internationally, further dampens the effects of government monetary policies. In Australia, Brash found that US foreign investors were re-investing 60 per cent of their profits in the country, and drawing much of the remainder from intra-company loans. The organization of international finance is often the most centralized of all international firm operations.[39]

There is accordingly a tendency for the process of internationalization to increase the potential economic instability in the world economy at the same time as decreasing the power of national governments to control economic activity even within their own borders.[40]

5. *States and the Balance of Payments.* If national capitalist governments increasingly lack instruments to control international capital, their policies do nevertheless have an important effect: namely, to further weaken their own national capital. We see here an important contradiction in any era of internationalization. On the one hand the disruptive effects of foreign take-overs, the internal re-organization of domestic industry, and the social and economic policies resulting from the balance of payments difficulties of an economy in the process of being incorporated (Britain, France, Ireland) all call for a firmer marshalling of the national capital, and a more sustained defence of its interests. On the other, the policies followed to correct a balance of payments deficit are often such as to further weaken the national capital and increase the domination of foreign capital within the national economy.

The clearest case of this is Ireland, where national planning acknowledges the country's dependence on foreign capital by leaving capital inflows as the residual in the planning process. Balance of Payments forecasts are made on the basis of a target rate of growth, and deficits in that balance are intended to be filled by the inflow of foreign capital, at the same time as domestic capital is restricted by deflationary measures. Similar curbing of domestic economic activity at the same time as welcoming foreign investment for

39. Brash (1966), pp. 91–2.
40. For a more detailed discussion of this point in relation to Britain see Murray (1971).

balance of payments purposes has been a feature of British policy, and now, to some extent, of the French.

## 4 Conclusion

I have been concerned to sketch out a framework which would allow a more substantial approach to the problem of the effects of an internationalization of capital on existing political organizations. In doing so, I have tried to show the importance of analysing the *interests vis-à-vis* the performance of state economic functions of various extended capitals, as well as the *powers* of the capital's domestic state to support its capital. I suggested that there was no necessary link between a capital and its state in the area of extension, that capital was rather a political opportunist, and that existing states often suffered a decrease in their powers as a result of internationalization. Thus while states may by their nature remain structurally opposed in economic rivalry, their powers, in terms of the capital they represent and the ability to perform economic functions, will vary. Where these powers increase there need be no contradiction between a nation state and its extended capital. But weaker states in a period of internationalization come to suit the interests neither of their own beseiged capital nor of the foreign investor.

For any analysis of imperialism, the elaboration of the connections between not only states, but the states and their capitals seems to me a first priority. Only then will we be in a position to present more fully what one might call the territorial dialectics of capitalism.

*References*

AHARONI, Y. (1966), *The Foreign Investment Decision Process*, Harvard Graduate School of Business Administration.

ALTMAN, O. (1960), 'Foreign Markets for Dollars, Sterling and Other Currencies', *IMF Staff Papers*, December.

ALTMAN, O. (1965), 'Eurodollars: Some Further Comments', *IMF Staff Papers*, March.

BALASSA, B. (1962), *Theory of Economic Integration*, Allen & Unwin.

BALASSA, B. (1965), 'Whither French Planning', in *Quarterly Journal of Economics*, November.

BARAN, P. A., and SWEEZY, P. M. (1968), *Monopoly Capital*, Penguin.

BRADSHAW, M. T. (1969), 'US Exports to Foreign Affiliates of US Firms', *Survey of Current Business*, May.

BRASH, D. (1966), *American Investment in Australian Industry*, Canberra.

BRUCK, N. K., and LEES, F. A. (1968), *Foreign Investment, Capital Controls and the Balance of Payments*, New York University Graduate School of Business Administration, Institute of Finance, *The Bulletin*, no. 48–9, April.

BYÉ, M. (1958), 'Localisation de l'investissement et Communauté Économique Européenne', *Revue Économique*, March.

DOBB, M. (1963), *Studies in the Development of Capitalism*, Routledge, revised edition.

ENGELS, F. (1968), *The Role of Force in History* (ed. and with an introduction by Ernst Wangermann), Lawrence & Wishart.

ERBES, R. (1966), '*L'Integration économique internationale*, Paris.

HIRSCH, S. (1967), *Location of Industry and International Competitiveness*, Oxford University Press.

KEMP, T. (1967), *Theories of Imperialism*, Dobson.

KEMP, T. (1969), *Industrialization in Nineteenth Century Europe*, Longman.

KIDRON, M. (1968), *Western Capitalism Since the War*, Weidenfeld & Nicolson.

KINDLEBERGER, C. P. (1969), *American Business Abroad*, Yale.

LENIN, V. I. (1915), *The Collapse of the Second International*, in *Against Revisionism*, Moscow, 1966.

LENIN, V. I. (1917), *Imperialism, the Highest Stage of Capitalism*, Foreign Languages Publishing House, Moscow (1970 edn.).

MANDEL, E. (1968), *Marxist Economic Theory*, Merlin Press.

MARX, K, (1867), *Capital*, Moscow, 1970 edn.

MARX, K. (n.d.), *The Poverty of Philosophy*, Foreign Languages Publishing House. Moscow.

MILIBAND R. (1969), *The State in Capitalist Society*, Weidenfeld & Nicolson.

MURRAY, R. (1969), 'Aid and the International Firm', *May Day Manifesto Bulletin*, nos. 16–17, November.

MURRAY, R. (1971), 'The Internationalisation of Capital and the British Economy', *Spokesman*. April.

PARKER, D. (1970), '*Capitalist Growth and the Formation of the German State*', Paper to the Second Socialist Economists Conference, Cambridge, October.

PARKES, N. (1969), 'The Failure of the European Headquarters', *Harvard Business Review*, March–April.

POULANTZAS, N. (1968), *Pouvoir Politique et classes sociales*, Paris.

ROBINSON, J. (1966), *The New Mercantilism*, Cambridge University Press.

ROLFE, S. E. (1969), *The International Corporation in Perspective*, Atlantic Council, mimeo.

SHONFIELD, A. (1965), *Modern Capitalism*, Oxford University Press.

TANZER, M. (1970), *The Political Economy of International Oil and the Underdeveloped Countries*, M. T. Smith.

TROTSKY, L. (1930), *The Permanent Revolution* and *Results and Prospects*, Pathfinder Press (1969).

TURNER, L. (1969), *Politics and the Multinational Company*, Fabian Society.

VERNON, R. (1966), 'International Investment and International Trade in the Product Cycle', *Quarterly Journal of Economics*, May.

VERNON, R. (1968), 'Economic Sovereignty at Bay', *Foreign Affairs*, October.

# 6 Bill Warren

## How International is Capital?

Bill Warren, 'The Internationalization of Capital and the Nation State: A Comment', *New Left Review*, no. 68, July–August 1971, pp. 83–8.

The central thesis of Robin Murray's essay in *New Left Review*, no. 67, is to the effect that the post-war 'internationalization of capital'[1] has tended to weaken the (capitalist) nation State. His argument may be summarized as follows. Since the Second World War there has developed an increasing territorial divergence between the activities of nation-states and those of large international firms, which are becoming the economically dominant institution of the capitalist world. An analysis of the economic functions of the nation State shows, firstly, that these functions need not always be performed by a firm's 'own' nation State and are in fact being progressively less so performed; and, secondly, that the increasing operational divergence of international firm and nation State significantly weakens the State and reduces its ability to control the major firms and the economy in general.

It should be noted that the discussion of territorial non-coincidence suffers from the lack of any preliminary definition of an 'international firm', or indeed of 'international capital', or even of the 'internationalization of capital'. Unfortunately, even with the utmost philological goodwill, this cannot be dismissed as simply a terminological nicety, since the absence of such a definition leads Murray to treat as something new a phenomenon long characteristic of British imperialism; and permits the inclusion of the EEC as an aspect of the 'internationalization of capital' even though it clearly represents an *extension*, via cooperation, of the power of the nation-states concerned *vis-à-vis* the large firms.

The point about British imperialism is, of course, that no one ever doubted that, however 'internationally' imperialist firms operated, they were *British*[2] and their fortunes were in a sense the fortunes of the British economy. Murray seems from time to time to have an inkling that something is wrong somewhere as his international Jekyll becomes on occasion an American Hyde, but in the absence of prior definition the two are

1. Variously dated by Murray from 1904 and from 1950.
2. i.e. they were owned by British capitalists and their profits contributed to British national income and foreign exchange.

necessarily indistinguishable and the difference between 'national' and 'international' firms disappears.

Nevertheless, something new has happened, even if a non-definitional approach tends to obscure it, and this is that within the post-war advanced capitalist world, the firms of individual nations, especially in the US and the UK, have increasingly tended to locate *manufacturing* activities in other advanced capitalist countries. This is not, of course, a completely unprecedented phenomenon either.[3] But it is new on the scale it has assumed since the Second World War, even though *compared with total domestic sales or investment that of subsidiaries located abroad remains an extremely modest proportion*.[4] This is the appropriate comparison if one wishes to gauge the significance of this phenomenon for the nation State. The figures are, in fact, quite remarkably low. Thus the annual average rate for the years 1960–64 of direct investment abroad as a percentage of gross domestic capital formation was only 3·5 per cent for the US, 4·7 per cent for the UK, 3·3 per cent for the Netherlands, 0·7 per cent for France and 1 per cent for Germany.

Apart from this development of overseas manufactures, the creation of the Common Market must also evidently be accounted a new phenomenon.

Now the crucial aspect of both the frontier-crossing productive activities of manufacturing firms and the creation of the Common Market is that *both were in large part the direct and intended consequences of deliberate policies adopted by nation States*. The post-war liberalization of world trade and finance was the consequence of deliberate state policy,[5] and it is this liberalization which underlies the ability and incentive of firms to locate productive activity abroad to take advantage of variations in market size and growth, of levels of cost and differences in technology. Furthermore, the merger movement of recent years in most advanced capitalist countries, associated

3. For example, between 1870 and 1914 branch industrial factories were established by German firms in many countries. 'The great establishments (Allgemeine Elektrizitäts Gesellchaft, Siemens and Schuckert) had plants in Austria-Hungary, Russia, Italy, Spain, and elsewhere, to make and instal electrical equipment. Electrochemical works were established in Russia, Austria-Hungary, Spain, Sweden, Norway and Switzerland.' Feis (1930), p. 78.

4. UN (1967), p. 65. The figures given by Murray are extraordinarily vague. Thus we are told of firms with productive facilities in six or more nations (why not 4 or 8 or 15?) and 'sales revenue from abroad' with no indication of whether or not this includes export sales or just sales of subsidiaries. 'Even more significantly,' Murray goes on, 'in 1965 81 US firms operating internationally had over 25 per cent of their sales or earnings derived from overseas operations with 11 others over 50 per cent and International Packers deriving as much as 96 per cent of their sales revenue from abroad.' The significance of this statistic escapes the present writer since no information is given which would permit a quantitative assessment of the importance of these firms in the US economy.

5. Especially it was the result of the policy of the US State.

with the expanded competition of the liberalized world capitalist economy, has been very much *a product of national State policy*, Britain itself being a notable example. The idea of national States cowering before the Paul Chambers of this world is wholly fanciful: the reality is national states deliberately encouraging the creation of gigantic competitive units.

Another equally widespread and yet incorrect notion is that the Common Market was the product of the 'demand' of European capital for a more effective State than the existing nations. The Common Market originated as a political initiative, whose underlying reasons related not only to the economic but also to the diplomatic-strategic interests of France and Germany. Subsequent economic developments owed little to business pressure as such and have occurred mainly as a result of developments in the political and bureaucratic superstructure of the EEC, which has evolved policy in part-response to US economic dominance.

## State economic policy

There seems little historical perspective in Murray's treatment of the 'internationalization of capital'. But at least it is characterized as a post-war phenomenon. Not so with State economic policy. Six economic policy functions are identified which are to be 'found in some form at all stages of capitalist development' in any century from the 16th to the 20th – and indeed for any country from Japan to Iceland. Since internationalization of capital is a post-war phenomenon while the six primary State economic functions have always been there, the implication is that the former must have recently grown while the latter have remained stationary through the ages and that the former is accordingly weakening the latter. Murray's unhistorical approach and impressionistic classification[6] of State economic functions has here led him seriously astray. Throughout their comparatively short lives industrial capitalist societies have suffered a series of shocks – war, revolution, competitive decline, international depression and many more. Those problems were and are not solved of their own accord. Their solution involved the *steadily increasing* intervention of the State in economic life generally – especially the post-war adoption of Keynesian policies which have helped sustain high employment levels and growth rates throughout the capitalist world, together with the public promotion by the State of individual industries and firms for competitive purposes on a scale never

6. There appears to be no principle of classification separating one category of economic policy function from another, so that the elementary logical principle of making the different categories mutually exclusive of one another is not followed. Thus 'economic orchestration' (e.g. full employment policy) overlaps with 'intervention for social consensus', and 'economic liberalization' overlaps with 'management of the external relations of the system'.

before seen. For ideological-psychological reasons, sections of the ruling class inevitably attempt to reverse this interventionist trend, but this cannot be done except on a limited and temporary basis. Because the solution of each economic contradiction eventually raises new ones, driving the State further along the road of control, so eventually the disappearance of steep trade cycles and mass unemployment in the long run remorselessly exerts pressure for control of wages, prices and profits to deal with the inflation which is the consequence of Keynesianism.

Indeed we may pause here to remark in passing that there are a number of reasons to argue exactly the opposite thesis to Murray's, i.e. that the power of the nation State *vis-à-vis* the large firms is *greater* now than ever before (and increasing). This indeed is what one might expect with the growing size of firms, accompanied as it is by *the expansion of state economic activities*, since the smaller the number of firms in an industry and the larger their size, the easier for the state to control them by administrative fiat, monetary and taxation policy and so on. [7] A glance at some of Britain's principal industries shows the powerful role of State policy.[8] The ship-building, aircraft, British computer and atomic energy industries would not exist without State support, or at best would be reduced to a fraction of their present size. The present shape of the textile industry is the result of government rationalization. The financial losses and consequent threat to the very existence of the British steel industry are the results of government policy in holding down prices. Large sections of heavy engineering are crucially dependent on government orders for their profitability, e.g. from the Central Electricity Generating Board. The steadily deteriorating international competitive position of the British motor-car industry has been in large part the result of a home market continuously depressed by government policy *despite never-ending protests from the industry*. This last point is crucial since it illustrates the fact that, while the relationship between large firms and the State is a two-way one involving a degree of mutual accommodation, the upper hand will generally be that of the State since it must of necessity look to the interests of the system as a whole (however imperfectly),[9] and will therefore be able to act with authority *vis-à-vis* individual industries or firms,[10] provided it is felt to be in fact looking to the general (capitalist) interest.

7. Compare the ease of controlling the motor-car industry with the difficulties of tackling the machine-tool industry.

8. That is, in relation to the constituent firms of an industry. But that is not necessarily to say that State policy is necessarily successful – only that its power *vis-à-vis* that of the firms is large and growing.

9. While the individual firms look to their market shares subject to minimum profit constraints.

10. e.g. Kennedy over steel prices.

## 'Extending capital' and its status

Returning to the main line of the argument, Murray is, of course, correct in pointing out that 'extending capital' can have various public functions performed for it by institutions other than its domestic state, including the states of other territories in which it operates. However, this is not a new phenomenon and it does not imply a weakening of either of the states concerned,[11] or that 'there is no necessary link between the extended capital and its home government'. To argue that one or other of the states concerned in such a relationship is weakened by it is to ignore the fact that many of the public functions needed by the firm abroad are simply the same as those it needs at home,[12] while governments are just as likely to play firms off against one another as the reverse. Moreover, contrary to Murray's belief, there is always necessarily a link between the 'extended capital' and its home government by virtue of the inter-connections between national taxation systems, international (company) law and private appropriation of profits – with their ramifications into the balance of payments and growth rate of the domestic economy.

This is not to say that there are no contradictions between the capitalist state and private firms (of a non-antagonistic variety in general) or that such contradictions are always resolved in favour of national states. There are and always have been such contradictions throughout the history of capitalism, for obvious reasons related to the difference between the whole and the sum of its parts. Moreover, post-war international free trade and macro-economic control have undoubtedly created certain new problems for nation-state economic policy. However, two points should be noted. First these new problems principally relate either to excess aggregate expansion (balance of payments and exchange rate difficulties, inflation) or to declining relative international competitiveness, and are not therefore problems generated by greater independence of large firms *vis-à-vis* the State.[13]

11. Indeed, since the War most advanced capitalist states have welcomed direct investment from other advanced economies as a direct accession of economic strength to them, except in the case of certain strategic sectors. It is also important to remember that the two states concerned in an act of direct investment may actually derive *mutual* benefit by improving their relative position as compared with third parties.

12. Foreign direct investment may thus in certain circumstances *strengthen* a host state.

13. Moreover, insofar as the new problems essentially concern aggregative control they do not throw into doubt the ability of the State to maintain full employment except insofar as competitive decline and balance of payment deficits lead to a special and new kind of government-created 'structural' unemployment, which is itself in principle solvable by a capitalism more prepared to control trade, payments, incomes and prices directly, besides stimulating production and productivity. However, for various reasons, the British ruling class or its agents seem unlikely to be capable of the necessary creative response to their problems.

Secondly, insofar as international economic liberalization has given some extra room for manoeuvre to large firms, State authorities have rapidly been evolving counter-measures. Thus the financial press reports that the tax authorities are rapidly getting control of the internal transfer price problem and it is clearly not going to be long before the central bankers, international organizations and State policy-making bodies chain down the Euro-dollar monster so that it is no longer available to do the bidding of large firms.

## The position of national economies

The central paradox of the important problem Murray has posed is this. The increasing economic interdependence between economies, which Murray so rightly emphasizes, precisely because it *does* make for greater uncertainty and new problems of economic control, forces the national States to become ever *more* active in their internal economies and their external economic relations. The declining room for manoeuvre of national economies, determined by the exceptionally rapid expansion of trade[14] and financial flows which render their fortunes constantly more dependent upon one another, provokes an ever greater degree of manoeuvring by the respective national states in resistance to the narrowing of their policy options. This in turn means both an ever closer relationship between the State and the large firms (both domestic enterprises operating abroad and foreign enterprises operating domestically) and, *on the whole*, a strengthening of the national capitalist State in relation to the constituent firms of the economies concerned.

The alternative interpretation – that increasing economic interdependence tends to weaken the national capitalist State – is incapable of explaining the developing pattern of increasingly acute economic rivalry and related governmental conflict between the USA, Japan and Europe – as well as the lesser, but growing conflicts within Europe and including Britain. The danger of the thesis that 'the national state is weakening *vis-à-vis* international firms' is that it may lend credence to the reformist belief that the capitalist State could have interests different from the national capitalist economy and society as a whole and may thus have to be defended against the cosmopolitan monopolies.[15]

14. Considerably faster than the growth of national products.
15. This is not to deny the relative autonomy of the state without which indeed it could not effectively perform its class functions.

## References

FEIS, H. (1930), *Europe: The World's Banker, 1870–1914*, Kelley.
UN (1967), *Economic Bulletin for Europe*, November.

# Part Three
# Integration and Imperial Rivalries

This section broadens the terms of the debate in Part Two, and moves on to the analysis of concrete patterns in imperialism today. Ernest Mandel (Reading 7) discusses the development of the European Economic Community in relation to the internationalization of European and American capital as a move in the direction of a 'super-state' enclosing a large enough economic space for the current degree of socialization of productive forces to remain compatible with a market economy. He argues (in 1967, but it holds true equally in 1974) that there is still no solid community of capitalist interests, and thus the EEC is still only an uncertain coalition; he also draws certain conclusions for socialist strategy.

Bob Rowthorn (Reading 8) discusses the effect of internationalization on the degree of unity in the capitalist bloc as a whole. He takes the view that the strength of US capital has declined relative to European and Japanese capital, and that this has sharpened the divisions between the major capitalist powers; interpenetration of capitals in the form of international firms in no way reduces these rivalries at present.

# 7 Ernest Mandel

## International Capitalism and 'Supranationality'

E. Mandel, 'International Capitalism and "Supranationality"', in R. Miliband and J. Saville (eds.), *The Socialist Register 1967*, Merlin Press, 1967.

It has long been a commonplace that the development of productive forces has outgrown the framework of the national state on the European continent. International cartels and international holdings steadily extend their control over important parts of the European economy. German industry – to take the most obvious example – cannot survive within the boundaries of the traditional German state. It is in essence expansionist, whether this expansionism takes the violent, military conquering road towards the East, as it did during the First and Second World Wars, or whether it takes the 'peaceful' commercial conquering path towards the West that it 'chose' after the Second World War, as a result of the changed political and military relationship of forces on the Continent. In this sense, one may say that the movement towards Western European economic integration *via* the Common Market is a product of capitalist concentration on an international scale: an attempt by capitalism to reconcile the level of development of the productive forces and the degree of monopolistic concentration with the survival of the national state. By creating a larger area in which commodities, capital and labour circulate freely, it thereby releases industry from at least part of the fetters which Malthusian cartels, tariff walls and short-sighted economic nationalism had imposed upon it in the inter-war years.

But the Common Market is not only a product of capital concentration; it is also the motor for a new phase in capital concentration on the Continent and beyond. Most of the large-scale Western European enterprises cater mainly for their national market; their export quota rarely exceeds 35 per cent. There are, of course, a few exceptions like the Belgian and Luxembourg steel industry or the Philips trust in Holland. But the rule generally applies to the main branches of manufacturing production, including the large machine-building and durable consumer goods sectors.

During the ten years of rapid economic expansion in Western Europe beginning with the Korean war boom, the problem of the relative size of the producing units did not really arise. The general tempo of expansion was such that there was a seller's market. Demand rose generally more quickly than supply: there was no severe cut-throat competition. Thus, the first phase of the Common Market, between 1958 and 1962, witnessed neither a strong process of concentration, nor a quick expansion of restrictionist cartels. It is true that employers' associations covered all industrial branches with cartel-like trade-associations,[1] but given the prevailing economic conditions, they were not obliged to take any measures of market apportioning or of restriction of production.

The year 1962 seems to have been the dividing line between this first phase of general euphoria and the next phase in the development of the Common Market, when problems started to arise. During the previous general boom, productive capacities had clearly outgrown effective demand in a whole series of key sectors, as we indicated in 1964.[2] Overcapacity started to appear and competition became fiercer. Rationalization and concentration therefore quickened their pace. And the logical direction which capitalist concentration took was towards the setting up of companies and units of production adapted not to the dimensions of any national market, but to the dimensions of the Common Market as such.

### Three forms of capital concentration

Three forms of capital concentration were theoretically possible, and all three have actually begun to occur in the Common Market.

The first of these is the fusion of existing national enterprises, the most spectacular of which so far has been the merger of the two top chemical trusts in Italy, *Edison* and *Montecatini*; the merger between two important French chemical trusts *Kuhlmann* and *Ugine*; the agreement of close co-operation between the two main West-German automobile trusts: *Volkswagen* and *Daimler-Benz*.

Secondly the fusion (or in most cases, one should more accurately say the absorption) of national companies in various Common Market countries, by large American companies: absorption of *Machines Bull* and *Olivetti* by *General Electric;* the recently announced, but not yet confirmed, purchase of the controlling interests of the Agnelli family in the giant *FIAT* works by the USA trust *General Motors*.

Thirdly, the fusion of national companies of the various Common Market countries into new units in which national capital is no longer predominant, but in which capital is now more or less equally dispersed over two, three or more Common Market countries (in a few cases even more

1. During the first years of the Common Market, trade associations and amalgamations on a Common Market level were established on an average of about one thousand a year. A Directory listing all employers' associations and trade associations created in the Common Market since 1958 covers 513 pages. Bilateral exclusive trade agreements between different firms inside the Common Market have been declared in 36,000 cases.

2. Mandel (1964), pp. 64–5.

Western European countries, with British, Swiss, Swedish and even Spanish capital participation). The most significant examples in this field have been the merger between the two most important trusts of photographic equipment and material on the Continent, the Belgian trust *Gevaert* and the West German trust *AGFA*; the merger between the Dutch steel trust *Hoogovens Ijmuiden* and the German steel trusts *Dortmund Hörder-Hütten-Union* and *Hoesch*; the merger between the French financial group *Schneider* and the Belgian financial group *Empain*; the agreement of close collaboration between the largest French chemical trust *Rhône-Poulenc* and the German trust *Bayer*; and so on.

The emergence of American capital within the walls of the Common Market, whether in the form of new direct subsidiaries of US companies, or through merger with or absorption of existing European units, always represents, in the last analysis, a means whereby part of the European market is taken away from European capital (except for the introduction of new products into that market, and then only to the extent that these do not automatically reduce the market for existing European products). It is unrealistic to assume that European capital will not react and defend itself against this process. Inasmuch as we are confronted here with a *process of intensification of international capitalist competition*, the amalgamation of European and American companies, in 99 cases out of 100, means in reality *a defeat* of European capital as a result of that competition. One cannot reasonably assume that European capitalists will accept their defeat as inevitable, and that they will not at least try to avert it. On the other hand, there are three reasons why the movement of financial and industrial amalgamation cannot take the form mainly of the merger of existing national companies or units, but will rather be the establishment of new companies and units based upon an *international interpenetration of capital*. In the first place, in certain industries, the amount of capital outlays and the risk of technological obsolescence before the invested capital has been depreciated – not to say before it has been valorized – are such that further developments in these branches become impossible on a national scale. Two striking examples are offered by the aircraft industry, which can only continue to keep abreast of the technical possibilities by embarking upon joint Anglo-French ventures (Concorde, for instance), and by the space industry, where the only realistic project, ELDO, depends upon a collaboration between all European capitalist powers. Already, the development of the nuclear industry has been proved impossible on a private enterprise basis; without state initiative and state financing, there would have been no nuclear industry in the West. Now the aircraft and space industries have offered further striking proofs of the old Marxist *dictum* that in our epoch the productive forces have obviously outgrown both the boundaries of private property and of the national state. In the second place, the problem of more vigorous international competition, especially of competition between North American and Western European industry, imposes upon European capitalism a furious pace of technological innovation, which the traditional national finance groups cannot maintain. Outlays and risks become so great that one mistaken decision might swallow up the whole of the reserves of some of the main holding companies or investment banks. The principle of spreading risks and reducing overhead costs logically leads towards the idea of international amalgamation: a trend which is facilitated by the habits of common consultation on all major problems facing each particular industry – habits which became firmly established in the early years of the Common Market. Thirdly, and again in order to keep pace with the giant North American monopolies, it becomes necessary to create financial and productive units inside the Common Market of such dimensions that they obviously are beyond the reach of any national trust. In the field of international competition, US capitalism still enjoys tremendous benefits from economies of scale. To neutralize these advantages, it will be necessary for the main Common Market companies and producing units to double or treble their size within a few years' time. Again, international amalgamation is here the obvious answer.

### National and 'supranational' state power

Formally, if one looks at the letter of the Rome Treaty, the Common Market is a free trade area surrounded by a common external tariff. The historical precedent which comes to mind is that of the German *Zollverein* of 1867 which had also its peculiar, indirectly elected Parliament and which became the last stage towards the constitution of a united German *Reich*. By itself, the Common Market is nothing but a means of facilitating trade expansion, and its impact on the national economies of the six member countries has still not yet outgrown these limits. Neither the price level nor the general trends of economic development, nor the location of industry, have been in any way decisively reshaped by the appearance of the Common Market institutions. But with the growth of international interpenetration of capital within the six member countries, new and formidable forces are at work which could completely modify that situation; and it is necessary to indicate the qualitative changes which will occur as a result of a breakthrough in international capital concentration in two important fields.

The State is viewed today as the main instrument of power of the bourgeois class, not only in defence of private property against the working classes, but also in an attempt to guarantee monopoly profits against the threats of severe economic crises. As long as the capital invested in the industry of a country is mainly national, the State is essentially the instrument of the native capitalist class. Whenever the capital invested in a country is mainly foreign, we are faced with a semi-colonial country, where the State to a large extent defends the interests of the foreign investors. But what would be the situation if the most important factories and banks of the six Common Market countries were owned neither by national nor by foreign capitalists, but by an amalgamation of the capitalists from the six countries? Obviously, from the point of view of bourgeois rationality, the State should then become the instrument of those capitalists taken together. But would it be possible to defend efficiently the interests of the amalgamated Germano-Franco-Italo-Belgo-Dutch capitalists within the framework of, say, the Italian or the Dutch state? Obviously not. To put the matter plainly: a recession threatening to grow into a severe crisis in the six countries could not be met by monetary, fiscal or economic policy measures of the Italian and the Dutch government alone. It could be met only – inasmuch as world economic conditions would still make such a temporary solution possible – by *common* monetary, fiscal and economic policies of all the six countries together. In other words: *the growth of capital interpenetration inside the Common Market, the appearance of large amalgamated banking and industrial units which are not mainly the property of any national capitalist class, represent the material infra-structure for the emergence of supranational state-power organs in the Common Market*. The larger the growth of capital interpenetration, the stronger the pull for transferring certain given powers from the national states of the six countries towards the Common Market supranational units. On the other hand, the more that commodities, capital and labour circulate freely among the Common Market countries, the more a tendency to locate industries as close as possible to the main group of consumers (or to ports from where the exported production is shipped overseas) will impose itself upon the large capitalist firms. This gives a predominant weight to the industrial heart of the Common Market: an area roughly identifiable with the triangle Paris-Amsterdam-Dortmund. Big shifts in location could occur as a result of this tendency, combined with moves determined by technological changes or modification in the source of raw materials (as for example the present trend towards establishing the steel industry near the sea). The big German chemical trust *Badische Anilin* has announced its intention of transferring its main plant and the firm's main offices from Ludwigshafen to Antwerp, where world chemical trusts are now building large plants catering for the needs of the Common Market countries. Similarly, the steel barons of the Ruhr are toying with the idea of a massive transfer of the West German steel industry to the Dutch seashore.

How far has international capital concentration advanced in the Common Market?

A question immediately arises: how strong is this movement of international capital interpenetration within the boundaries of the Common Market? What point has it reached today? The answer is, of course, that it is only in its inception, and that its results have so far only been marginal upon the global socio-economic situation in the Common Market countries. Undoubtedly today, the main plants and banks of the five main countries of the Common Market are still predominantly national.[3] Statistical data are notoriously inadequate in this field. But from a French government publication we learn that during the last few years, foreign investment has been less than 10 per cent of current investment in plant and equipment of French industry. As for Western Germany – where foreign capital is most concentrated, as a result of military defeat and occupation – the *Deutsche Bundesbank* estimates that at the end of 1964, total foreign capital investment in German firms amounted to nearly 3,000 million dollars, representing a little more than 15 per cent of total capital invested in that country. The percentage was much higher in the automobile, the petroleum and the electronics equipment industries. Roughly 60 per cent of these foreign investments were American and 25 per cent belonged to Common Market countries. At the same time, the movement towards international amalgamation of financial, industrial and commercial companies has started, and is today gaining momentum, for the reasons indicated above, which are linked with the trends both of neo-capitalist expansions and of neo-capitalist recessions.[4] A striking example is the creation of an international finance group[5] which dominates the leasing of industrial equipment to individual firms (a relatively new technique) in the whole of Western Europe. Another example is the creation of a common export company by eight European chemical trusts, three of which are French, three German, one Italian and one Belgian.

The longer the present stage of intensified competition and isolated national recessions in the Common Market countries lasts – France and

3. With the exception of course, of Luxembourg, whose economy is dominated by the ARBED steel trust, in which French and Belgian capital occupy a larger place than Luxembourg capital.

4. Mandel (1964).

5. *Interlease*, created by the Belgian *Banque de Bruxelles*, the French *Banque d'Indochine*, a West German and a Dutch bank, the Italian *Banca Commerciale Italiana*, the Spanish *Banco Español de Crédito*, and the British merchant bank of *Hambro Bros.* Other European ventures undertaken in common by finance capital of different nationalities are, to give just two examples, the *Syndicat Éuropeén d'Études et de Financement* created by six banks from five different countries and the trust *Euro-Finance* created by the Belgian *Société Générale*, the West German *Deutsche Bank*, the Italian *Banca Commerciale Italiana*, the Swiss *Crédit Suisse* and a Dutch bank.

Italy went through such a recession for most of 1964 and the beginning of 1965: Germany, Holland and Belgium are experiencing them at this moment – the stronger will be the momentum towards an inter-nation concentration of capital within the six countries. When a general recession breaks out in all the six countries (and this seems to us inevitable), the 'moment of truth' for the Common Market will arrive. It will either be pulled apart by the forces of 'national self-defence' of the respective national bourgeois classes, which will imply at least some forms of relapse into economic nationalism, protectionism, etc., or it will be pushed forward towards anti-recession measures on a Common Market scale, in which case the supranational institutions will take over some of the main monetary and fiscal functions from national states. *A single Common Market currency and a single Common Market taxation system would thereby be unavoidable. Their appearance would be a decisive proof of the fact that, in the eyes of the leading groups of the Western European bourgeoisie, supranational state power had become a more efficient anti-recession instrument than the national state.* The struggle between these two tendencies will be decided by the relative strength of the bourgeois forces interested in or opposed to international capital amalgamation *at the particular moment of time.* For that reason, it is impossible to make concrete predictions today as to the outcome of that struggle. Neither is it prudent to state today that the Common Market has become irreversible. *The main test will be a general recession in Western Europe.* Until this happens, it is too early to decide which of these tendencies will ultimately prevail. During the French and Italian recession of 1964, certain measures taken were of a typically protectionist character (e.g. in favour of the Italian automobile and of the French refrigerator industry). These measures did not cause a grave crisis in the Common Market only because they were *partial* measures coping with a *partial* recession. In the case of a general recession, it is very hard to vizualize a general reversal towards protectionist measures which would not involve a disintegration of the Common Market.

The general crisis of the steel industry in which the Common Market countries are involved is a good indication of the kind of tensions which a general recession would quickly build up inside the Common Market. Until now, the High Authority of the European Coal and Steel Community has quite failed as an efficient instrument to combat the crisis: in the same way as it had failed previously to prevent, stop or even slow down the general decline in the coalmining industry. Capitalist interests are conscious of this failure, and do not mince words on the subject.[6] Rationalization plans that are drawn up or implemented are guided by the national governments; at best the Luxembourg High Authority combines them into international

6. A recent document drafted by the Belgian steel employers' association considers the ECSC a 'nearly complete failure'.

cartel measures. But the efficiency of these national plans is extremely limited, given the stage already reached in international capital interpenetration. If the ECSC does not succeed in imposing international discipline on its members, it might very well fall apart. As against this, however, the European Parliament in Strasburg has already openly raised the demand for a single Western European currency (the *euro-franc*). Consultations between the finance ministers of the six Common Market countries towards a unification of the taxation system progress slowly but continuously. The international monetary crisis, in which France takes a stand different from that of the other Common Market countries, seems to be a great stumbling block on the road of monetary unification. But this would be a factor of minor importance, if the Six were tomorrow confronted with a serious general recession.

## Supranationality and American competition

It was not accidental that de Gaulle provoked the memorable crisis in the Common Market in 1965 around the question of the financing of the common agricultural policy of the EEC. The choice of this 'breaking point' reflected much less the (rapidly declining) importance of the peasantry in the French electorate than the decisive importance, in de Gaulle's eyes, of a qualitative strengthening of the supranational powers of the Common Market authorities. The initial plan of the Common Market Commission was to concentrate in the hands of the supranational organs the important funds which would be collected through special duties on agricultural imports from countries outside the Common Market. Today, the Common Market budget is financed by subsidies by the Six governments. If the Commission's initial plan had been successful, the supranational organs would have collected funds to the amount of 2,300 million dollars by 1 January 1972; *and they would have become financially independent of the national governments*. This de Gaulle wanted to avoid at all costs. But the objective of de Gaulle – preserving France's sovereignty, and establishing its supremacy on the European continent – appears self-defeating. For by opposing amalgamation between French, German and Italian industrialists, he only prepares the ground for them to be swallowed up by the Americans! The fate of the main French firm making electronic computers – *Machines Bull* – which has been absorbed by *General Electric*, and which could certainly have been resisted if it had amalgamated in time with Italian, British and West German firms, is typical of the situation.[7] De Gaulle is caught in

7. *The Economist* of 19 November 1966 indicates that negotiations to produce a single Anglo-French electronic computer had been conducted secretly and had broken down at the end of 1965. They could, of course, start again, the day Britain joins the Common Market. Such a perspective is one of the main forces pushing British capita-

the dilemma between his anti-Americanism and his opposition to supra-nationality. The impulse towards capital concentration which is now assuming an ever-more pronounced international character will eventually break his resistance.

From 1964 onwards, the supranational Commission of the Common Market began a systematic campaign to draw the attention of European capitalists to the tremendous differences in scale between the main North American and the main Western European enterprises. In 1964, among the 100 largest companies of the capitalist world, 65 were American, 5 Japanese, 11 British and only 19 from the Common Market countries. The largest automobile company in the Common Market manufactures five times less cars than the largest one in the USA, although the total car industry of the Common Market has already nearly reached 70 per cent of the USA automobile production. The largest steel trust in Western Europe has a business turnover 3·5 times smaller than the largest one in the USA; and so on. Combined with this difference in scale, there is a difference in outlays and employment for research which, in an age of permanent technological revolution, is a tremendous handicap in the competitive struggle. According to a study recently published by the OECD, expenses for research and development amounted in 1962, *per capita*, to 93·7 dollars in the USA against 33·5 in Britain and an average of hardly 20 dollars in the Common Market; personnel actively engaged in research amounted to 10·4 persons per 1,000 of the active population in the USA against 6·1 in Britain and an average of less than 4 in the Common Market. In 1965, it was estimated that $13·4 billion were spent on research in the USA, against $5·8 billion in Western Europe, Britain included. For all these reasons, the Common Market Commission tried to encourage a process of amalgamation and concentration not only through propaganda means, but by re-interpreting the Rome Treaty and actively preparing the legal framework for the creation of so-called European companies. This would imply the creation of a new type of commercial law applicable to the six Common Market countries as a whole, for which the Court of Justice of the Common Market would become

---

lism towards that 'solution' for its current problems, the other one being the fear that, in case there is an actual merger between the main European trusts, British firms would then be crushed between the American and the Common Market giants. Both the prospect and the fear hover behind Mr Wilson's call for a 'European technological community', capable of reducing the growing gap between Western European and North American 'know-how'. Recently, Sir Paul Chambers, chairman of ICI, speaking in Paris, insisted on the importance of Britain joining the Common Market in order to strengthen the struggle against American technological predominance. He revealed that 75 per cent of the drugs distributed through the British Health Service are sold through American licences.

the supreme legal authority. Efforts are at the same time being undertaken to create a European finance market, advocated by the Bankers' Federation of the Common Market countries. This would be a typical demonstration of the tendency, well-known to Marxists, of the legal superstructure adapting itself to changed property relationships, i.e. the appearance of a type of capitalist property having outgrown the limits of the old national state on the European continent.[8]

This is by no means an ideological game, played by the supranational Common Market Commission for obvious *pro domo* reasons. The direct representatives of the capitalist class vigorously push in the same direction. The official Employers' Association inside the Common Market, UNICE (*Union des Industries de la Communauté Européenne*) addressed a memorandum to the Common Market Commission in April 1965, in which it asked for legislation facilitating the international amalgamation of firms, and in which it explicitly stated that the increase in the size of enterprises should be considered one of the essential objectives of the European Community. Another memorandum on the same subject was published in the summer of 1966. In the same vein, the International Chamber of Commerce published a declaration in October 1965, calling for an elimination of all legal and fiscal barriers to concentration or to joint ventures between enterprises.[9]

### An 'open' or a 'closed' Common Market?

The question of the Common Market's external custom tariff must be considered in terms of the same basic trend which explains the international amalgamation of capital: accelerated technological innovation and increased international competition. From the outset, the different national

8. The French daily *Le Monde* published an amusing series of articles by Paul Fabra ('Comment faire naître des sociétés européennes?') indicating the difficulties for 'European' companies to be set up within the framework of the existing national systems of commercial law (29 June 1965 et. seq.). A recent study appearing in the same newspaper (20–21 November 1966) also suggests that these 'European companies' are still some way off.

9. Baran and Sweezy (1968) note that the term 'multinational corporation' or 'multinational company' was first used by David E. Lilenthal, and was then widely publicized by a special report in *Business Week* (p. 193). The chairman of IBM's European subsidiary, M. Jacques Maisonrouge, made a candid analysis of the 'multinational company' in a speech delivered in Brussels in October 1966. He called for multinational capital and subsidiaries which should be preferably led by 'nationals' of the countries in which they were established (*L'Echo de la Bourse*, 11 October 1966). This is very far from actual reality if one examines the US 'multinational firms', which are not 'multinational' at all but completely dominated by US capital. But it does represent fairly well what happens in those firms set up by capitalists from various Common Market countries.

industries inside the Common Market did not find themselves in the same position. The industries of the Benelux countries, and to a large degree of Western Germany, were accustomed to light tariffs and to looking outwards to the world market; Italian and especially French industry was on the contrary accustomed to heavy tariff protection and to catering essentially for the home market. Inevitably, these latter countries clamoured for strong protection against competition by countries outside the Common Market. The Rome Treaty awarded them partial protection through a common tariff which, while lower than their own national tariff, was decidedly higher than the former tariffs of the traditional free-trade countries.

Behind these different attitudes towards the problem of customs protection and the exterior tariff of the Common Market, there are of course differences in competitive capacity. And from these differences flow inevitable conclusions as to the preference for an 'open' or a 'closed' Common Market. For French industry, which at the beginning of the Common Market was weaker, less concentrated and technologically more backward, the ending of protection inside the Common Market was considered a gamble, and is even considered so today. Episodes like the severe blow inflicted upon the French refrigerator industry by Italian competition [10] partially confirmed these fears, although the efforts at concentration and specialization, vigorously supported by the Gaullist régime, have had some results. But it is evident that French industry, while unwilling to give up the very real profits drawn from the Common Market, [11] is not ready and will not be ready for a long time to undertake any expansion outside of the Common Market boundaries. For that reason, French industry and French government continue to insist upon the need for a real tariff protection against the inflow of industrial goods from competitive areas abroad, and are unwilling to move in the direction of a broadening of the Common Market towards any important industrial country (though they would accept the inclusion of countries like Spain, which would present no serious threat of industrial

10. The output of refrigerators in France declined from 913,000 in 1960 and 978,000 in 1961 to 834,000 in 1962 and 953,000 in 1963. Recovery came in 1964 with 1·06 million units. During the same period the Italian refrigerator industry witnessed a sensational expansion: 977,000 units in 1960, 1·53 million in 1961, 1·77 million in 1962, 2·19 million in 1963 and 2·18 million in 1964.

11. Between 1958 and 1965 (first three quarters), French quarterly exports to Common Market countries rose from $284 million to $987 million, i.e. by 347 per cent. Comparative increases for Belgian exports were 278 per cent, and for West German exports 253 per cent. Exports to Common Market countries amounted to only 22·1 per cent of total French exports in 1958; they amounted to 40 per cent of total French exports for the first three quarters of 1965. For West Germany, the part of the Common Market in total exports rose only from 27·3 per cent in 1958 to 35·1 per cent in the three first quarters of 1965.

competition). West Germany finds herself in an entirely different position. Her exports outside the Common Market are much more important than her exports towards the Common Market. Her industry, in full growth, feels itself able to tackle any competitor, including American industry itself. Export figures indicate an astonishing march forward. Between 1958 and 1965, exports of machinery and transport equipment rose from an annual figure of less than $4 billion to more than $7 billion; exports of chemicals rose from less than $1 billion to more than $2 billion. These figures are coming within reach of those of the United States, which has three times the population of West Germany! It is therefore understandable that West Germany is much more sanguine than other members of the Community about plans for the extension of the Common Market towards Britain, the other EFTA countries or even Canada and the USA: an Atlantic Free Trade Area is not a project to inspire fear between the Rhine and the Elbe. Again, by a strange paradox, the French protectionist plans (which in this field conform nicely with de Gaulle's political schemes) are rather self-defeating. Threatened with being locked out from the Common Market by the high external tariff, American industry simply bypasses this protective barrier by establishing business inside the frontiers of the Common Market.[12] And France has become the Common Market country which has in recent years attracted more American capital than any of the other five member countries. In fact, at the same time as de Gaulle has accentuated his anti-American calls in favour of a return to the gold standard, he has been quietly encouraging American capital investments in France.[13]

## Socialists and the Common Market

The position of socialists towards the Common Market can best be derived from the traditional Marxist position towards capitalist concentration. Marxists are not in favour of trusts as opposed to small business; at the same time, they understand that to try artificially to protect small business against capitalist concentration is a reactionary policy. Socialists therefore point to small businesses being gobbled up by large trusts as indications of an inevitable process of capitalist concentration, which should increase the pressure in favour of collective ownership of the means of production.

In the same perspective, it would not make sense from a Marxist point of view to call either for bourgeois supranational powers over the national state, or to defend the bourgeois national state against the growth of supranational powers. Both the tendencies of capital concentration and of obso-

12. A study by the EEC Commission estimates that American subsidiaries produced 24 per cent of the automobile production, 15 per cent of the synthetic rubber and 10 per cent of the petrochemical production of the Common Market countries in 1965.
13. *Le Monde* (14 December 1966).

lescence of the national state on the European continent are indications of over-ripeness for socialist solutions: the need for a planned economy based upon collective ownership in the framework of a Socialist Federation of Europe (which would not be limited, of course, to the six Common Market countries). But this general theoretical approach to the problem does not automatically furnish an answer to the tactical problems arising out of the present *combination and conflicts of trends* towards national economic programming on the one hand, and international amalgamation of capital (with the parallel rise of supranational powers) on the other hand. In order to answer these tactical problems while avoiding the dual pitfalls of dogmatism and pragmatism, one has to take into consideration a series of *permanent trends of the class struggle* in Western Europe which will remain valid at least for a whole historical period:

1. Economic, social and political development in Western Europe continues to be determined by the *law of uneven development*. The degree of economic integration of Western European capitalist countries, while having the tendency to increase, will not be such, in the immediate and medium-range future, as to result in a complete parallelism of economic, social and political developments in these countries.

2. Combined with the historical differences in structure and in the dynamic of the labour movements in the various Western European countries, the uneven socio-economic and political development in these countries creates uneven developments in the relationship of forces between the classes, and uneven chances for a conquest of power by the working class and a break-through towards socialism.

3. Refusal to exploit temporarily favourable conditions for a break-through towards socialism on a national scale, under the pretext that conditions are not yet ripe in neighbouring countries, would only lead to great disappointment and demoralization of the working class in that country, and thereby favour reaction, nationally as well as internationally. Under the given conditions, internationalism does not mean for socialists to wait till 'conditions' are favourable everywhere and the same moment, (which might very well mean to wait a long time indeed!). Internationalism on the contrary involves exploiting favourable opportunities for a socialist break-through whenever they occur in one country, in order to help improve conditions in favour of socialism in the neighbouring countries. This point was made by Lenin against the Mensheviks as early as 1917; there are no reasons to take another position today in the Common Market.

4. It follows therefore that socialists should continue to work for the overthrow of capitalism within the boundaries of 'their' own country inside the

Common Market, as long as this is *objectively possible* (i.e. as long as international capital amalgamation, international economic integration and growth of supranational powers have not reached the point where it is no more possible to break the stranglehold of private property and the bourgeois state over that country's resources on a national scale). The international dimensions of that struggle would then arise essentially through the efforts of the labour movement of the other member countries to prevent international capital and the Common Market institutions economically strangling, or militarily threatening, the country where the working class has conquered power. The pace and range of this defensive action would depend upon the relationship of forces, and the presence of organizations capable of leading the working class in that direction.

5. While therefore maintaining their general traditional attitude towards collective ownership, nationalization, workers' control and conquest of political power, socialists should use all available *possibilities* for educating the workers towards an *internationalization of the class struggle*, which results from the growing trend towards an internationalization of capital. This implies among other things a study of the possibilities for setting up *international trade-unions* where they face a single international company and fighting for an *international collective contract*, which would prevent the employers from exploiting international wage differentials. As a first step in this direction, we need an international coordination of wage and other demands among the workers who are employed by the same trust or company. It need hardly be said that the contradictions between the complete top-level unification of all employers' associations within the Common Market, and the hopeless ideological and national division of the trade unions, has led and will lead to a deterioration from the workers' side of the balance of forces between employers and workers inside the Common Market.

6. When the process of international amalgamation and interpenetration of capital, and the growth of supranational powers has reached the point where quantity turns into quality, and where the workers of the six countries are faced actually with a new 'European' employers' class, the whole struggle for socialism will have to be lifted to the new international dimension. It is to be hoped that the preparatory phase indicated under point 5 will be used sufficiently well to create favourable conditions for this new form of struggle for socialism: otherwise this might lead, at least in its first phases, to serious setbacks for this struggle. One should not underestimate the tremendous difficulties on the road to the practical, international co-ordination in a struggle for political power, if only because of the differences in language and the levels of centralization needed for such a struggle. But

when the objective conditions leave no choice, socialists will have to measure up to the new needs, rather than hide their heads in the sand.

*References*

BARAN, P. A., and SWEEZY, P. M. (1968), *Monopoly Capital*, Penguin.
MANDEL, E. (1964), in R. Miliband and J. Saville (eds.), *The Socialist Register 1964*, Merlin Press.

# 8  Bob Rowthorn

## Imperialism in the 1970s – Unity or Rivalry?

B. Rowthorn, 'Imperialism in the Seventies – Unity or Rivalry?', *New Left Review*, no. 69, September–October 1971, pp. 31–51.

This essay will discuss the effects of recent economic trends on the unity of the imperialist bloc and on the autonomy of its constituent elements – the individual nations.[1] Three broad possibilities may be distinguished:

*US super-imperialism* in which all other capitalist states are dominated by the United States and have comparatively little freedom to choose their policies and control their economies in ways opposed by the American state. America acts as the organizer of world capitalism, preserving its unity in the face of socialism. This domination may not, of course, operate smoothly – for antagonisms will not be eliminated but merely contained.

*Ultra-imperialism* in which a dominant coalition of relatively autonomous imperialist states performs the organizing role necessary to preserve the unity of the system. For this to work the antagonisms between the members of the coalition must not be so severe that they overcome the interest they have in maintaining the coalition.

1. Articles by Robin Murray (Reading 5) and Bill Warren (Reading 6) have analysed the relationship between capital and the nation state. Although this is not the place to discuss these articles at length, one particular aspect of them is directly relevant to the present paper. Broadly speaking, with many qualifications, Robin Murray takes the view that the internationalization of capital is leading to the weakening of the nation state *vis-à-vis* large firms. For this he is criticized by Bill Warren, who says that in many ways states have *strengthened* their power over large firms and that the formation of the EEC will shift the balance still further in favour of the state. Unfortunately, although correct, Bill Warren's criticism does not take us very far, for he is largely concerned with the *independent* power of the large firm *vis-à-vis* the individual nation state considered in *isolation*. As I have tried to show in this paper, however, the central questions arise when we consider situations in which more than one nation state is involved. In particular:

a. How does the state best serve the capital whose general interests it is defending? What policies should it adopt when dominant sections of this capital are operating in economic or territorial spaces where they are subject to the power of foreign states? These questions arise even where the state has absolute dictatorial power over individual capitals.

b. How far does the ability of certain firms to call upon the support of foreign states place them effectively beyond the control of the domestic state? In other words, how far does the power of foreign states serve to offset the increasing power of the domestic state so rightly stressed by Bill Warren?

*Imperial Rivalry* in which the relatively autonomous states no longer perform the necessary organizing role, or perform it so badly that serious conflicts break out between them and the unity of the system is threatened. For this to happen the antagonisms between states must be severe.

Recent Marxist writers have been divided in their views on which of these three variants of imperialism is most likely. The majority, amongst whom are to be found Sweezy, Magdoff, Jalée and Nicolaus, believe that the United States is not only the dominant imperial power today, but that it will become increasingly dominant in the future.[2] Their argument runs, with variations, roughly as follows. American firms are much bigger, more advanced and faster growing than their foreign rivals. They are using this strength to take over key sectors of European industry, and are using American state power to force their way into Japan. Eventually American firms will dominate the economies of Europe and Japan, and, as a result, large sections of the national bourgeoisies of these countries will be de-nationalized, becoming objectively – if not subjectively – representatives of American capital. Moreover, European and Japanese capital surviving this process will be weak and completely subordinate to American capital. Even today, they argue, a coalition of dominant American and subordinate foreign capital is creating a unified imperialism under the hegemony of the United States and the contradictions between national capitalisms are becoming of increasingly little significance. The significant contradiction is more and more between a unified imperialism and the 'third world'. These writers have been criticized, in my opinion fairly, as 'third-worldists' by Ernest Mandel. For convenience I shall also use this term.

On the opposite side stand Mandel (1969, 1970a, 1970b) and perhaps

2. Magdoff (1969), Sweezy & Magdoff (1969), Jalée (1969), Nicolaus (1970). In a subsequent article, Paul Sweezy seems to have changed his position and now admits the ability of European and Japanese firms to mount some kind of challenge and resistance to American firms (see *Monthly Review*, June 1971). On an economic level he recognizes the existence of a genuine and growing rivalry between the big firms of various capitalist countries. He does not, however, seem to believe that this has any significant implication for the political relations between capitalist states, or for the class struggle *within* the advanced capitalist world. Indeed, he reiterates his long-held view that 'Since the Second World War, it has become increasingly clear that the principal contradiction in the system, at least in the present historical period, is not *within* the developed part but *between* the developed and underdeveloped parts.' In the 1950s this was a plausible view. In the 1970s it is not, for it ignores both the increasing intensity of class struggles in almost every advanced capitalist country and the growing imperial rivalry between these countries. This does not mean, of course, that the national liberation struggles in underdeveloped countries have become unimportant. On the contrary, they will continue to play a crucial role in determining the future of the imperialist system. So too, however, will contradictions within the developed capitalist world. To elevate either kind to the level of a permanent principal contradiction would be both dangerous and misleading.

Kidron (1968), who believe that the hegemony of the United States is being challenged by the Europeans and the Japanese. Mandel argues as follows. A combination of mergers, accumulation and rationalization is destroying the size advantage of American firms, and as a result non-American productivity levels are catching up with those of the Americans. The formation of a supranational state in Europe would speed up this process considerably, but even in the absence of such a state the Europeans are closing the gap. Since non-American wages are much lower than American wages, increases in productivity could make goods produced in Europe and Japan so cheap that exports from these countries could flood American markets, creating severe contradictions within that country as American capitalists try to hold down wages in an attempt to stem this flood. Moreover, American penetration of Europe or Japan has by no means reached the point where the bourgeoisies of these countries have been denationalized. National states still defend the interests of national capital. Neither Europe nor Japan are anywhere near to being neo-colonies. As the struggle for world markets intensifies there will be increasing conflict between nation states as they attempt to defend their respective firms. In particular, the non-Americans will come into conflict with the Americans. Indeed the European states may even form an alliance or perhaps a supranational state to enable them to stand up to the Americans on equal or near equal terms. Internally, within the non-American nations, contradictions will become increasingly severe as states try to hold down wages to enable their firms to compete more effectively. Thus Mandel's view is of an imperialism increasingly wracked by internal contradictions, although he does not believe these will be severe enough to break out into wars. The need to defend the system as a whole will be too great to allow this to happen.

Somewhere in between these two poles hovers the Soviet economist Varga (1968) who, appealing to the law of unequal development, argues that European and Japanese capital will break the hegemony of American capital, and that the United States will be forced to share its leadership of the imperialist world. Antagonisms between national capitals, however, will be of comparatively little importance in determining the future of the imperialist system. They will be adequately, if not smoothly, contained by the rapidly proliferating supranational institutions, whose aim is both to resolve the economic antagonisms between national capitals and to preserve the unity of imperialism against the challenge posed to it by the revolutionary movements of the third world. Apart from his notion that the leadership of imperialism will be shared by a number of states, Varga's ultra-imperialism does not differ greatly in content from the super-imperialism of the third-worldists.

## Points of difference

It is clear that there are three central issues on which the various schools of thought differ: 1. the relative strength of US capital and the related question of the degree to which it can dominate Europe and Japan by capturing most key industrial sectors; 2. the severity and nature of the antagonisms between different national capitals; 3. the extent to which the common fear of socialism can overcome those antagonisms which do exist.

It is impossible in the space of this article to discuss in depth all of these points of difference. On the third, I shall content myself with the following observations. The degree to which the common fear of socialism can overcome antagonisms depends on the nature and severity of these antagonisms, and the extent to which states perceive that in pursuing the interests of their national capitals they are putting the entire system in jeopardy. China and Eastern Europe would never have been invaded if the Japanese and German imperialists had realized that the outcome would not be the colonization of these areas but their detachment from the imperialist system as a whole. To ascribe this myopia to madness, as does Varga when he says that capitalism will no longer be dominated by madmen like Hitler, is to ignore the objective conditions which determine whether or not 'madmen' are in control. Amongst these objective conditions must be counted the nature and extent of the antagonisms between national capitals. A high degree of antagonism may induce a high degree of myopia. Indeed this may even be 'structural' myopia in the sense that those concerned may individually understand what is happening but be powerless to prevent it. We do not, of course, need to take such an extreme example as that of imperialism and war. The system may be put in jeopardy by contradictions between capital and labour within the imperial countries, contradictions brought to explosion-point by antagonisms between national capitals. A crisis caused by the collapse of the international monetary system might, for example, lead to a socialist revolution in Italy or France. So might competitive attempts by the imperialist states to contain inflation, attempts which had their roots not in a contradiction between imperialism and the third world but in antagonisms between national capitals. Rather than pursue such an obvious, if neglected, line of argument, let us pass on to the remaining two questions at issue.

## The strength of US capital

The relative strength of US capital and its advantages in the struggle for world markets have been greatly exaggerated by the 'third-worldists'.

First, although American firms are still, on average, larger than their foreign rivals, mergers, takeovers and high rates of accumulation in Europe and Japan have done much to close this gap. In many industries, such as chemicals, machinery, oil or steel, the differences in size have ceased or are rapidly ceasing to be significant. In others, such as computers or automobiles the differences are still significant, although in most cases they are being lessened by the continued concentration and centralization of capital in Europe and Japan. Indeed, if the Common Market, with or without Britain, can develop a common company law facilitating mergers between European firms of different nationalities, all but a few of the existing inequalities in size will be eliminated or reduced to the point where they no longer matter.

Secondly, although it is true that American firms are the leading innovators and have monopolies or near-monopolies in the production of many advanced or 'modern' products, the third-worldists' almost exclusive focus on these products and the research and development expenditures associated with them is seriously misleading. It ignores both the temporary nature of technological monopolies and the faster growth of European and Japanese capital in products other than the most advanced. As leaders, American firms must spend enormous amounts making mistakes which others can avoid and discovering things which others can imitate or adapt cheaply. Within a few years of their introduction, 'modern' products in which the Americans initially had monopolies become 'traditional' and are produced efficiently and in bulk by European and Japanese firms. To maintain their lead, therefore, or to prevent it being eroded too rapidly, American firms are forced to spend far more on research and development than their rivals overseas. This is the price they pay for being leaders.

As the gap between the Americans and the non-Americans closes, the scope for catching up will, of course, diminish and the non-Americans will be increasingly forced to become innovators themselves and competition will become increasingly centred on advanced products. Indeed the growing chorus of demands in Europe and Japan for technological cooperation and for more state expenditure on research and development suggests that this is already happening, and that non-American capital is preparing to challenge the Americans in areas where they have, until now, reigned supreme. It is quite wrong, therefore, to see these demands as evidence of a desperate last-ditch attempt on the part of weakening European and Japanese capitals to resist 'technological colonization' by the Americans. Their growing need to become innovators themselves and not merely imitators is a direct consequence of their past dynamism and the increasing sophistication of both their markets and products. If the European and Japanese challenges fail these firms will, of course, be compelled to tail along behind the Americans. However, their failure is by no means a foregone conclusion, as the third-worldists seem to believe. On the contrary, the growing strength of European and Japanese capital, caused by mergers and accumulation, together with the growing size and sophistication of their markets, suggests that they will be able to mount an effective challenge in most, if not all, advanced products.

Finally, the third-worldists have over-emphasized the offensive aspects of American direct investment overseas and under-emphasized its defensive aspects. With the exception of a brief period in the late sixties, when the United States experienced a boom at the same time as Germany experienced a recession, continental Europe has grown substantially faster than the United States during the last two decades. Japan has grown even faster than continental Europe, its GNP rising from one twentieth of the American GNP in 1953 to nearly one sixth in 1968. This growth has affected American firms in two ways. On the one hand, growing markets overseas have offered them the chance to expand overseas, often in products for which American demand has begun to level out as domestic markets become saturated. On the other hand, the growth of overseas economies has enabled many foreign firms to strengthen themselves to the point where they have begun to threaten the world position of American giants. American investment in Europe and other areas can only be appreciated if both these aspects of non-American growth are taken into account. In addition to increasing the sales of American firms, overseas investment has served to frustrate foreign competition and preserve American monopolies. If American firms had not taken over actual or potential foreign rivals and established subsidiaries overseas, they would have been forced to rely upon exports – not a very effective means of penetrating foreign markets – and today would be faced with an even greater foreign challenge.

Despite their phenomenal expansion overseas, however, big American firms are having and will have increasing difficulty in keeping ahead of their foreign rivals. The fast growth of American firms in the late sixties was based largely on an accelerated growth of the US economy and a rapid increase in the level of concentration in that economy, neither of which is likely to last. The US economy is once again stagnating and American giants will experience increasing difficulty in raising their share of the domestic economy. Thus, viewed in a longer perspective, the cause of the American invasion of Europe must be seen as the erosion of a previously impregnable position. So long as they were absolutely superior American firms could rely mainly on exports, and could regard European and Japanese recovery with a certain indulgence. With European and Japanese recovery, however, the firms of these countries have become dangerous challengers and American firms are forced to invest overseas for their own defence. Hence their massive investment in Europe and their increasing pressure on Japan to allow the entry of foreign capital. So much for the supposedly overwhelming and increasing superiority of American capital. Let us now turn to the question of antagonisms.

## Antagonisms

Relations between capitals are always to some extent antagonistic, the degree of antagonism depending both on the area of actual or potential competition and on its intensity. Thus, in the present case, where we are concerned with relations between capitals of different nationalities, it is important to know: 1. over what areas the firms of North America, Europe and Japan are or will be in competition with each other; 2. what form this competition will take – will, for example, Continental and Japanese capitals create or at least attempt to create international firms of their own or will they rely mainly on exports as a means of penetrating foreign markets? To answer these questions, let us begin by discussing international trade and investment.

### 1. *International trade and investment*

The post-war economic growth of advanced capitalist countries has been accompanied by an increasing dependence on international trade as both imports and exports have risen considerably faster than output. Much of this increase has consisted of manufactured goods either sold to or imported from other advanced capitalist countries. As a result, trade within the advanced capitalist bloc is now three times as large as between this bloc and the rest of the world, and exports account for a significant proportion of the output of many manufacturing firms.

Exports have not, however, been the only way in which firms, particularly big firms, have penetrated foreign markets. Direct investment, whereby firms establish and operate production and distribution facilities overseas, has played an important role in the penetration of foreign markets by the firms of at least five countries – Britain, the United States, the Netherlands, Canada and Switzerland. Indeed, it has been more important than exports in the case of Britain and the United States. Between 1957 and 1965, direct investment accounted for five-sixths and three-fifths respectively of the overseas expansion of the average American and British manufacturing firm (see Table 1). Moreover, since big firms account for the bulk of overseas investment, the proportions given in Table 1, which reflect the experience of the *average* firm, understate the extent to which big firms in the five major investing countries rely on overseas production for their expansion. For these firms, overseas investment has become the characteristic means of serving important markets. Exports are reserved for lesser markets or products for which overseas demand is not yet large enough to justify local production. For the firms of the remaining countries, such as France, Italy, Germany and Japan, overseas investment has not until recently played a significant role in the penetration of foreign markets. Even the big firms have relied mainly on exports.

Table 1 Expansion overseas 1957–65: percentage of sales increase accounted for by manufacturing firms

|  | Exports | Overseas production | Overseas sales |
|---|---|---|---|
| US | 2 | 13 | 15 |
| UK | 12 | 20 | 32 |
| France | 6 | 1 | 7 |
| Germany | 14 | 2 | 16 |
| Italy | 24 | 5 | 30 |
| Netherlands | 27 | 17 | 43 |
| Canada | 33 | 13 | 46 |
| Japan | 17 | 2 | 20 |

Source: Rowthorn (1971), Table 22.

Overseas investment has enabled the firms of certain countries to establish powerful and sometimes dominant positions in foreign markets, even where their export performance has been poor. Indeed, it is only by looking at overseas production as well as exports that one gets an idea of the penetration of American or British firms into such areas as Europe, South Africa, Australia or Canada.

The role of investment becomes particularly clear when one examines the economic relations between the United States and other advanced capitalist countries. In 1966 American exports to Europe were not much different from European exports to the United States (see Table 2). American penetration of European markets by means of exports was thus more or less matched by European penetration of American markets by means of exports. When we look at investment, however, the situation is quite different. The sales of American manufacturing and petroleum affiliates in Europe were equal to approximately $US36,000 millions, a figure which is two and a half times as large as the total value of all American exports to Europe including food and raw materials. The sales of European manufacturing and petroleum affiliates in America were, by contrast, fairly small, being equal to less than $US9,000 millions, which is considerably less than the value of European exports to America, and less than one quarter of the sales of American affiliates in Europe. As a result of this imbalanced investment the total sales of American firms in Europe, including both exports and local production, were two and a half times the total sales of European firms in the United States. In absolute terms this meant that American firms extended their markets by a *net* amount of around $US30,000 millions, i.e. US sales in Europe exceeded European sales in the United States by this amount.

A more detailed breakdown of the figures by country would reveal wide variations in the degree to which American penetration of particular foreign markets had been matched by non-American penetration of the American markets. British, Dutch and Swiss firms have invested heavily in the United States and their affiliates account for the bulk of European production in that country. Indeed the Netherlands and Switzerland have positive investment balances with the United States, with the result that Swiss and Dutch firms actually sell more in the United States than American firms sell in Switzerland and the Netherlands. Other European countries such as France, Germany or Italy have not invested much in the United States, and American sales in these countries are considerably greater than the sales of their firms in the United States.

Table 2 **Exports and local production** ($US millions)

|  | X | P | P/X | X | P | P/X |
|---|---|---|---|---|---|---|
| *Out of US* | 1957 | | | 1966 | | |
| Europe | 6,940 | 10,762 | 1·55 | 14,440 | 36,000 | 2·50 |
| Japan | 1,851 | 555 | ·30 | 3,545 | 2,000 | ·62 |
| *Into US* | 1959 | | | 1966 | | |
| UK, Netherlands, & Switzerland | 2,320 | 4,657 | 2·01 | 3,740 | 7,400 | 1·97 |
| Other Europe | 4,580 | 559 | ·12 | 8,050 | 1,271 | ·16 |
| – France | 690 | 92 | ·13 | 1,050 | 123 | ·12 |
| – Germany | 1,380 | 47 | ·03 | 2,700 | 138 | ·05 |
| Japan | 1,543 | 29 | ·02 | 4,444 | 50 | ·01 |

*Source:* For European figures see R. E. Rowthorn and S. Hymer in Kindleberger (1970).
Japanese figures have been calculated in the same way.
*Definitions:*
X = exports (all countries).
P = manufacturing and petroleum sales of local subsidiaries.

Turning now to Japan, we find a completely different picture. Foreign investment in Japan has been restricted and until recently Japanese firms did not invest much overseas. Moreover, trade with the United States is *roughly* balanced, just as it is in the case of the Europeans. Indeed, Japan exports slightly more to the United States than the United States exports to Japan. The result of this combination – roughly balanced trade and little investment – has been that American firms have not been able to penetrate Japanese markets to any great extent, and what gains they have made have been more or less offset by Japanese gains in American markets.

The significance of overseas investment in international competition goes far beyond the example we have just been discussing. An examination would reveal:

(i) Trade in manufactures between industrialized capitalist countries is usually in rough balance. Collectively, the manufacturing firms of one of these countries lose about as much of their domestic markets to foreign imports as they gain by exporting to other industrialized capitalist countries. Only in trade with underdeveloped and other resource-producing countries do industrialized countries have substantial surpluses in manufactures.

(ii) Overseas investment is becoming the most effective means of penetrating the world's major markets. It is becoming increasingly important both as a means of defending existing markets and of capturing new ones.

(iii) Direct investment, unlike trade, is often highly unbalanced. Britain, the United States, the Netherlands and Switzerland have invested far more overseas than foreign firms have invested in these countries. As a result, their big firms have made considerable net gains, capturing markets overseas without sacrificing an equivalent amount of home markets in return.

If Lenin's words were something of an exaggeration when he wrote them in 1916, they have become true today: 'Under the old capitalism when free competition prevailed, the export of *goods* was the most typical feature. Under modern capitalism, when monopolies prevail, the export of *capital* has become the typical feature.'[3]

## 2. *European and Japanese capital*

A well-established, if not so well understood, feature of capitalism is the tendency for capital to expand outwards and seek new markets overseas. Since European and Japanese firms are manifestly not exceptions to this rule, it follows from the above conclusion regarding the role of direct investment in overseas expansion that these firms will be forced to rely increasingly on overseas investment if their objectives are to be attained.

As well as what might be called the universal reasons for overseas expansion, however, European firms have an added reason in the form of an already massive American investment in Europe. As we have shown above, this investment has enabled American manufacturing and petroleum firms to penetrate European markets to such an extent that their sales in Europe exceeded European sales in the United States by $US30,000 million a year in 1966. Clearly, American firms derive a considerable advantage from this net penetration of European markets and to eliminate or greatly reduce the deficit will be one of the future objectives of European big capital.

The deficit can, in principle, be tackled in one of two ways: *defensively* by reducing the size and growth of American sales in Europe, or *offensively* by

3. Lenin (1917), p. 723.

increasing European sales abroad, both in the United States and elsewhere. Since American capital is already well-established in Europe, a defensive approach would have to be based on drastic state intervention if it were to have any real effect. The result would be a confrontation with America on a scale which, for obvious reasons, European capital wants to avoid; although as we suggest below, such a confrontation may eventually come about if America protects its domestic capital against the incursion of European and other foreign capital. We can assume, however, that European capital will not initiate such a confrontation and that, until the American state initiates it, American firms will be allowed to operate fairly freely in Europe. In so far as European capital attempts to reduce the American advantage it will adopt, therefore, an offensive approach and counter-attack overseas either by exporting more or by establishing more overseas subsidiaries.

Exports cannot, however, provide anything like the necessary increase in overseas sales. Quite apart from what might be called the micro-reason of rising European wage costs, there is a crucial macro-reason relating to the equilibrium of the world monetary system. Annual European *exports* would have to increase by a gigantic amount, $US20,000 million to $US30,000 million over and above any offsetting increase in *imports*.

Europe as a whole would have, therefore, to run massive current account surpluses with the rest of the world. Moreover, since the bulk of non-European purchasing power is located in America, a large proportion of the extra exports would have to be bought by that country, and America would have to run massive current account deficits. Thus, if the Europeans were successful in their export drive, the result would be European surpluses and American deficits of unprecedented magnitude, qualitatively larger than the surpluses and deficits which have plagued the capitalist world during the last few years. Within a short time either the world monetary system would collapse and with it trade, or else a major realignment of currencies, in which some were revalued and others devalued, would take place, thereby destroying the cost advantage of European firms and restoring the equilibrium of the world monetary system. In other words, the very success of the export drive, by creating huge surpluses and deficits, would undermine the conditions which made it successful. This argument, it should be noted, applies quite generally to the question of overseas expansion by means of exports. Any country which exports so successfully that it obtains massive surpluses tends to undermine the conditions of its own success.

It seems then that a defensive approach, although technically possible, would do more harm than good to European firms and that an offensive approach based on exports could not provide surpluses large enough to compensate for more than a small proportion of the enormous American sales in Europe. Only by investing heavily overseas, establishing production facilities in other countries, could European firms hope to compensate for losses to American firms in Europe.

Thus for both general reasons relating to the outward expansion of capital and particular reasons relating to the already massive American stake in Europe, European firms must invest heavily overseas. For the same general reasons Japanese firms will have to follow suit. As yet, however, the incentive for the latter to do so is not quite so great, for they have managed to pursue a successful defensive strategy in which the operation of American capital in Japan has been severely circumscribed. American pressure is, however, causing Japan to relax some of its restrictions and, should the stage be reached where American capital has more or less free entry into Japan, Japanese firms will be forced to adopt an offensive strategy which seeks to compensate for domestic losses by investing overseas.

It is important to notice that any compensation for American sales in Europe must come about through sales outside of Europe. If, for example, the manufacturing firms of one European country increase their sales in another European country, the gains of the firms of the first country are exactly cancelled by the losses of those of the second. Taking in each other's washing in this way, whatever its other vices or virtues, does nothing to compensate for the American presence in Europe. If American firms succeed in penetrating the Japanese economy, then collectively European and Japanese firms will only be able to compensate for American penetration by expanding into areas other than Europe or Japan. Since the bulk of the world's markets outside of these two areas are to be found in America, any substantial improvement in the net position of European and Japanese firms would imply a massive penetration of American markets. Thus an offensive strategy, which aimed to compensate for a large part of the American gains in Europe and perhaps one day Japan, would entail massive expansion into American markets, which could only come about through direct investment.

The overseas expansion of Continental and Japanese firms by means of direct investment has, in fact, already begun. The overseas investment of German, Italian and Japanese firms has increased dramatically in recent years (see Table 3). Between them these three countries invested an average of $US230 million a year during 1957–60. By 1961–4 the figure had risen to $US480 million a year, in 1967 it was $US600 million and by 1968 it had reached $US840 million. Between them these three countries invested as much overseas as Britain in 1968. Germany provides the most striking case. After rising steadily for the last few years, German direct investment overseas was substantially more in 1969 than foreign direct investment in Germany.

These are, however, no more than signs. Annual American direct invest-

Table 3 **Direct investment overseas** ($US billions)

|  | 1957–60 | 1961–4 | 1967 | 1968 |
|---|---|---|---|---|
| USA | 2·83 | 3·21 | 3·15 | 3·03 |
| UK | ·51 | ·67 | ·74 | ·89 |
| subtotal | 3·34 | 3·88 | 3·92 | 3·92 |
| Germany | ·12 | ·22 | ·25 | ·39 |
| Italy | ·06 | ·17 | ·23 | ·23 |
| Japan | ·05 | ·09 | ·12 | ·22 |
| subtotal | ·23 | ·48 | ·60 | ·84 |
| Belgium | — | — | ·05 | ·03 |
| France | ·01 | ·10 | ·20 | — |
| Netherlands | ·71 | ·12 | ·21 | ·22 |
| Canada | ·06 | ·10 | ·08 | ·16 |

Sources: IMF, OECD.

ment is still far greater than that of Japan and the major Continental countries combined. Moreover, much of their investment is going to countries other than the United States, so that exports still provide their main way of penetrating American markets.

The question is, therefore, whether European and Japanese direct investment overseas will continue to grow rapidly and whether much of it will be directed towards the United States. Before attempting to answer this question, it is necessary to make clear at what level the response will be cast. A complete answer could take into account a whole range of political and other factors, such as the reaction of the American state to heavy foreign investment in the United States. Since, however, it is part of our aim to understand the forces which may lead the American state to act against foreign capital, we shall assume that the existing liberal policies are maintained. This will enable us to understand the economic tendencies at work within the current situation, although it will not, of course, tell us the extent to which these tendencies will be realized in practice.

The problem has both macro and micro aspects. On a macro level, if Europe and Japan are to finance heavy overseas investment, they must be able to guarantee a substantial surplus somewhere else in the balance of payments. Only a world banker such as America (or, at one time, Britain) can finance direct investment overseas by accumulating short-term and portfolio liabilities. During the last few years such a surplus has appeared. Between them Germany, Italy and Japan now have on current account alone a surplus of over $US6,000 million a year (see Table 4). This is over twice the annual net direct investment overseas of all American firms com-

bined. Thus if only half of the European and Japanese surplus was channelled into direct investment, the firms of these countries would invest overseas as much as American firms. So far, however, this has not happened.
The surplus has instead been devoted to the accumulation of short-term
dollar liabilities and gold, and the purchase of American securities. Indeed,
European holdings of American corporate stocks alone now stand at
$US13,000 million (1968) and are almost enough to offset the enormous
American direct investments in Europe. To understand how this situation
has arisen, we must look at the problem on a micro-level. Until fairly
recently, there were two reasons why Continental or Japanese firms did not

Table 4  **Current Account Balances** ($US millions)[1]

|  | 1966 | 1967 | 1968 | 1969 |
|---|---|---|---|---|
| Japan | 1254 | −190 | 1048 | 2185 |
| Germany | 119 | 2464 | 2838 | 1770 |
| Italy | 2117 | 1599 | 2627 | 2368 |
| Total | 3490 | 3873 | 6513 | 6323 |
| *For comparison* | | | | |
| Net US Direct Investment Abroad[2] | −3639 | −3154 | −3025 | −3060 |

Source: OECD.
[1] indicates deficit.
[2] indicates a net outflow of US direct investment.

invest very much overseas, and relied mainly on exports to serve foreign
markets. First, wage costs were lower at home than in many other countries,
in particular than in the United States. Although these were partially offset
by the higher cost of capital goods, it was still cheaper to produce at home.
A survey conducted amongst American firms on behalf of the National
Industrial Conference Board, for example, revealed that for the year 1960
costs in the European Common Market were only about 0·85 of costs in the
United States.[4] Secondly, to invest overseas a firm must be able to establish
an efficient-sized plant and must be able to sell the output of that plant. To
build or buy a large plant may be very expensive, and to be sure of selling its
products the firm must either have already built up a market by exporting
or must have the funds to finance a costly programme of sales promotion
and to cover the losses incurred whilst demand for its products grows. Until
a few years ago, all but a few Continental and Japanese giants were unable
to command the necessary funds, hence had not penetrated overseas markets
to any great extent. As a result, they had no alternative but to export when

4. Gates and Linden (1961), pp. 14–15.

they could and forego markets when they could not. Thus, by exporting, these firms could exploit cheap labour and economies of scale at home, whereas by producing overseas, particularly in North America, they would have been compelled to pay high wages and would have been unable to exploit economies of scale.

In recent years, however, the situation has begun to change. Money wage costs in Europe and Japan are rising rapidly, so that the advantage of cheap labour is being lost. Continental and Japanese firms have established markets for many of their products by exporting. Mergers and high rates of accumulation have strengthened them to the point where many can now afford to build efficient-sized plants overseas and can finance the promotion of their products where necessary.

The notion of an efficient-sized plant depends not only on technical conditions but also on the scale of production of rival firms. In a small economy like Australia, for example, a firm may be able to operate quite happily with a scale of one fifth, one tenth, or even less of what would be necessary for survival in the United States. Thus initially the growing ability of Continental and Japanese firms to finance overseas investment will manifest itself, indeed is already manifesting itself, in an expansion into areas other than the United States. As the process of merger, rationalization and accumulation continues, however, it is inevitable that these firms will turn increasingly to the United States itself. To help them they may have state aid, disguised wherever possible to prevent American retaliation. If international mergers such as that between Dunlop and Pirelli become the fashion, European investment in America will take place on an enormous scale. Similarly, if Japanese industry consolidates still further and the Japanese economy continues growing at its present rate, Japanese firms will invest heavily both in the United States and elsewhere.

We may sum up this argument by saying that rising costs at home, greater strength, and established overseas markets for European and Japanese products are all combining to make the big firms of these countries move towards investment as the most effective way of penetrating foreign markets, both in America and elsewhere. European-wide mergers would accelerate this process but it will occur even without them. This does not, of course apply to all products or all firms. It is likely that we shall see both a more intensive export drive by some firms, particularly those too small to invest, and a massive investment drive by others.

This discussion has been concerned with manufacturing firms. For obvious strategic and economic reasons, however, a similar growth of non-American investment overseas will occur in the field of natural resources. Indeed, it is already beginning.

## 3. Conclusions

The above discussion, although by no means definitive, points to the following conclusions:

(i) European and Japanese capital is strong enough not only to fight back against American capital but also to counter-attack by expanding overseas.

(ii) The overseas expansion of big European and Japanese firms will increasingly take the form of direct investment in other countries, including the United States itself. Exports will, however, continue to be important both for small firms and certain products.

(iii) Continent-wide mergers in Europe and further consolidation in Japan would accelerate the process considerably and the firms of these countries would invest overseas on an enormous scale.

These conclusions, it will be noticed, are broadly similar to those of Ernest Mandel, who stresses the growing challenge of European and Japanese capital to American hegemony. One important difference, however, lies in the emphasis given here to direct investment by the Europeans and Japanese, in contrast to Mandel's emphasis on exports.

## Capital and the Nation State

Before discussing what the above conclusions imply about the future development of the capitalist system, it will be helpful to discuss the relationship between the strength of capital and the autonomy of a state *vis-à-vis* other states. All of the writers mentioned above, no matter whether they believe in US super-imperialism, ultra-imperialism or imperial rivalry, take for granted that the autonomy of a nation state is determined by the strength of capital based on that nation – i.e. that a state with strong capital is autonomous and that one with weak capital is subordinate. Thus, those who believe that American capital is overwhelmingly stronger than European or Japanese capital see Europe and Japan being and remaining subordinate to the United States, and, conversely, those who believe that European and Japanese capital is challenging American capital see Europe and Japan becoming increasingly autonomous. In reality, however, things are not so simple; for although strength and autonomy are related to each other, there is no one-to-one correspondence between the strength of capital and the autonomy of the state.

British *big* capital is still among the strongest in the world. Of the 100 largest businesses in the world 11 are British, compared with 18 for the EEC as a whole; of the 200 largest non-American companies 53 were British at the end of the sixties, compared with 43 Japanese, 25 German and 23 French.[5] British companies have always operated on a global scale and are flanked by

5. Ernest Mandel (1970a), p. 63.

a major banking complex and financial centre in the City. Yet the British *state* has not aggressively pursued the interests of a specifically British capitalism. The economic policies of British governments have, on the contrary, been highly sensitive to the advice of the international institutions of the capitalist world and of the largest imperialist power, the United States. The policies adopted by British governments during the recurrent balance of payments crises were, in fact, quite different from those which would have been pursued by a more independent capitalist state and have aggravated the stagnation of British capitalism. Paradoxically the weakness of the British state is to be explained not by the simple decline of British capitalism as such, but by the very *strength* of the cosmopolitan activities of British capital, which has helped to undermine further its strictly domestic economy. British big capital has always had a major international dimension and the conditions of the post-war world led to an *accentuation* rather than modification of this pattern. While capital in Europe and Japan had less experience and few facilities for direct investment overseas, combined with great opportunities in a rapidly growing home economy, British big capital found itself with unexciting domestic prospects but a plethora of overseas opportunities and contacts. The relative decline of the home-base of British capitalism was thus reinforced and the relative independence of the British state further undercut. Between them, these trends – the international expansion of British big capital coupled with the contraction of the British state and the domestic economic base of British capitalism – have led to a situation where many British companies now conduct a large part of their business in areas where the British state exercises no control and little influence, and where it can offer them little or no protection. As a result both they and British capitalism generally have become extremely vulnerable to retaliation should Britain follow economic policies not to the liking of other imperialist powers.

Coherent policies for advancing the indigenous interests of British capitalism would in the last decades have entailed such measures as import controls, severe restrictions on overseas investment and the freezing of certain sterling balances. Each of these would have in turn inhibited the international operations of British firms, either by interfering with their ability to move capital freely across frontiers and perhaps denying them the funds necessary for investment, or else by provoking retaliation on the part of other capitalist states. In return, British companies would have been offered the benefits of growth in their home economy. However, the dubious and difficult prospects of growth in the single domestic market could not match those of expansion into varied overseas markets. Thus as the British economy became more integrated into a global capitalism over which the British state had no control, it became increasingly vulnerable internationally and the potential benefits to big capital of a straightforwardly aggressive nationalist development have dwindled accordingly. Thus, faced with the threat of massive losses in their foreign business in exchange for doubtful gains in their domestic business, those sections of British capital which operate internationally, and this includes the bulk of finance capital and many large industrial companies, have opposed the measures necessary for dynamizing British capitalism, preferring – if not actually liking – the alternative of stagnation and deflation in response to the demands of the other imperial powers.

Thus, leading sections of the British bourgeoisie have been effectively 'denationalized', not through their own weakness but through the weakness of the British state and their own home base. The overseas strength of British big *capital* has compounded the debility of British *capitalism*. If the dominant British corporation had been smaller they would not have been able to expand overseas to anything like the same extent. Overseas production and international finance would now account for a far less important part of their income, British companies and the British economy would be less vulnerable to retaliation, and, as a result, the benefits and possibilities of domestic growth would be much greater. Alternatively, if the British state and the domestic British economy had retained their former power, foreign retaliation would be far less likely and attempts to stimulate and restructure the domestic economy would not jeopardize the international operations of British firms. British firms would not then have to choose between domestic and overseas expansion. They could have both. *If the discussion of Europe and Japan above showed that there are inherent limits to expansion solely through exports, the British case demonstrates the perils of expansion via direct investment unsustained by a sufficiently strong sponsoring state and home base.*

## Perspectives

Let us now return to the prospects for the European Economic Community and Japan. As European and Japanese firms expand overseas, they will increasingly threaten the position of American firms, both in the United States and elsewhere. Initially the American state is likely to respond to this threat, indeed is already responding, by restricting certain kinds of imports, aiding domestically controlled firms and attempting to obtain or maintain American privileges in overseas markets. If these measures prove inadequate as they probably will in the face of heavy European and Japanese investment, the American state will be tempted to restrict the operations of foreign capital in the United States, and where possible persuade its more dependent allies to do the same.

Thus, as non-American capital counter-attacks, the American state will intervene more vigorously on behalf of American capital. To penetrate the

United States and other areas under its hegemony non-American capital will, therefore, be forced to rely increasingly on the use of its own state power: financial and technological support to lower costs of production and to provide the funds for expansion; economic or even military inducements to weaken America's grip on its satellites; and, finally, counter-threats against American capital in Europe. If these measures fail, European and Japanese expansion in the United States and its satellites will be severely hampered, and European and Japanese capital will be forced to operate mainly outside the US sphere of influence. Thus, the medium-term prospect is one of increasing intervention by the American state in the face of a growing non-American challenge, threatened or actual retaliation by non-American states, and perhaps a partial reversal of existing tendencies towards interpenetration as the capitalist world fragments into more self-contained regions.

The extent to which the American state can be deterred from intervening on behalf of American capital depends on the extent to which non-American states are able to act in a concerted fashion and to form effective alliances. A European bloc, for example, embracing virtually the whole of Western Europe would have tremendous bargaining power with the United States. With sales in Europe of over $US60,000 million a year, American subsidiaries would be extremely vulnerable to retaliatory action by the combined European powers in the event of a conflict with the United States, and at the present time the loss of a substantial proportion of these sales would far outweigh the benefits to American firms of vigorous state intervention on their behalf. Thus, although not enough to guarantee that America would continue to follow liberal policies, the threat of retaliation by the combined European powers would, in the short run, be enough to guarantee the existence of a powerful liberal lobby in the United States. In the medium run, however, the formation of a European bloc would have the opposite effect, for by facilitating European-wide mergers and mobilizing massive state resources on behalf of European firms, this bloc would so strengthen European capital that it could expand overseas on an enormous scale, both into the United States and elsewhere. Before long the Europeans would pose such a serious threat to the operations of American firms in Latin America, Canada, Australia, the Middle East and even the United States itself that many firms of formerly liberal views would be forced to call upon the American state to defend their interests in these areas, even if the price of such defence was a restriction of their activities in Europe. Thus, although in the short run the formation of a European bloc might deter the American state from acting too vigorously on behalf of American capital, in the medium run it would have the opposite effect and would only serve to intensify the pressures for state action.

It is clear from the above discussion that the ability of firms to compete internationally, both in capturing new markets and sources of supply and in defending existing ones, will come to depend increasingly on the use of state power. If, for one reason or another, the state power available to capital is nowhere near commensurate with its needs, then not only will this capital be at a serious disadvantage in world competition, but even the state power it does command will not be exploited to the full for fear of provoking retaliatory action by other states.

To overcome this disability there are several obvious courses of action. The state concerned can ally itself or even merge with other states, thereby placing greater state power at the disposal of its capital. Britain's application to join the Common Market, for example, is intended to serve both of these objectives. British capital, being highly international in its operation and perspectives, needs a greater state power than Britain alone can provide, and at the same time is frightened that, if Britain remains outside the Common Market, the state power of continental countries will be used against it. Alternatively, failing an alliance or merger of states, capital can change its nationality. For example, provided the British state agreed, certain British firms operating mainly within the US sphere of influence might change their nationality and become American. Under certain circumstances even the agreement of the British state would be unnecessary.

These two courses of action are not, of course, mutually exclusive. Indeed alliances may actually facilitate changes of nationality. Within the Common Market, for example, it may become relatively easy for say a French firm to merge with a German firm and gradually shift the balance of its activities and eventually its headquarters into Germany, becoming thereby effectively and one day legally German. Given a merger between states, on the other hand, the situation is less simple, for then all capitals adopt the 'nationality' of the new unit. This change will not, however, affect the original nations and national capitals equally and the degree to which it can be considered a true change of nationality will vary from country to country.

Although changes of nationality may eventually turn out to be important, alliances or mergers of states are likely to be of more immediate significance in view of the growing unity of the Common Market and Britain's application for membership. At its widest, an extended Common Market might cover virtually the whole of Western Europe, and, at its most complete, so many basic economic and military decisions would be irreversibly centralized that the resulting 'United Europe' would be a single nation. As well as increasing considerably the state power at the disposal of European capital, this unification would have the effect of 'renationalizing' the operations of many European firms and of giving them a much greater interest in the health of the newly created 'home' economy. All West European markets would be brought under the control of what amounted to a single state power, and, from the point of view of European firms, many formerly overseas markets, i.e. those located in other European countries, would become home markets. Many firms which were previously international under the old system of separate European states would become 'national' under the new system – most of their production and sales would be located within the 'national' boundaries of a United Europe. As a result, these firms would have a strong interest in a fast-growing 'national' economy, even where the price of this growth was conflict with America or some other capitalist state. This does not imply, of course, that all of these firms would have a corresponding interest in their growth of their original national economies. On the contrary, capital based on the more backward areas of Europe or those where the working class was particularly militant would migrate to more prosperous or more congenial parts of Europe, with possibly disastrous consequences for the areas left behind.

Since European big capital would depend closely on the health of the West European economy and would derive considerable benefits from the use of European state power, it would act as a 'nationalist' force, supporting an autonomous economic development for Western Europe and relying on the use of state power overseas. The relationship of European capital to the European 'state' would be much the same as that of American capital to the American state and this European state would, therefore, be autonomous *vis-à-vis* other states and would act vigorously on behalf of its own capital when necessary. Thus, a United Europe would constitute what, for want of a better name, we may call an 'imperialist metropolis', i.e. it would be autonomous and imperialist.

It is not necessary to assume such an all-embracing West European unity in order to deduce the existence of imperialist metropolises other than the United States. If the existing Common Market unified to the point where crucial economic and military decisions were irreversibly centralized, then capital would have much the same relationship to the 'state' as we observed in the case of a United Europe, and the Common Market would constitute a single imperialist metropolis.

At the present time of writing, of course, a number of existing nations constitute imperialist metropolises in their own right. Most firms, big or small, based in such countries as France, Germany or Japan are and will remain closely dependent on their home economies for some years to come. In times of economic crisis these firms will have an overriding interest in domestic growth and will, therefore, support an autonomous economic policy. Moreover, these states are able to extend substantial, if not entirely adequate, protection and support for the relatively limited overseas operations of their firms, either in the form of direct economic and even military aid, such as Japan is likely to offer its firms in South East Asia, or else in the form of retaliatory measures against foreign interest in the home economy, such as continental Europe may take if America restricts imports from Europe. Thus, even in the absence of European unification, an ideal solution from the point of view of most big European firms, there will be autonomous non-American states which will use their power vigorously on behalf of their own capital.

## Conclusions

We shall make no attempt to summarize what is contained above, other than to say that the prospect is one of imperial rivalry, in which a number of relatively autonomous states, which we have called 'imperialist metropolises', are in conflict with each other as they try to support their respective capitals. Whether these metropolises will consist of certain of today's nation states or of wider units will depend on a number of political and other factors, most of which have not been discussed. There are strong forces pushing European states into closer and closer alliance with each other, but whether this alliance will become sufficiently close to constitute a single true metropolis is not yet clear. Unless they can find allies, certain nation states, of which Britain is the leading example, will become, or perhaps already are, relatively subordinate. In contrast to the imperialist metropolises they might be called 'imperialist satellites'.

The reason these countries are or will be satellites is not necessarily to be found in the weakness of their capital, but in some cases may be in a lack of correspondence between the needs of this capital and the state power available to it. Where big capital operates internationally on a large scale and the state is relatively powerless, one of its prime needs is to keep on good terms with powerful foreign states. Thus, in economic affairs it will oppose the policies necessary for an indigenous solution to economic crises, for such policies may lead to foreign retaliation, and in foreign affairs it will not want the state to antagonize those states upon whose goodwill it depends.

Although these conclusions have important implications for the future of the imperialist system, we shall not discuss them here. One point is, however, worth making. The problems and prospects facing the working class and revolutionary movements in advanced capitalist countries will depend partly on the extent to which big capital is prepared to support an indigenous path of economic development in times of crisis, i.e. on the extent to which it acts as a nationalistic force, where the term 'nationalist' must be interpreted widely to include such phenomena as Common Market or European 'nationalism'. In a metropolis where this is the case, the danger exists of a new kind of 'social imperialism', whereby – in return for the benefits of an indigenous development – the working class accepts the capitalist system and

B. Rowthorn    179

supports or at least acquiesces in imperialist policies. 'Benefits' need not, of course, mean an actual increase in the standard of living of the working class. On the contrary, in a severe world crisis, the main benefit of an indigenous development would be to cushion the shock rather than actually to improve the workers' position. In a satellite, by contrast, where big capital is not prepared to support an indigenous development and acts, therefore, as a cosmopolitan force, the state's room for manoeuvre is greatly reduced and at times of crisis it is correspondingly more difficult to provide any benefits for the working class. Indeed, within the constraints imposed by the international needs of big capital, the state may be compelled to tackle the crisis by making a frontal attack on working-class living standards.

## References

GATES, T. R., and LINDEN, F. (1961), *Costs and Competition*, The National Industrial Conference Board, New York.

JALÉE, P. (1969), *L'Imperialisme en 1970*, Paris.

KIDRON, M. (1968), *Western Capitalism Since the War*, Weidenfeld & Nicolson.

KINDLEBERGER, C. P. (1970), *The International Corporation*, Harvard University Press.

LENIN, V. I. (1917), *Imperialism, the Highest Stage of Capitalism*, in *Selected Works*, Moscow, Vol. 1 (1967 edition).

MAGDOFF, H. (1969), *The Age of Imperialism*, Monthly Review Press.

MAGDOFF, H., and SWEEZY, P. (1969), 'The Multinational Corporation', *Monthly Review*, October and November.

MANDEL, E. (1969), 'Where is America Going?', *New Left Review*, no. 54, March–April.

MANDEL, E. (1970a), *Europe versus America?*, New Left Books.

MANDEL, E. (1970b), 'The Laws of Unequal Development', *New Left Review*, no. 59, January–February.

NICOLAUS, M. (1970), 'The Universal Contradiction', *New Left Review*, no. 59, January–February.

ROWTHORN, R. (1971), *International Big Business 1957–67*, Cambridge University Press.

VARGA, Y. (1968), 'The Problem of Inter-Imperialist Contradictions and War', in *Politico-Economic Problems of Capitalism*, Moscow.

# Part Four
# Technological Dependence in Less Developed Countries

Almost all writers on international firms have emphasized the importance of their ownership and control over technology, and they agree that the firms capitalize on this control in their investments in less developed countries. If LDCs are especially weak in bargaining power, the pursuit by international firms of their own interests may lead them to supply outdated or irrelevant technology at monopoly prices. Constantine Vaitsos (Reading 9) has pioneered the study of this relationship in the countries of the Andean Pact, and he details thoroughly the extent and depth of the abuse of monopoly power through technology. John Roberts and Jacques Perrin (Reading 10) describe the development of engineering consultancy in the Indian iron and steel industry. Engineering consultancy (the rather awkward English equivalent of the American, and French, term 'engineering') might be best described as the 'industrial technology industry'. If LDCs are to gain control over the technology they need, steel is an important sector in which to do this, since it is a basic producer-goods industry; it should also be relatively easy since most of the technology is well-established and slowly changing.

In the Andean Pact countries, and in the Indian iron and steel industry, there appears to be some progress towards indigenous control over technology. First, however, so long as *capitalist* participation in the capitalist world economy is envisaged, this may have little impact without the accompanying growth of worldwide marketing networks, political leverage, etc. – in short, capitalist development generally. A socialist planned economy may be better placed to benefit from importing technology for industrialization, as Russia did on a large scale in the 1920s and 1930s. Secondly, is control over technology in iron and steel, or machinery of most kinds, of much use if electronics and organic chemistry are now the mainstays of technological progress in the advanced countries?

# 9 Constantine Vaitsos

## The Process of Commercialization of Technology in the Andean Pact

Extracts from C. V. Vaitsos, *The Process of Commercialization of Technology in the Andean Pact; a Synthesis*, mimeo, Lima, 1971. Parts of this document were also included in C. V. Vaitsos, *Intercountry Income Distribution and Transnational Enterprises*, Oxford University Press, Oxford, 1974.

## Characteristics of the market for technology commercialization

The literature that evaluates issues related to the process of know-how importation by developing countries generally identifies the subject under the heading of 'technology transfer'. Terminology, although an inadequate index, is often illuminating to the extent that the concepts it represents have been adequately analysed and understood. The term 'transfer' indicates here the existence of a very limited comprehension of the market for technology. In commercial or economic terms we do not talk about the 'transfer' of copper or cotton, or television sets. We refer instead to the sale (or purchase) of these commodities. Similarly, in the case of factors of production, meaningful analysis has been undertaken by distinguishing and evaluating the characteristics of foreign direct investment, portfolio investments, international indebtedness, worker migration, the brain drain, etc. The term 'transfer' could represent a rather loose usage of the word; or it could be an indication of insufficient knowledge of the phenomena involved; or it could even fall within what Myrdal called 'diplomacy by terminology'. In the present paper we thus prefer the term *technology commercialization* and our purpose will be to evaluate the characteristics of its market. In that sense, technology is removed from the R&D laboratory or from the sphere of national policies for education, science and technology, by entering the arena of the commercial world. Technology viewed as an economic unit, a merchandise, has a special market (even a market 'place') with particular structure and properties, mechanisms that settle prices and 'quantities', rules of exchange and market impurities. The general principles of the determination of market prices, based on relative scarcities and the definition of market performance (number and size of buyers and sellers, relative bargaining power, degree of available information, etc.), govern also the market for technology commercialization *given its own particular characteristics*. We proceed to evaluate these special characteristics by dividing our presentation into three broad areas of analysis: (A) the supply of contractually sold technology; (B) characteristics of the demand for technology and some institutional constraints, and (C) three properties of technology and their economic implications.

## (A) *The supply of contractually sold technology*

First we need to distinguish between the concept of availability (or non-availability) of technology and that of supply of technology. The former has to be qualified by inquiring: available to whom? As in the analysis of availability of credit (as distinct from the cost of credit), answers to the above question will depend on the understanding of the concentration and captivity of technology on the one hand, and the factors that affect access to it by potential users on the other. As far as concentration is concerned, internationally traded industrial technology is to a large extent localized in corporations which, basically through product and process innovation and imitative or adaptive research, are able to bring into commercial usage the fruits of knowledge. It should be emphasized that a large part of that technology (certainly most of the sort sold to developing countries) implies on the part of the sellers 'cutting and taping together' bits of knowledge which, when appropriately combined and promoted, could lead to the successful commercialization of modified or new products and processes. This form of innovative activity, with its own form of scarcity, requires technical and other skills (with respect to the search for existing knowledge, systems of information diffusion, evaluation, improvement, etc.) which are quite distinct from the activities of the so-called 'centres of excellence' of research, oriented towards the frontiers of scientific know-how. A systematic study undertaken in the petrochemical industry indicated that, during the period when technology was most likely to be sold to developing countries, the original producers of a particular product or process accounted for only one per cent of the total licensing of know-how. The remaining 99 per cent was divided between 'followers' of commercial producers (52 per cent) and engineering firms (47 per cent)[1]. Similarly, know-how in electronics sold to developing countries by technology-intensive companies like Philips International or General Electric generally includes know-how on products that have been in commercial usage for some time (such as transistorized components for TV or radio). Such technology is available to other firms, which are not necessarily technology-intensive, in Belgium, Spain, Japan, etc. Furthermore, this know-how corresponds to technological activities quite different from those of a later vintage and for different products, such as satellites, for which present R&D budgets are allocated by Philips or General Electric. Thus, when we talk about the availability of the technology which is currently sold to developing countries, it is more relevant to talk about the *kind* of technological activities pursued (which could in-

1. See Stobaugh (1970), p. 5.

clude 'inverse technology', product testing, imitation, even product servicing) than about the size of the R&D budget. The economics of technology at this stage are more closely related to the broader issues of the economics of information and its usage for commercial purposes.

As far as captivity is concerned, this is related to legal monopoly privileges granted through patents by countries, and to technical captivity acquired through experience, product testing and improvement, guarded use of knowledge, etc. Access to knowledge and its use (outside of impediments imposed legally through patents or commercially by other barriers to entry) are related, among other things, to the capacity of potential users to search for knowledge and to their ability to translate it into competitive product and process innovations. The elements that enter here are quite diverse and include the size, ownership, structure and organization of firms, the market protection for the 'final' goods produced, the ease by which know-how is acquired embodied in intermediate products and capital goods, etc. For example, high tariffs, by influencing the risk perception of firms with respect to competitive pressures, could affect the motivation of existing firms to search for and use new forms of technology. On the other hand, restrictions on imports have been identified as a significant stimulus for exporters of the restricted products to undertake foreign investments or to sell technology through licensing arrangements.[2]

The elements listed above with respect to the availability of technology are related to, but also need to be distinguished from, the supply of technology. By supply, we mean the cost structure of technology sold to a given firm. Although potentially much more competitive, the present market of technology in relation to developing countries approaches the characteristics of bilateral oligopoly, that is, those of oligopoly-oligopsony. In such a market structure, bargaining appears to be the determining mechanism for prices and 'quantities' of the technology exchanged. The reasons for such a market structure are related to (a) the intrinsic properties of technology as a traded economic entity, which we will explain later in the paper; (b) the concentration of contractually sold technology in relatively few transnational enterprises which, through policies of cross-licensing or of similar nature, further accentuate the geographic or regional concentration; and (c) the limited initiative on the part of potential buyers to look for technology which is available but not sought after and which does not reach the stage of being supplied.[3] In a bilateral oligopoly market with the special marginal

2. See for example Horst (1969).

3. Research in Indonesia indicated that the technology used by foreign investors in that country could have been obtained without necessarily being attached to foreign investment, had the Indonesians searched the world market adequately. In the absence of such initiative by the local firms, technology reached Indonesia through foreign direct investments.

cost considerations that are involved in the development and commercialization of technology, *its supply cannot be determined* a priori. We can refer to the supply of technology (as distinct from its availability) only with respect to the supply facing a given firm with a particular size and ownership structure, confronting a given effective market protection related to goods produced as well as those imported for further processing, operating within a particular tax (and even monetary) system, and confronting specific government policies with respect to access to and negotiations for technology acquisition. Thus, for the same know-how a Chilean-owned firm faces a different supply of technology than a Brazilian-owned firm or than a foreign-owned firm in Chile or Brazil. The issue becomes even more complex if one considers the fact that the supply of more of the same technology is meaningless for a given firm once it has mastered that technology and it is contractually and legally permitted to use it.

The following example will help to clarify the reasons for the *a priori* indeterminacy of the cost (or supply) of technology. The predominant form in which the price of technology is denominated is through a percentage rate on the sale of goods or services incorporating the respective know-how. To start with, such a percentage for a given technology will depend, among other factors, on whether the recipient firm is owned by the licenser or by third parties. If it is owned by the licenser and the local government does not intervene in the process of negotiations, the percentage of royalty payments will depend on the global financial management of the parent-licenser. For example, if the corporate tax rate in the host country of the subsidiary is higher than in the home country, the parent will be induced to increase royalty receipts so as to reduce overall tax payments for the firm. Similarly, the higher the *ad valorem* tariff rates for intermediate products sold by the parent to a subsidiary, the lower will tend to be the (transfer) pricing of such products, which in turn will prompt higher royalty payments as a mechanism of income transfer. The considerations involved in the supply of the same technology to a firm not owned by the licenser will be quite different. Furthermore, the cost of technology (whether in terms of percentage rates or absolute amounts) will depend on the number of units sold and the price of the product incorporating the respective know-how. Also, given a royalty rate, the higher the *ad valorem* tariff rate on the products produced by a given know-how, the higher the absolute cost for obtaining that technology.

(B) *Characteristics of the demand for technology and some institutional constraints*

In the formulation of the demand for technology by a prospective buyer, it is necessary to distinguish three different elements that enter jointly into such a decision making process. First, one needs to evaluate the expected benefits to be derived from the imported technology. The introduction of new technology could be cost-saving by reducing the total cost of other inputs necessary for a given amount of output. That cost reduction will represent the benefit to be obtained by utilizing more efficient know-how. Similarly, the introduction of technology could mean the competitive survival of a firm which confronts others in a given market situation. In that case, the benefit resulting from the application of new technology would be not the costs saved, but the opportunity offered to the firm of meeting competitive pressures successfully. Furthermore, the introduction of new technology could bring about the establishment of new production activities, products or processes. The benefits from such utilization of technology will be represented by the series of net earnings resulting from the new activities. Cost reduction, competitive survival and additional net earnings resulting from new operations accrue over a period of time. Equally, payments for a given technology are registered for various periods of time, while the actual learning period and absorption of new technology could take place during a different and generally shorter time range.

All these diverging time factors which create different forms of demand and supply relations necessitate a discounted present value analysis for meaningful comparisons of the magnitudes involved. Furthermore, for the individual firm the relevant magnitudes refer to effective profitability, while for countries they refer to value added.

Thus, the *upper limit* of the demand for technology should represent the net benefits resulting from its use, appropriately measured. Under competitive market conditions such a result will tend to be almost self-regulating. Since, though, the market for technology is highly imperfect and non-competitive and encompasses products that are equally non-competitive among firms that often do not operate at arms-length, the demand for know-how will tend to differ from its benefits in actual market behaviour.

A second factor in the formulation of the demand for technology by a firm or country concerns the cost involved for developing such know-how, or a close substitute, internally within that firm or country. If that cost is lower than the expected benefits from the use of technology, then the upper limit of the demand for know-how will be set by such a cost. The argument here is equivalent to that involved in make-or-lease decisions for equipment. Thus, even if the imputed value of technology is higher, the demand for it will be set by the lower opportunity cost of developing it internally in the firm or country.

Finally, the demand for technology will also depend on the alternative sources of supply for the same or similar technology. Given our analysis above of the *a priori* indeterminacy of the supply of technology and the fact that technology is treated within an imperfect bargaining framework rather than a competitive market structure, alternative supplies affect (or should affect) a firm's demand for technology. With a set of existing alternative sources of supply and a cost of developing a given technology within a firm, the upper limit of demand for technology for new sources will be set by the *lowest* cost involved from such existing ones *if* the imputed value of the benefits accruing from such technology is higher. If, on the other hand, the imputed value of benefits is lower, then the upper limit of demand will be represented by that imputed value.

We come now to consider some institutional factors that affect the formulation of demand for technology.[4]

1. Technical know-how in the process of its commercialization appears to be the least identified and understood factor of production. The form of its exchange takes place by the most vague means, at least in the minds of the purchasers. Countries have developed specific definitions as well as elaborate systems (which still leave a lot to be desired) for the classification and evaluation of the commercialization of other resources. One need not spend very much time in a central bank or a customs office to notice the elaborate mechanism of registration, classification, etc. in the interchange of financial capital or goods among countries. Generally, technical know-how is still commercialized under the broad, vague and tautological definition of 'technology'. The question arises as to what, at least operationally, is the technology that a country is importing for a given industry or process or product. Is it a production manual, or a patent (which is not technology but the legal captivity of technology), or technical assistance transmitted through experts, or production processes embodied in machinery, or designs of factory layouts and work programmes, or specifications already incorporated in intermediate products, or what? In order to understand the effects of technology, the type of dependence that exists between its buyer and seller, its potential substitutability and the process of its negotiation, one needs to define, itemize and qualify that which one imports. Furthermore, one needs to quantify the economic value of what one intends to purchase, in order to determine its imputed value. Clearly, technology lacks units of measurement, at least in the traditional sense. Its quantification can thus be estimated only by trying to determine the economic equivalent of its effects.

Furthermore, of great importance to developing countries is the fact that there are many different sources of supply, with different prices, that can offer a given type of technology for the majority of the industrial needs of these countries. (France, for example, might need computer technology that only I B M has and Japan might need know-how that only Texas Instruments Company has. But textile technology, fertilizer plants, components for

4. See Vaitsos (1971).

television sets and processes for producing tyres have no great secrets and are available from different sources world-wide). As indicated above, an adequate and rational specification of the demand for technology requires information on these alternative sources. This implies an effort to identify and disaggregate the various components included in technical know-how and an attempt to discover and evaluate alternative sources of their supply. At the present time, technological inputs are demanded and sold in a *package form*, in which a supplier sells together various inputs and forms of know-how,[5] achieving through this process various degrees of monopoly control.

2. The process of information handling in the 1960s in the developing countries on the commercialization of technology appears quite similar to that of the early concession agreements in the extractive industries during the first part of this century. During that time, concession contracts were kept secret and 'only a great deal of detective work – combing legal libraries of universities in developed countries, scanning trade journals for clues, trading information with other governments, etc. – could yield much information'.[6] It took some time to understand the necessity of exchanging information as an explicit policy by governments of developing countries. This, together with other factors, led to the establishment of such institutions as the Organization of Petroleum Exporting Countries (OPEC), which has as one of its main functions the dissemination of information to the definite interest of the member countries. The result of this enhanced availability of information, together with market and risk factors, led to the signing of 'model contracts' in the 1960s and 70s.

Reflecting on the process and procedures with respect to the handling of information about technology commercialization during the 1960s, one encounters cases which are similar or parallel to the standards practised during the initial concession agreements. In the process of technology commercialization, due to mis-specified concepts of confidentiality and secrecy, contracts of technology transfers are kept completely secret. In countries that do not apply an exchange control mechanism in contractual agreements, information is restricted to the two contracting parties.

In countries where governmental regulating bodies intervene in the contractual processes between private parties, inadequately functioning administrative procedures limit the degree of knowledge of contractual terms. The members of royalty committees usually 'know' overall industry terms in an intuitive sense and by memory only. Of course, no explicit mechanism exists for inter-country comparisons. Government

5. See Cooper (1970).
6. Wells (1968).

agencies guard very scrupulously the contractual agreements of their nationals from other neighbour countries, thinking that in that way they preserve national interests. Effectively, what they are jointly achieving is a reduction of their own knowledge and bargaining power by segmenting the market of information and accentuating problems of relative ignorance.

Clearly, one cannot ask for something if one knows neither what it is nor how to ask for it. The degree of availability of information will determine one's negotiating strategy with maximum and minimum conditions, and also the areas within which the other party is most or least likely to give way. Secrecy is clearly one of the elements implicit in a contract. (Conditions are established so as to respect the secrecy or confidentiality of technical or marketing know-how that is purchased.) Yet, if this secrecy is misdefined and misused, damage to at least one of the negotiating parties could certainly result. Government agencies in groups could certainly proceed to inform themselves about market conditions in technology commercialization around the world, as well as informing each other about them and about terms of agreements in their own countries. The benefits derived from such a policy would certainly outweigh the actual or imaginary benefits of secrecy among nations in their contracts with foreign technology suppliers.

(C) *Three properties of technology and their economic implications*

(1) Technology in the process of its commercialization is usually embodied in intermediate products, machinery and equipment, people's skills, whole systems of production (like turn-key plants), even systems of distribution or marketing (like cryogenic technology in ships that transport liquid gas), etc. Thus, know-how represents a part integrated in a larger whole. As a result, the market for the former is not independent but constitutes part of the market for the latter. This market integration of various inputs creates non-competitive conditions for each one of them since they are sold in a package form.

(2) In the formulation of the demand for information, as in all other markets, a prospective buyer needs information about the properties of the item he intends to purchase so as to be able to make appropriate decisions. Yet, in the case of technology, what is needed is information about information which could effectively be one and the same thing. Thus, the prospective buyer is confronted with a structural weakness intrinsic to his position as purchaser, with resulting imperfections in the corresponding market operations.

(3) The usage of information or technology by a company or person does not in itself reduce its availability, present or future. Thus, the incremental cost in the use or sale of an already-developed technology is close to zero for

someone that already has access to that technology. In cases of minor adaptation (due to scale, taste, differing local conditions, etc.) the firm incurs certain costs that can be estimated and usually do not exceed a figure in the tens of thousands of dollars. From the point of view of the prospective purchaser, though, the relevant incremental cost for developing the same type of an alternative technology with his own technical capacity might amount to millions of dollars. Given market availabilities, the price between zero or tens of thousands of dollars, on the one hand, and millions of dollars, on the other, is determined solely on the basis of crude bargaining power. The range between the corresponding cost considerations is so wide that no price between them can be claimed to be more or less appropriate.

## Empirical results and their interpretation

### Analysis of contracts of technology commercialization

In order to understand the terms of technology commercialization, 451 contracts in various sectors were analysed and compared in the five Andean countries. The country breakdown was as shown in Table 1.

Table 1 Technology commercialization contracts analysed

| Country | Number of contracts | Number of sectors |
|---------|---------------------|-------------------|
| Bolivia | 35 | 4 including 'others' |
| Colombia | 140 | 4 |
| Chile | 175 | 13 |
| Ecuador | 12 | 5 |
| Peru | 89 | 2 including 'others' |

Despite the fact that the basic methodology pursued was a common one, different administrative and legal requirements existing in the countries prior to Decision No. 24 of the Andean Pact necessitated diverse procedures so as to obtain the requisite information. For example, in Chile and Colombia, due to prior legislation, contracts of technology commercialization were deposited in corresponding government agencies. In Ecuador some contracts were available to the Central Bank, while in Peru and Bolivia the researchers had to contact the private sector directly. As a result, data was not equally available and some of the information not totally comparable. Thus, data in Chile and Colombia included the results of government negotiations with foreign technology suppliers, while in the other countries the terms reflected the agreement reached between the two contracting parties. The latter has important repercussions in the case of contracts established between subsidiary firms and foreign parent corporations, since, in the absence of government intervention, terms of agreement reflect here a totally one-sided preference set by the parent. The absence of arms-length negotiations results in terms that either reflect overall company strategy or could even be redundant since control can also be achieved through ownership ties.

The clauses that we will be discussing immediately below raise important economic and legal issues about the way in which private contracting (*contratación privada*) extends into areas where private economic benefits derived by the parties involved are in conflict with the overall economic and social interests of the country in which they operate. Some answers to this type of question have long been provided in the industrialized world through antimonopoly and antitrust legislation, as well as through the establishment of public regulatory agencies. Many developing countries have still to demonstrate an awareness of these issues and their implications for private and public economic interests. Furthermore, the terms to be discussed below raise questions about the concept of liberty or sovereignty to make contracts between unequals. In a bargaining structure with highly unequal participants, with limited information and imperfect overall market conditions, the sovereignty of the 'technology consumers' becomes an inapplicable concept.

## Export-restrictive clauses

One of the most frequent clauses encountered in contracts of technology commercialization is that of export prohibition. Such restrictive practices generally limit the production and sale of goods utilizing foreign technology solely within the national boundaries of the receiving country. Some allow exports only to specific neighbouring countries. From the total of 451 contracts evaluated in the Andean Pact, 409 contained information on exports which appeared as follows in Table 2.

Table 2 Export-restrictive clauses

| Country | Total number of contracts | Total prohibition of exports | Exports permitted only in certain areas | Exports permitted to the rest of the world |
|---|---|---|---|---|
| Bolivia | 35 | 27 | 2 | 6 |
| Colombia | 117 | 90 | 2 | 25 |
| Ecuador | 12 | 9 | — | 3 |
| Peru | 83 | 74 | 8 | 1 |
| total | 247 | 200 | 12 | 35 |

In Chile, from 162 contracts with information on the matter, 117 prohibited totally any form of exportation. Of the remaining 45, the majority limited export permission to certain countries. The exact number of these partial export permits was not possible to estimate from the data offered by Chile. Thus, in the four countries where precise figures were available, about *81 per cent of the contracts prohibited exports totally and 86 per cent had some restrictive clause on exports*. In Chile more than 72 per cent of the contracts prohibited exports totally.

The country breakdown in Bolivia, Colombia and Peru by sector and by ownership structure of the contracts containing information on possibilities of exports of goods utilizing purchased technology can be seen in the following table:

Table 3 Export-restrictive clauses by sector and ownership structure

| Countries | | Colombia | | | Bolivia | | | Peru | | |
|---|---|---|---|---|---|---|---|---|---|---|
| Sectors | Ownership structures | Exports prohibited | Partial permission | No export restriction | Exports prohibited | Partial permission | No export restriction | Exports prohibited | Partial permission | No export restriction |
| *textiles* | foreign (wholly owned) joint ventures national firms | 11 | 0 | 1 | 4 | 2 | 1 | | | |
| *pharma-ceuticals* | foreign | 31 | 2 | 13 | 1 | 0 | 0 | 13 | 5 | 0 |
| | joint ventures | 3 | 0 | 0 | | | | | | |
| | national | 34 | 0 | 4 | 3 | 0 | 1 | 52 | 0 | 0 |
| *chemicals* | foreign | 3 | 0 | 2 | | | | | | |
| | joint ventures | 2 | 0 | 2 | | | | | | |
| | national | 6 | 0 | 3 | | | | | | |
| *food and beverages* | foreign | | | | 8 | 0 | 2 | | | |
| | national | | | | 0 | 0 | 1 | | | |
| *others* | foreign | | | | 10 | 0 | 1 | 5 | 1 | 1 |
| | joint ventures | | | | | | | 1 | 0 | 0 |
| | national | | | | 1 | 0 | 0 | 3 | 2 | 0 |

The above data indicates that no significant differences exist among countries. For example, contracts with complete prohibition of exports as a percentage of the total number of contracts with relevant information were as follows:

Bolivia:    77 per cent;
Colombia: 77 per cent;
Ecuador:   75 per cent;
Peru:      89 per cent.

With the exception of Peru, where figures were biased upwards by the large number of cases belonging to the pharmaceutical sector in the sample taken, the figures indicate similar percentages in the upper seventies. These contrast with an average of 53 per cent reported in Japan by the Agency of Industrial Science and Technology published in 1962.[7] If one takes into account, furthermore, that certain key sectors in Japan reported much higher percentages on export prohibition than the overall country average, it is probable that for the sectors included in the Andean study the export restrictive clauses on Japanese firms in the 1950s could be much smaller after taking into account differences in the types of technology sold within a given sector. For example, in contrast to the country average of 53 per cent, the following percentages were reported in various Japanese sectors:

Metallic products:            90 per cent;
Non-transport machinery: 85 per cent;
Transport machinery:        80 per cent;
Paper products:               65 per cent.

Restrictive clauses on exports are based on relative bargaining power, given market conditions on alternative sources of supply of technology. Thus, countries like the Andean ones, despite the diverse size and relative strength of their firms, do not achieve major concessions in terms of their negotiations with foreign transnational corporations that sell industrial technology. The bargaining power of a relatively large firm in Medellin, Colombia, *when confronting a transnational corporation*, does not seem to differ that much from a smaller firm in Cochabamba, Bolivia. There appears to be a necessary critical mass of bargaining power, which also depends on concomitant government policies. On the other hand, (larger) firms with access to information about world market availabilities, and aided by government action (like the policies pursued by MITI in Japan), can achieve better conditions.

In terms of ownership structure, the following percentages were noted in the Andean countries for the various forms of export restrictions with respect to the total number of contracts providing relevant information:

Wholly-owned foreign subsidiaries: 79 per cent;
Nationally-owned firms:               92 per cent.

7. See OECD (1967).

The lower percentage figure noted for wholly-owned foreign subsidiaries is of limited significance since control through ownership can dictate export possibilities. The reasons for the inclusion of export restrictions in contracts signed between parents and subsidiaries are various: (a) a parent through export restrictive clauses can protect future operations in other markets in case it decides or has to sell part or all of the subsidiary to a third party; (b) an export restrictive clause could provide a 'legal' basis for refusing local government's pressures to export (e.g. France and Japan explicitly request foreign technology suppliers to export from these countries); (c) export restrictive clauses set clear 'rules of behaviour' for local managers in decentralized transnational corporations or in ones having cross-licensing and cartel agreements with other firms; and (d) sheer redundancy.

The figure, though, of great significance, is the one referring to nationally owned firms. *In our sample it indicated that 92 per cent of the contracts of Andean owned firms were prohibiting the exportation of goods produced with foreign technology.* This occurred at the time when the Andean nations with the establishment of their common market were trying to integrate their economies by, for example, increasing inter-country trade. Agreements reached between governments are, in the case of technology commercialization, greatly conditioned by the terms reached among private firms whose relative bargaining power is totally unequal. Also, efforts by UNCTAD and individual governments to achieve preferential treatment for the export of manufacturing goods from developing countries have to be considered within a market structure which among other things forbids such exports through explicit restrictive clauses.[8] Technology, an indispensable input in industrial development, becomes through the process of its present form of commercialization a major factor limiting such development.

In terms of sectorial comparisons, the following figures were noted in the Andean countries, with respect to the number of contracts that included export restrictions as a percentage of the total contracts availing relevant information:[9]

Textiles:          88 per cent;
Pharmaceuticals:   89 per cent;
Chemicals:         78 per cent;
Food and beverages: 73 per cent;
Others:            91 per cent.

8. Export restrictive practices have been observed by the governments of Iran, El Salvador, Mexico, Chile, India, Colombia, Philippines, Kuwait, etc., in the process of purchase of foreign technology. See UNCTAD (1969), pp. 4–6.

9. In the statistics for chemicals, we added to the figures of Bolivia, Columbia, Ecuador and Peru those provided by Chile, which included 51 contracts with complete export prohibitions in of a total 62 contracts. The rest of the percentages refer only to the former four countries.

The above percentages indicate no major differences by sectors. Irrespective of industrial activity, suppliers of technology to the Andean group limit the possibilities of exports. Through market segmentation, as far as Andean-owned firms are concerned, foreign know-how suppliers can take advantage of different elasticities of demand for technology in the various countries. As for foreign owned subsidiaries, inefficiency due to small scale production is offset by monopolistic margins achieved through special discriminatory practices, aided by the import substitution strategy of local governments.

*Tie-in clauses on intermediate products*

A large percentage of the contracts in the commercialization of technology includes obligatory terms which designate the purchase of intermediates and capital goods from the same source as that of know-how. Even in the absence of such explicit terms, control through ownership or technological requirements and specifications, stemming from the nature of the know-how sold, could determine uniquely the source of intermediate products. Thus, as in the case of tie-in arrangements in loans, benefits for the supplier and costs for the purchaser are not limited only to the explicit payments such as royalties or interest rates. They also include implicit charges in various forms of margins in the concomitant or tied sale of other goods and services. Furthermore, at the aggregate level, flows of technology between countries imply the joint accompanying flow of intermediates, equipment and capital.[10]

As far as tie-in arrangements are concerned, these take various forms in technology commercialization contracts. The majority explicitly require the purchase of materials from the technology supplier. Some of them also make such tied purchase conditional on a maximum price being paid for the goods purchased. For example, contracts signed by Colombian-owned firms stipulated that the prices of the tied products should not exceed by more than 10 per cent 'world market prices'.[11] No such conditional tie-in arrangement was encountered in contracts between foreign-owned subsidiaries and their parents. Other contracts, in addition, prohibit, limit or control the use of local materials. Still others can achieve indirectly similar results in the purchase of intermediates through quality control clauses. A factor that often strongly affects the tied purchase of materials is the question of patents (or trade marks). The types of technology or of intermediate products imported by developing countries have generally several alternative sources of supply, if an adequate search for them is undertaken. On the

10. For a fuller analysis on this last point see Gruber, Mehta and Vernon (1966).
11. The extra benefits accruing to the supplier are determined by the difference between the price of sale and the marginal cost of producing such goods. The extra cost for the purchaser is determined, in turn, by the difference between the sale price and that of alternative sources of supply. The two are, obviously, not the same.

other hand, monopoly privileges through patents restrict such supply to the patent-holder.

Tie-in clauses on intermediates for Bolivia, Ecuador and Peru appeared as shown in Table 4.

Table 4 Tie-in clauses on intermediates

| Country | Contracts with tie-in clauses | Contracts explicitly permitting free importation |
|---|---|---|
| Bolivia | 29 | 6 |
| Ecuador | 8 | 4 |
| Peru | 55 | 34 |
| total | 92 | 44 |

*Thus, 67 per cent of the contracts with relevant information have tie-in clauses in these countries.* The industry break-down in Bolivia was as shown in Table 5.

Table 5 Tie-in clauses by sector: Bolivia

| Sector | Contracts with tie-in clauses | Contracts explicitly permitting free importation |
|---|---|---|
| food and beverages | 11 | 0 |
| textiles | 4 | 3 |
| pharmaceuticals | 4 | 1 |
| others | 10 | 2 |

In Colombia, 100 per cent of the contracts of foreign-owned subsidiaries and above 95 per cent of nationally-owned firms in the pharmaceutical industry included tie-in clauses. In the Colombian chemical industry, three out of five contracts had such clauses. In all countries it appeared that the pharmaceutical industry had the highest or among the highest percentages of tie-in arrangements. We will be dealing with the price effects of these clauses later in the paper.

*Other types of restrictive clauses*

To understand the meaning and repercussions of a contract, one has to evaluate it in its totality. Often terms that are defined in clause X are conditioned or modified in clause Y. Also, without explicitly stating something that would violate local legislation, one can achieve the desired end through indirect, legally accepted means. For example, through certain quality clauses one can indirectly affect volume of production or control sources of intermediates; or, through control of the volume of production (which is permissible under certain patent legislations), one can control the volume of exports (which is not permitted by the same patent legislations).

Restrictive clauses in contracts for technology commercialization are of various types. For example, in Bolivia, out of 35 contracts analysed (and in addition to the export restrictions and tie-in clauses on intermediates cited above), the following terms were included: 24 contracts tied technical assistance to the usage of patents or trade-marks and vice versa; 22 tied necessary additional know-how to the present contracts; 3 fixed prices of final goods; 11 prohibited production or sale of similar products; 19 required secrecy of the know-how involved in the contract, and 16 after the end of the contract also; 5 specified that any controversy or arbitrage should be settled in the courts of the country of the licenser. Also, 28 out of the 35 cases contractually put quality control in the hands of the licenser. Similarly, in Chile, out of 175 contracts, 98 had quality-control by the licenser; 45 controlled the volume of sales; and 27 the volume of production. In Peru, from 89 contracts, 66 controlled the volume of sales of the licensee. Some clauses prohibited the sale of similar or identical products after the end of the contract. Others tied the sale of technology to the appointment of key personnel by the licensor.

The list of clauses included in contracts for technology commercialization and the impact they have on business decisions prompt the question of which crucial policies are left under the control of the ownership or management of the recipient firm. If the licenser retains control of the volume, markets, prices and quality of goods sold, the sources, prices and quality of its intermediates and capital goods, the hiring of key personnel, the type of technology used, etc., then the only basic decision left to the licensee is whether or not to enter into an agreement to purchase technology. Technology, through the present process of its commercialization, becomes thus a mechanism for control of the recipient firms. Such control supersedes, complements or substitutes that which results from ownership of the capital of a firm. Political and economic preoccupations that have been voiced in Latin America concerning the high degree of foreign control of domestic industry can properly be evaluated, not only within the foreign direct-investment model, but also within the mechanism of technology commercialization. It is for this reason that the term 'technology *transfer*' is considered in the present paper as one that inappropriately represents the phenomena involved and their implications.

An additional issue needs, furthermore, to be mentioned. The type of clauses encountered in contracts for technology commercialization violate basic anti-monopoly or antitrust legislations in the home countries of the licensers. Since the extra-territoriality of laws is in general not applicable (at least operationally), it befits the technology-receiving countries to legislate and regulate accordingly, so as to protect the interests of the purchasing firms. Industrialized countries have in the last half-century, or even earlier, undertaken to define in one way or another in their legal structure the extent to which private contracting and the exercise of business power can operate within a market mechanism.[12] Developing countries have still to show an adequate understanding of the issues involved in their commercial laws, which regulate the application of industrial property matters, etc. As will be seen in the next section, the mechanism of technology commercialization cannot function adequately, so as to protect the interests of the comparatively smaller and weaker national firms, without the existence of concomitant legislation that defines the extent of acceptance of terms negotiated by large foreign transnational corporations.

## The role of governmental negotiating committees

On various occasions earlier, it was pointed out that the market for technology commercialization is best described within a bargaining framework. Given this premise, and the fact that a large part of foreign know-how is introduced through the establishment of foreign-owned subsidiaries, it can be concluded that such firms lack even a minimum negotiating position, since their interests are, presumably, identified with those of their parent corporation and not with the host country. For example, it is not uncommon to encounter cases where a wholly-owned foreign subsidiary has capitalized in its books technology that originated with the parent corporation. As a result it could be (a) paying royalties; (b) reducing its tax payments through depreciation 'charges' of intangible assets; (c) having lower tax coefficients in countries where taxable profits are related to 'invested' capital; and (d) claiming higher capital repatriations, all for the same know-how. Clearly a foreign-owned subsidiary does not need to capitalize technology since 100 per cent of its capital is already owned by its parent. Thus, unless a government body intervenes between the 'private contracting' of a parent and a subsidiary, the distribution of returns from the usage of technology are likely to be only one-sided.

Similarly, even among independent firms the relative size of transnational corporations and companies in developing countries is such, and the relative cost considerations are so different, that the strength of the bargaining power of the purchaser can only be achieved through corresponding government action. Such action is based on the power a government enjoys in permitting

12. For tie-in restrictions see Section 1 of the Sherman Act and Section 3 of the Clayton Act in the US. For similar and related issues (such as export restrictions), see Article 85 (1) of the Rome Treaty establishing the European Economic Community, Article 37 of the 1945 Price Ordinance of France, the Economic Competition Act of 1958 of Netherlands, the Antimonopoly Law of Japan, etc.

C. Vaitsos 199

or rejecting access to the domestic market. This type of power seldom resides within the limits of private firms and its usage can be quite effective in the confrontation of the different types of power at the disposition of transnational corporations. From the second half of 1967 to June 1971, the Comité de Regalías of Colombia had evaluated 395 technology commercialization contracts. Of these, 334 were negotiated, modified and finally approved and 61 were rejected. In the process of negotiations, payments of royalties were reduced by about 40 per cent or about $US8 million annually. The size of the annual royalty reduction in Colombia brought about by government negotiation is equivalent to the total annual payments for technology reported for the whole economy of Chile. Furthermore, it was estimated in Colombia that the average absolute size of royalties paid by foreign subsidiaries was three times as large as that paid by national firms. This can be attributed to differences in the volume of sales of given products, differences in the number of products included in contracts and differences in percentage royalty rates agreed. In the negotiations that took place between the middle of 1967 and end of 1969, of the contracts that were approved as presented (rather than being modified or rejected), 75 per cent had as licensees nationally-owned firms. Unless the Comité de Regalías were applying easier standards to nationally-owned firms, this would tend to suggest that such firms were undergoing a much more rigorous negotiating process with their foreign licensers before presenting contracts for approval to the Comité de Regalías. Or it could equally suggest that foreign-owned subsidiaries in Colombia were using royalty payments as an alternative means to profit repatriation and not for the compensation of 'strictly defined' technical services, with significant fiscal and balance of payments effects for Colombia.

Also, during the latter part of 1970 and the beginning of 1971, negotiations by the Colombian Comité de Regalías:

(1) Reduced by 90 per cent the tie-in clauses in the purchase of intermediates;
(2) Eliminated by 100 per cent the restrictive export clauses;
(3) Eliminated by 80 per cent the clauses on minimum royalty payments;
(4) Prohibited payments on taxes by the licensee on royalties remitted to the licenser;
(5) Established maximum percentage royalty rates by sectors.

These significant achievements by the Comité de Regalías have to be qualified in the following way. As far as foreign-owned subsidiaries are concerned, the reduction in royalty payments could result in higher profits, which could be remitted after payment of local taxes or could be passed on to the parent firm through inter-affiliate transfer pricing. Furthermore, the exclusion of clauses from the contract of a subsidiary does not mean that the practices involved will be abolished, since control through ownership could still dictate the same practices. As far as nationally-owned firms are concerned, it is known that in some cases, after such government intervention, 'gentlemen's agreements' exist, extra-contractually, between licensers and licensees. Nevertheless, in other cases government intervention has resulted in known benefits for nationally-owned firms.

Up to the end of 1970, when Decision No. 24 of the Andean Pact was approved, only Colombia and Chile had governmental negotiating committees for technology, patents and trademarks, while Bolivia, Ecuador and Peru lacked corresponding bodies. Some of the major negotiating deficiencies of the Colombian and Chilean committees were the following: first, such committees lacked an adequate legal backing to confront restrictive business practices imposed through bargaining by foreign know-how and patent licensers. For example, up to 1969 the Colombian Comité de Regalías was not oriented to control the major restrictive practices in the negotiated contracts. Yet, in 1970, through specific government action and reinforced by the provisions on commercial and other practices included in Decision No. 24 at the end of that year, the Comité de Regalías was able to enhance its negotiating scope and power. Chile's experience was similar. The name itself of these committees (Royalty Committee) indicates the initial limitations of their orientation. They were directed only towards control of payments or fees and that only with respect to balance of payments considerations, excluding thus the broader and often more important effects of other clauses in technology commercialization. Second, as the evaluation of contracts in the rest of the Andean Pact has confirmed, payment of royalties in more than 95 per cent of the cases examined is set as a percentage of sales and not with respect to profits or value added. One result of this is that the more inefficient a firm is and/or the higher the protective tariff levels are on the goods produced, the higher the royalties paid for foreign technology! Articles incorporated in Decision No. 24 (as in very recent legislation in Argentina) have attempted to correct this situation. Finally, a major limitation of existing government negotiating committees rests on the fact that their bargaining power is significantly limited by very inadequate information systems. For example, there is no institutionalized prior search for alternative sources of supply of technology by studying international market availabilities. Similarly, minimum conditions exist for the evaluation of the technological and broader economic impact of the imported technology.

*Some considerations of the structure and effects of patents.*[13]

The economic impact of patents stems from the *monopoly privileges* granted by the state to innovations that are industrially useful. Such privileges are

13. The basic ideas of this part have been borrowed from Vaitsos (1972).

granted on the basis of the traditional assumption that patents provide a
necessary incentive for inventive activity and/or compensate for it. Also,
through patent disclosure, or the guarantee of monopoly, etc., it is assumed
that sufficient incentives are given so as to introduce innovations into
commercially-beneficial industrial activities. In addition, in terms of overall
country effects (leaving distributional effects aside), it is assumed that the
monopoly costs to consumers and to other producers are smaller than the
benefits that accrue from promoting inventive and investment activitie
through patents. It is important to clarify that the above arguments are no
with respect to inventions and investments *per se*, but with respect to the
role of monopoly privileges on such activities. Monopoly privileges granted
by patents are clearly intended to introduce the production of inventions in
a market price framework. Prices exist when scarcity exists. Patents, granting
monopoly of usage (or usage under licence), create scarcity by limiting the
availability of inventions, although an invention is by its nature an 'in
exhaustible' entity in terms of number or times of usage. To a certain extent
prices are put on the usage of inventions not because of their scarcity but *i,
order to make them* scarce to possible users. A patent diminishes the possible
usage of an innovation, with the intention of generating an economic rent.

In order to understand the effect of patents on developing countries w
need to stress the following three aspects:

(1) *The patents granted in developing countries are almost all of foreign
origin.*

The following table presents comparative data on the number of patents o
foreign origin as a percentage of the total patents granted by variou
countries between the years 1957–61.

Furthermore, if the number of patents granted by developing countries i
weighted by their economic value (for example, by the volume of sales the

Table 6 **Patents of foreign origin as percentage of total granted**

| 'Large' Industrial Countries | | 'Smaller' Industrialized Countries | | Developing Countries | |
|---|---|---|---|---|---|
| USA | 15·72% | Italy | 62·85% | India | 89·38% |
| Japan | 34·02% | Switzerland | 64·08% | Turkey | 91·73% |
| West Germany | 37·14% | Sweden | 69·30% | Arab Rep. | 93·01% |
| United Kingdom | 47·00% | Netherlands | 69·83% | Trinidad | |
| France | 59·36% | Luxemburg | 80·48% | & Tobago | 94·18% |
| | | Belgium | 85·55% | Pakistan | 95·75% |
| | | | | Ireland | 96·51% |

Source: United Nations (1964), pp. 94–5.

represent or their value added), the percentage of patents of national origin will probably be less than 1 per cent. Thus, whenever we talk about patents granted by developing countries and the policies that should regulate them, we really refer to patents belonging to foreign companies or foreign nationals in these countries.

The experience of the large industrialized countries has not indicated any relatively major change in the percentage of patents of foreign origin. For example, the following table shows the patents of foreign origin as a percentage of total patents granted by each country.

Table 7 **Patents of foreign origin as percentage of total granted**

| Countries | 1940 | 1957–61 |
|---|---|---|
| USA | 10% | 16% |
| Japan | 25% | 34% |
| Germany | 25% | 37% |
| United Kingdom | 50% | 47% |
| France | 50% | 59% |

Sources: Diegger (1948), p. 257; table 6 above.

By contrast, the patents granted by developing countries have experienced a progressive denationalization during recent periods. Table 8 indicates the Chilean experience in this respect.

Table 8 **Percentage of patents granted in Chile according to origin**

| | National | Foreign |
|---|---|---|
| 1937 | 34·5% | 65·5% |
| 1947 | 20·0% | 80·0% |
| 1958 | 11·0% | 89·0% |
| 1967 | 5·5% | 94·5% |

Source: CORFO (1970b).

## (2) *Patents and concentration of economic power*

An important change has taken place in the structure of ownership of patents in the industrialized countries as well as in developing ones. The majority of patents have left the world of the individual inventor and have become the property of large transnational corporations. The latter use patents for their global business policy. This change in the structure of ownership of patents has, in turn, resulted in the concentration of patents under the control of a relatively very small number of transnational firms. For example, 50 per cent of all patents obtained by companies whose corresponding investigations were financed by the Federal Government of the US between 1946 and 1962 belong to 20 firms.[14] Furthermore, of all patents resulting from research that was financed by private firms as well as by the Federal Government during the same period in the US, 35·7 per cent belonged to less than 100 firms. Since the patents granted in developing countries are almost all of foreign origin, they also reflect the same type of concentration. In Colombia less than 10 per cent of all the firms that obtained patents in the pharmaceutical industry controlled in 1970 more than 60 per cent of all the patents in that sector. The same percentage existed for samples of patents in synthetic fibres and chemicals.[15]

The concentration of patents in the hands of a small number of firms results in patents being to a large extent oriented towards the control of the market, in order to maximize the overall interests of a small number of firms who have industrial property privileges. This market control and oligopolistic concentration is reinforced by the system of cross-licensing between companies, which in turn reduces a world-wide oligopolistic structure into a regional monopoly.

(3) *Lack of direct exploitation of patents in developing countries*

Patents granted by developing countries not only belong almost totally to foreign companies but, in addition, are hardly ever exploited in such countries. For example, in Peru, of 4,872 patents granted between 1960 and 1970 in the electronic, textile, machinery and equipment, chemical, food processing, pharmaceutical, fishing, metal processing and transport equipment sectors, etc., only 54 were registered as being exploited. Working or exploitation of patents was thus less than 1·1 per cent of the total. Similarly, in Colombia, out of a total of 3,513 patents evaluated (2,534 belonging to the pharmaceutical sector, the rest to the textile and chemical ones), only 10 were exploited in that country. The lack of exploitation of patents in developing countries contributes basically to the preservation of secure import markets for transnational corporations, limiting to that extent any possible competition with other companies, foreign or national. The repercussions of this lack of competitive forces could imply significant price increases, with negative income and balance of payments effects on the recipient countries.

To a large extent, technology is sold to developing countries, and foreign investments take place, as a defensive strategy to avoid loss of markets for the technology and capital owners. Thus a company will tend to sell technology to a given country not because of assured monopoly privileges but

14. See Holman and Watson (1967), p. 1.
15. Deduced from data collected by Timoléon López and F. Castaño from the Colombian Industrial Property office for the studies of technology commercialization in the Andean Common Market.

because if it did not, another company would have done so and in this manner replaced it. In view of the fact that monopoly privileges extended through patents restrict competition, and since almost all patents appear not to be exploited in the patent-granting developing countries, patents in this sense restrict the flow of technology and limit the factors that induce foreign investment to take place. When foreign investment takes place, patents become one of the instruments by which national companies are acquired by foreign ones, due to the monopoly privileges extended through the presently-existing patent system.

The mechanisms that have been introduced in the legal systems of the Andean Countries (which more or less reflect world wide practices) to correct existing policies in the patent system have proved to be inefficient or inoperative. One of the basic reasons for such inefficiency (like that of the process of obligatory licensing) stems basically from the long and expensive legal procedures through which the present patent system is administered. The lack of automatism in the corrective measures and the long and costly legal procedures tend to favour the financially stronger transnational corporations rather than the relatively weaker national firms in the recipient countries. The above considerations lead to the conclusion that the presently existing patent system needs a total re-evaluation to correct inadequacies which appear to have negative effects, particularly on the economies and interests of developing countries.

## Overall financial analysis of market structures

The strategy pursued by developing countries in the process of their industrialization has meant basically the substitution of imports of *final* products. As distinct from the process of industrialization of the 'late-comers' (Japan, Russia, etc.), developing countries advance in industrialization by becoming *increasingly* dependent on the importation of intermediate products and capital goods. Only a few countries, finding themselves between the stages of developing and developed economies, have in certain industries (e.g. Brazil in the automotive and capital goods industries, Argentina in parts of the electronics industry, etc.) through backward linkages achieved significant domestic content in the range of goods produced. Also, due to lack of sufficient and appropriate domestic resources, industrialization has meant the *concomitant and joint* importation of foreign technology and foreign direct investment. These three elements – imports of intermediates, foreign technology and foreign capital – are jointly sold to developing countries in a package form. An analysis of one of them immediately implies the analysis of the others and, even more, the analysis of all of them in the package they constitute.

Evaluating the payments to foreign suppliers of intermediates, technology and capital by Chilean licensees in 399 contracts for the purchase of technology in the manufacturing sector indicated the following distribution in 1969:

| | |
|---|---|
| Royalties | $US8,203,000 |
| Profit remittances | 2,676,000 |
| Purchases of intermediates | 25,844,000 |
| Total | $US36,723,000 |

The above figures, referring to about 75 per cent of the total number of contracts for technology in Chile, present the following picture. In 1969 in Chile royalties amounted to more than three times the remitted profits by foreign subsidiaries. The higher royalty payments are due to the fact that (1) some of the licensees are Chilean-owned and thus do not pay dividends outside the country and (2) foreign-owned subsidiaries for tax, political and other reasons could be understating their profitability and dividend remittances by increasing royalty payments to their parents. Purchases of intermediates, equipment, etc., by the licensees from their licensers amounted to about 70 per cent of the total payments made. These purchases include coverage of the costs incurred by the licenser for producing such products, as well as a contribution to his effective profitability in his country of origin.[16]

Using the Chilean case as an example, we proceed to analyse three forms of *concentration* that throw further light on the description of the phenomena involved. Such concentration has significant impact on the prices or income effects that result from the purchase of resources by developing countries.

First, there is a concentration in the total payments involved by sector with respect to the country of destination of such payments. Chilean licensees (national- and foreign-owned), in the 399 contracts analysed, paid for royalties, profit remissions, intermediaries, etc., percentages of the total outlays by sector to certain countries as shown in Table 9.

This type of very high country concentration of destination of payments from the various sectors (which in turn is the mirror image of the concentration of origin of resources) depicts basically two interrelated causal factors. On the one hand, it indicates the lack of diversification or lack of attempts to diversify potential sources of supply on the part of the purchaser. Quite often *he* prefers to receive resources in package form from the same origin, since an alternative strategy of diversification would involve the cost of obtaining information, stress on initiative, etc.[17] A rational decision

16. The above figures do not include payments of interest charges for interaffiliate loans which also constitute part of the package of the resources exchanged.

17. J. Sábato has also commented on the distinction between the package of resources that the receiver tends to favour as a convenience and the package of resources that the supplier prefers to sell for monopoly rent objectives.

would necessitate a comparison between these costs and the ones involved in purchasing inputs in a non-competitive manner from the same origin. Such rational decisions are not always made. Anyhow, complicated issues are involved in defining a 'rational decision' in the absence of adequate information or under uncertainty. The second causal factor involved stems from the fact that the country concentration, expressed above, often reflects a company concentration. Arrangements of patent cross-licensing among transnational corporations, cartel agreements and tacit segmentation of markets (particularly of developing countries whose size prompts such arrangements) often constitute common behaviour rather than the exception.

Table 9 Country concentration in licensee payments from Chile

| Sector | Countries | Percentages of total payments by the whole sector going to these countries |
| --- | --- | --- |
| food and beverages | Switzerland and USA | 96·6% |
| tobacco | United Kingdom | 100·0% |
| industrial chemicals | West Germany and Switzerland | 96·6% |
| other chemicals | USA, W. Germany, Switzerland | 92·0% |
| petroleum and coal products | USA and United Kingdom | 100·0% |
| rubber products | USA | 99·9% |
| non-metallic minerals | USA | 97·0% |
| metallic products (except equipment) | USA | 94·0% |
| non-electric machinery | USA | 98·7% |
| electric equipment | Holland, USA, Spain | 92·0% |
| transport equipment | France, Switzerland | 89·0% |

Source: Data from the Chilean study analysed by Oxman (1971).

A second type of concentration involved reflects the joint existence of technology contracts, foreign investments (direct as well as loans) and the purchasing of intermediates and capital goods. See, for example, Table 10, which lists by order of importance the countries that have the highest number of technology contracts and the largest volume of foreign direct investments in Chile, the largest credits extended by foreign private firms and the largest receipts from the sale of intermediates and capital goods to their Chilean licensees, from whom payment of royalties and/or receipts of dividends are also obtained.

Table 10 indicates an almost complete one-to-one correspondence in the order of countries appearing in each of the four columns. Since the

Table 10 Ranking of foreign sources of licences, investments, loans and receipts in Chile

| Number of licences | | Total volume of foreign direct investments 1964–8 | | Total volume of foreign private loans 1964–8 | | Total receipts from intermediates, capital goods, royalties and profits in 1969, corresponding to 399 technology contracts | |
|---|---|---|---|---|---|---|---|
| USA | 178 | USA | $43,103,000 | USA | $120,299,000 | USA | $16,849,000 |
| West Germany | 46 | Canada | 25,181,000 | West Germany | 28,181,000 | West Germany | 4,238,000 |
| Switzerland | 35 | West Germany | 14,517,000 | Switzerland | 18,250,000 | Switzerland | 3,949,000 |
| United Kingdom | 30 | Switzerland | 2,941,000 | United Kingdom | 8,121,000 | United Kingdom | 3,896,000 |
| France | 17 | United Kingdom | 2,264,000 | France | 6,051,000 | France | 2,606,000 |
| Italy | 12 | | | Canada | 4,789,000 | Holland | 2,575,000 |
| Holland | 10 | | | | | | |

Sources: ODEPLAN (1970), also Chilean study on commercialized technology as analysed by Oxman (1971), p. 35.

listing of countries reflects in practice the firms involved, the table indicates once more the existence of a collective exchange of factors of production and intermediates in a package form. Foreign direct investment implies the concomitant 'sale' of technology from parent to subsidiary.[18] Also, the propensity to use technology commercially prompts foreign direct investment. Furthermore, the sale of technology and capital generates the sale of products embodying the former or tied to them. This concentration of resources in a package form creates special monopolistic conditions due to the absence of competitive forces for each one of the inputs involved, which are exchanged jointly in a collective unit.

The third form of concentration concerns the market structure of the recipient countries. In a sample taken of foreign-owned subsidiaries in Chile, 50 per cent of them had a monopoly or duopoly position in the host market. Another 36·4 per cent were operating in an oligopoly market where they had a leader's position. Only 13·6 per cent of the foreign subsidiaries in the sample controlled less than 25 per cent of the local market.[19] Similar concentration indices were noted in Colombia. Thus, foreign resource suppliers operating within high protective tariff walls[20] are able to pass to the final consumer, through market domination, monopoly rents that are related to the other two types of concentration examined above.

Thus, the three kinds of concentration are intimately connected. Market concentration and control in the host country, coupled with high tariff protection, enables the realization of high effective returns in such markets. These returns, then, are passed on through tied arrangements of inputs to foreign suppliers of collective units, often resulting in domestic tax avoidance (as distinct from tax evasion). Furthermore, country or firm concentration prevents competitive forces even among alternative packages of inputs. Thus, the markets for technology commercialization and for foreign direct investments, due to their high and compounded imperfections through various forms of concentration, necessitate particular counter policies by the host governments to protect their national interests.

18. The term 'sale' of technology from a parent to a subsidiary is as artificial an expression as the 'sale' of services by the marketing division to the manufacturing one within the same company. We can certainly talk about the sale of technology from one country to another. Yet interaffiliate 'sales', although registered separately in an accounting sense, constitute operations of parts within a presumed whole where the absence of arms-length relationships creates special characteristics and behaviour. The distinction between sale of technology among countries and 'sale' among affiliates is certainly an important one to make.

19. See CORFO (1970a), p. 16.

20. The infant industry argument and tariff protection certainly need a reevaluation if 'infancy' is ascribed to companies like General Motors, ICI, Philips Int., Mitsubishi, etc., whose subsidiaries dominate the market of key industrial sectors in developing countries.

*Prices of imported inputs and their implications*

In previous pages, reference was made to the increasing dependence of developing countries on the importation of intermediate products and capital goods as they advance in the first stages of their industrialization. Thus, in Colombia two-thirds of the total import bill for 1968 comprised imports of materials, machinery and equipment for the industrial sector, while the other one-third included final products for consumption and intermediate goods for the agricultural sector.[21] Similar dependence and structure of imports is to be expected in Chile and Peru and other nations of comparable industrial development. Also, Bolivia and Ecuador, following the same road (particularly in the manufacturing sector), are likely to find an increasing dependence on imports of intermediates and capital goods as their industrialization advances. For the whole of Latin America, it has been estimated that during the period 1960–5 about $US1,870 million were spent annually on the importation of machinery and equipment. These imports amounted to 31 per cent of the total import bill of the area. They also constituted about 45 per cent of the total amount spent by Latin America on capital goods during the same period. For individual countries this relationship amounted to 28 per cent for Argentina, 35 per cent for Brazil, 61 per cent for Colombia and 80 per cent for Chile.[22] As far as intermediates are concerned, industry samples in Colombia have indicated that imported materials represented in 1968 between 52–80 per cent of total materials used by firms in parts of the chemical industry. For rubber products, the corresponding ratio was 57·5 per cent and for pharmaceuticals 76·7 per cent. It was only in textiles that the ratio of imported intermediates to total materials used fell to 2·5 per cent.[23] Similar figures were reported for Chile. For example, imported intermediate products amounted to more than 80 per cent of total materials used in the pharmaceutical industry and between 35–50 per cent of total sales of the firms involved.

This heavy dependence on imports of intermediates and capital goods has important repercussions on the recipient countries, if one considers the fact that the largest part of such imports are exchanged between affiliated firms and/or tied to the purchase of technology. For example, it has been estimated that about one-third of the total imports of machinery and equipment in Latin America are realized by foreign subsidiaries.[24] The prices of those imports traded among affiliates correspond more to the global strategy of

21. See data from Banco de la República, tabulated by INCOMEX (1969).
22. Preliminary estimates by CEPAL presented by F. Fanjzylber (1971), pp. 91–94.
23. See Vaitsos (1970), pp. 48–54.
24. Estimates were based on figures of OECD and the Survey of Current Business, as analysed by Fanjzylber (1971), pp. 94–5.

the transnational firm, given related government policies, than to any adherence to prices, competitive or otherwise, established in markets that are characterized by arms-length relationships among firms. Furthermore, as indicated above, about two thirds of the contracts evaluated in the commercialization of technology in Bolivia, Ecuador, Colombia and Peru included tie-in clauses that required the purchase of intermediates from the supplier of technology or his affiliates. The price differentials of such tied purchases can constitute an important implicit cost in the commercialization of technology which, in some cases, could completely overwhelm other considerations with respect to the payment of royalties, remission of profits, etc. The Andean studies of the measurement of FOB price differentials of imported intermediate products above market prices in different parts of the world were mainly concentrated in the pharmaceutical industry. This was primarily due to the availability of information on world market prices which were specially reviewed and collected for the present study in that industry.[25] Defining as 'overpricing' the following ratio

$$100 \times \frac{P_M - P_W}{P_W}$$

where $P_M$ is FOB price of imports in Andean countries, and $P_W$ is FOB price in different world markets, the results for each country presented the following indicators:

In the Colombian pharmaceutical industry, the weighted average overpricing of products imported by foreign-owned subsidiaries amounted to 155 per cent while that of national firms was 19 per cent.

The absolute amount of overpricing for the foreign firms studied amounted to a figure of six times the royalties and twenty four times the declared profits. For national firms, the absolute amount of overpricing did not exceed one-fifth of the declared profits.[26] The sample evaluated included 25 per cent of the imports of foreign firms controlling about half the Colombian market, and 15 per cent of the imports of the most important nationally-owned firms.

The small samples studied in the other four countries for the same industry do not permit extrapolation of the estimates obtained nor any estimates of weighed averages. The absolute figures of these studies were reported as follows:

In Chile, from 50 products for which international prices were available corresponding to the imports of 39 firms:

25. The time requirements for the international review of prices for the Colombian study, used later in the other countries, amounted to about one man-year.
26. For a full analysis of the above see Vaitsos (1970).

Table 11  Overpricing of imports, pharmaceutical industry, Chile

| Percentage overpricing | Number of products | Number of firms | |
|---|---|---|---|
| | | Nationally-owned | Foreign-owned |
| 0% | 11 ⎫ | 13 | 6 |
| 1–30% | 9 ⎭ | | |
| 31–100% | 14 | 5 | 3 |
| 101–500% | 12 ⎫ | 2 | 10 |
| Over 500% | 2 ⎭ | | |

In Peru imports of 22 firms were studied, with the results shown in Table 12.

Table 12  Overpricing of imports, pharmaceutical industry, Peru

| Percentage overpricing | Number of nationally-owned firms | Number of foreign-owned firms |
|---|---|---|
| 0– 20% | 4 | 3 |
| 20– 50% | 1 | 5 |
| 50–100% | 1 | 2 |
| 100–200% | 1 | 2 |
| 200–300% | 0 | 2 |
| Over 300% | 0 | 1 |

In all three countries studied, overpricing registered on imports of foreign-owned subsidiaries was on average consistently and significantly higher than that of nationally-owned firms. Foreign subsidiaries apparently use transfer pricing of products as a mechanism of income remission, thus significantly underdeclaring their true profitability.[27]

In the electronics industry in Colombia, comprehensive samples corresponding to firms that controlled about 90 per cent of the market indicated overpricing which ranged between 6 per cent and 69 per cent. In the Ecuadorian electronics industry, 29 imported products that were evaluated in relation to the Colombian registered prices indicated that sixteen of them were imported at prices comparable to the Colombian ones; seven were overpriced by up to 75 per cent; and six were overpriced by about 200 per cent. Earlier studies undertaken only in Colombia presented a weighted average of 40 per cent overpricing in the imports by foreign-owned subsidiaries in the rubber industry and zero overpricing by nationally-owned firms. Also

27. For an extensive comparison of the Chilean, Peruvian and Colombian pharmaceutical sectors see Diaz (1971), pp. 19–28.

smaller samples in the Colombian chemical industry indicated weighted average overpricing that ranged between 20–25 per cent.

A significant point needs to be added. The above investigations and their results were based on comparisons of 'overpricing' or discriminatory pricing, which in turn imply the comparison between two different prices. Yet income flows occur on the basis of *pricing* and not just of 'overpricing'. The former implies the comparison between price and costs while the latter that between prices. In addition to questions of relative magnitude, important conceptual and measurement considerations are involved. It has been correctly pointed out that there is no such a thing as an international market for Volkswagen doors by which to estimate overpricing.[28] Similarly, there is no world price for a revolving ball for Olivetti typewriters. In areas of standardized products, such as natural or synthetic rubber, certain chemicals, specific synthetic fibres, various electronic components, etc. 'overpricing' is an attainable estimate. But, in cases of highly differentiated goods, obtaining estimates is extremely difficult and those arrived at are in practice probably meaningless. Furthermore, one can ask what is the relevance of 'overpricing' in the case of a monopoly or a cartel market structure where prices or mark-ups are fixed accordingly. On the other hand, the comparison between prices and costs to determine net generated income begs the question of the definition of the costs. How should overheads be allocated at the international level? To place the question in a more crude form and in a manner that leads to value judgements, one can ask: how far should a country (in our case a developing country) contribute not only to the financial, entrepreneurial and monopoly rents of a transnational corporation, but also to the coverage of 'fixed' costs of goods and services obtained by it *and* the parent *as well as* the rest of the world?

The above conceptually-perplexing questions indicate the need for further work on the subject, placing the issue of technology purchase and foreign direct investment within a bargaining framework. Diverse and complementary policies, such as top price limits on standardized products or direct negotiations on the pricing of diversified ones, etc., constitute some of the necessary steps to be taken by recipient countries, *given the particular characteristics of each industry*. The major indirect mechanism that appears to reduce overpricing rests on tariff levels on imported intermediate products. Yet such tariff levels cannot be considered independently from the final product ones, nor from the overall commercial policies directed towards an acceptable competitiveness of domestic production. What remains evident, though, from our analysis is that the cost of technology (particularly when it is obtained through foreign-owned subsidiaries) cannot be limited to explicit payments such as royalties, but should also include considerations

28. See Cooper (1970).

for the often much more important implicit charges through import product pricing.

## References

COOPER, C. (1970), *Transfer of Technology from Advanced to Developing Countries*, study prepared for the secretariats of ACAST and UNCTAD.

CORFO (1970a), *Comportamiento de las Principales Empresas Industriales Extranjeras Acogidas al DFL 258*, Publication no. 9–A/70, Santiago.

CORFO (1970b), *La Propriedad Industrial en Chile y su Impacto en el Desarrollo Industrial*, Santiago.

Dîaz, P. (1971), 'Análisis Comparativo de los Contratos de Licencia en el Grupo Andino', Lima, mimeo.

DIEGGER, J. A. (1948), 'Patent Policy: A Discussion', *American Economic Review, Papers and Proceedings*, vol. 38, May.

FANJZYLBER, F. (1971), *Elementos para la Formulación de Estrategias de Exportación de Manufacturas*, ST/ECLA/Conference 3/L.21, Santiago.

GRUBER, W., MEHTA, D., and VERNON, R. (1966), 'The R&D Factor in International Investment of United States Industry', *Journal of Political Economy*, Autumn.

HOLMAN, M. A., and WATSON, D. S. (1967), 'Concentration of Patents from Government Financed Research in Industry', *Review of Economics and Statistics*, vol. 49, August.

HORST, T. O. (1969), *A Theoretical and Empirical Analysis of American Exports and Direct Investment*, unpublished Ph.D. dissertation, University of Rochester.

INCOMEX (1969), *Clasificación Económica de las Importaciones*, Bogotá.

ODEPLAN (1970), *El Capital Privado Extranjero en Chile en el Período 1964–1968 a nivel Global y Sectorial*, Santiago.

OECD (1967), *Reviews of National Science Policy: Japan*, Paris.

OXMAN, G. (1971), *La Balanza de Pagos Tecnólogicos de Chile*, mimeo.

STOBAUGH, R. (1970), '*Utilizing Technical Know-How in a Foreign Investment and Licensing Program*', paper delivered to the National Meeting, Chemical Marketing Research Association, February.

UN (1964), *The Role of Patents in the Transfer of Technology to Developing Countries*, New York.

UNCTAD (1969), *Restrictive Business Practices*, TD/B/C2/93.

VAITSOS, C. V. (1970), *Transfer of Resources and Preservation of Monopoly Rents*, Economic Development Report no. 168, Harvard University.

VAITSOS, C. V. (1971), 'Estrategias Alternativas en la Comercialización de Tecnologia: El Punto de Vista de los Paises en Desarrollo', forthcoming in *Comercio Exterior*.

VAITSOS, C. V. (1972), 'Patents Revisited: their Function in Developing Countries', *Journal of Development Studies*, October.

WELLS, L. T. Jr. (1968), *The Evolution of Concession Agreements*, Harvard Development Advisory Service Conference, Sorrento.

# 10 John Roberts and Jacques Perrin

## Engineering Consultancy in India: the Public Sector Steel Industry*

John Roberts and Jacques Perrin, *L'Engineering en Inde*, mimeo, Institut de Recherche Économique et de Planification, Grenoble, 1970, pp. 1–21. Translated by Hugo Radice and John Roberts.

## Introduction

1. In studying the functions of engineering consultancy in the industrialization process, a number of lessons can be learnt from the Indian experience. Briefly, our interest in the Indian case is based on:

(i) the existence of an old industrial tradition starting long before overall economic development became an important political objective;

(ii) the fact that Indian leaders realized very early on (before the Second World War) the necessity of basing the country's industrialization on heavy industry and on a public sector including the key industries;

(iii) the fact that the planners, while emphasizing the production goods sector, did not take sufficient account of linkages, first between the organized, modern industrial sector and other sectors (i.e. the need to remove the 'enclave' character of the modern sector), and secondly between various investment projects within the modern sector itself.

The consequential problems still affect the way in which investment activities (e.g. development of heavy industry and engineering, creation and application of technical knowledge, engineering consultancy, etc.) are organized, and these may be of some interest.

Although she has achieved a certain degree of industrialization, India is not a major technical innovator; this is another reason why Indian engineering consultancy is an interesting case study. We can think of engineering consultancy as an organic link between equipment manufacture and original R&D on the one hand, and the commissioning of individual investment projects on the other. Is this link broken if the technology is substantially imported? It is no coincidence that engineering consultancy is more developed in India in civil engineering and perhaps also in the metallurgical industries than for example in petrochemicals, where technical progress is

* Numbered footnotes to the text are from the original. Asterisked footnotes have been added in translation to bring certain information up to date.

rapid and innovations (new products) often imply an entirely new process technology, requiring a long and expensive research programme.

2. In an underdeveloped country, engineering consultancy's role is to increase the efficiency of investments, both by reducing the initial cost of capital-formation and by increasing yields once the plant is operating, under conditions which are very different from those in the country of origin of the techniques being used. There are examples in India in which, through consultancy work, applied research has led to reductions in costs and increases in returns from investments (e.g. the work of the National Metallurgical Laboratory on iron ores, which has increased the pig-iron output of blast furnaces). In India we can consider by looking at actual cases the extent to which this 'normal' process is impeded by technological dependence and by the existence of technological enclaves connected to research and development, design and equipment manufacture conducted abroad, and to production organized from abroad.

### Engineering consultancy and command over technical knowledge in the Indian steel and heavy engineering industries

The aim of this section is to highlight the progress made in India in engineering consultancy, equipment and plant design and manufacture, following the considerable investments carried out since the beginning of the 2nd Five Year Plan in steel and heavy engineering. It would seem strange for a country – even one underdeveloped in other respects – which possessed a significant core of industrial complexes constantly demanding maintenance and enlargement not to be led to control for itself the technology needed to construct new plants and projects. India has undoubtedly sought the same kind of 'self-sufficiency' in this respect as she has in industrial production generally. She is well aware of the dynamism and potential which the possession of technical knowledge tied to her existing industrial strength would bring. However, it appears that she is not yet always technically equipped to obtain optimum yields from the productive capacity which she has built up at such cost.

This section reviews the principal public sector projects in steel and heavy engineering, in an attempt to characterize the relationship with foreign owners of technical knowledge, and looks at the attempts made to create an engineering consultancy sector in India. There are also some comments on other efforts made by the industries in question to improve the technical level of their staff and workers.

# 1. Review of projects completed or under construction

## 1.1. – Steel

The three existing steel plants in the public sector belong to Hindustan Steel Ltd (HSL), founded in 1954 with headquarters at Ranchi. We can distinguish between the first-generation plants and later developments:[1]

### (i) first-generation plants:

Bhilai: Soviet assistance: girders, rails, heavy structural steels, etc. Initial capacity 1 million tons (ingots).

Durgapur: British assistance: light sections, merchant products, wheels and axles for railway wagons. Initial capacity 1 million tons.

Rourkela: German assistance: flat products and tubes: 1 million tons.

### (ii) expansions

Bhilai: first expansion finished around 1967. Capacity increased to 2·5 million tons by adding blast-furnaces nos. 4 and 5, open-hearth furnaces nos. 7 and 8 and a wire-drawing mill. A second expansion with a sixth blast furnace should increase capacity to 3·1 million tons in 1970.

Durgapur: first expansion completed in 1968 with 4 additional blast furnaces, some supplementary soaking-pits, a sinter plant and a skelp mill.

Rourkela: first expansion bringing capacity to 1·8 million tons completed in 1968 with the addition of a fourth blast furnace, a fifth LD converter and various improvements to the rolling mill, including a galvanized sheet mill and an electrolytic tin-plating department.

### (iii)

The factory at Bokaro: completion announced for 1972: Soviet assistance: initial capacity 2·5 million tons to be increased soon to 4 million. Basically flat products. 3 blast furnaces and 4 LD converters with hot and cold rolling mills.[2]

### (iv)

Other HSL undertakings: alloy steel plant at Durgapur (completed), special steels plant at Rourkela (under way).

1. The private sector consists of two main plants: one at Jamshedpur belonging to Tata Iron & Steel Co. (TISCO) (capacity 1·5 million tons of finished steel) and the other at Burnpur owned by the Indian Iron & Steel Co. (IISCO) (capacity 0·8 million tons finished steel, i.e. 1 million tons ingots). The first dates from 1906 and the second from 1918. Their recent expansions took place in the 1950s, i.e. before any Indian capacity existed for designing and constructing steel plant. The IBRD helped finance the expansions.

2. Since the decision to decentralize the management of the public sector steel industry because of HSL's poor financial results, the Bokaro project has been controlled by Bokaro Steel Ltd.

## 1.2. – Heavy engineering

The Heavy Engineering Corporation (HEC) has been responsible for four projects, all more or less complete:

Foundry-Forge Project (FFP) at Ranchi, 80,000 tons capacity.

Heavy Machine Building Project (HMBP) at Ranchi: equipment for the steel industry, large construction works and oil wells, capacity 80,000 tons per year.

Heavy Machine Tools Project (HMTP) at Ranchi.

Coal Mining Machinery Project at Durgapur: mining and blast-furnace equipment, capacity 45,000 tons per year; now reorganized as the Mining and Allied Machinery Corporation (MAMC).

## 2. Types of contract agreed with foreign suppliers

There are two main types of contract for consultancy services for industrial projects: the first is the consultancy contract in which the activities of the firm are strictly controlled by the owner, and the second is the turnkey contract where the consultant engineers are part of a larger firm or a consortium entrusted with all the stages of design and construction with the minimum of external control.[3] The Indian experience in steel and heavy engineering shows an attempt to move from an almost pure turnkey system to a much less clear-cut arrangement in which a foreign engineering consultancy firm works with increasing Indian participation, both in designing the plant and equipment and in machine building and project execution. Clearly, once the foreign supplier allows some of the investment goods to be constructed in India, the takeover of certain functions by local design offices follows logically.

Experience gained on even the most trivial work, especially in the relations which they have to build up with local construction firms, allows the firm's own engineers, and consultant engineers from outside, to prepare eventually much more far-reaching projects.[4]

All the three first-generation steel plants were designed and constructed along virtual turnkey lines. The integrated plant at Bhilai was first put forward in a preliminary report made by a Russian mission in 1954–5. After the inter-governmental agreement which followed, the Russian firm Gipromez prepared a detailed report on the project and provided drawings, equipment and technical supervision during the construction stage. The Russians also undertook the commissioning of the plant. The Indian government for its part (and after 1957 HSL) undertook site preparation, the provision of certain materials and infrastructural work on roads and

3. Judet, Perrin and Tiberghien (1970), p. 20.
4. ibid., p. 35.

railways, etc.; hence there had to be some coordination between Russian and Indian engineers and planning teams.

The first and second expansions to Bhilai showed from the start a quantitative and a qualitative difference in the procedures followed. The quantitative difference consisted in the inclusion of an increasing proportion of Indian-produced materials and equipment: for the second expansion, 100 per cent of the building work (including steel girders, etc.) and 58 per cent of the equipment were to be provided locally, which implied also a growing collaboration between Indian manufacturers and Russian engineers. The qualitative difference lay in the establishment of a 'Design Cell' at Bhilai consisting of ten Russian engineers and a larger number of Indians, whose job was to perform modifications on existing plant and to prepare and oversee the expansion projects. The Design Cell worked very closely with Gipromez, and had to submit plans to it for approval at least when Soviet credits were involved.

The UK consortium ISCON in charge of the Durgapur project agreed a contract much closer to a turnkey arrangement, with complete responsibility right up to completion, and only very limited responsibility after the initial commissioning. The consortium, set up after the Coates Mission's preliminary report in 1955, took charge of all the work from design onwards, and also monitored the work until the commissioning. It did however allow Indian participation in the project in two ways: first, the government (again, HSL after 1957) was able to have changes made in the specifications and design, which of course delayed completion of the project; and secondly, certain tasks were entrusted to Indian sub-contractors (e.g. building coke ovens). The disadvantages of this type of contract emerged very clearly in the difficulties encountered after commissioning: responsibility for training teams of technicians and for managing the enterprise during start-up had not been laid down in the contract, and when technical problems arose (for example, a shortfall in the surplus gas from the coke ovens, which was to be supplied to the neighbouring power station of the Damodar Valley Corporation), they took a long time to solve.

The Rourkela plant, which was undertaken by the firm of Krupp-Demag, was done in similar turnkey fashion. Its execution differed considerably from Durgapur since a large role was given to sub-contractors (about sixty in all), some of whom were Indian. However, the Germans maintained a considerable number of engineers and technicians in the enterprise after commissioning, and even increased this presence in 1960–61 following the difficulties encountered in using the LD converters. A problem analogous to the coke-oven gas one arose at Rourkela: the project envisaged a nitrate fertilizer factory which would use as feedstock the gas from the LD converters. The design engineers' study turned out to be too optimistic, and the gas surplus was not enough to feed the fertilizer factory. It was not until 1967 that a complementary plant was installed allowing the factory to use naphtha as an alternative feedstock.

We shall see in the following section that for the expansions made to the Durgapur and Rourkela plants, carried out with the help of foreign credits but without foreign control over and coordination of the whole work, the design and construction procedures were completely different: the feasibility studies and some of the detailed drawings were prepared in India, and foreign technical assistance was only called in for setting up certain new installations or for making new products on the basis of specific agreements (for example, with a German firm for repairs to the Durgapur coke ovens, and the Luxemburg firm Tor Isteg for manufacturing cold-twisted bars for reinforced concrete).

With the Bokaro plant we find considerable progress in the participation of Indian engineering consultants, in a project which still remained the over-all responsibility of the Russian firm Gipromez. It was thought, before 1965, that the private engineering consultants M. N. Dastur & Co. would make the necessary studies and plans for the factory. A special team was set up for this, but it was dissolved after the decision was taken to entrust the project to the Russian firm.[5] This was due not only to a lack of confidence in Indian technical capabilities, but also to the pressing need for credits. However, if the basic design work, planning and supervision were entrusted to the Russian firm, Dastur & Co. were still able to participate as a consultancy sub-contractor for certain secondary parts of the project. Indian equipment manufacturers (such as HEC and MAMC) and civil engineering firms associated with the project (such as HSL's subsidiary Hindustan Steel Works Construction Co. Ltd) were to collaborate closely with the Russians who provided the plans and drawings, because 86 per cent of the structural steel, 100 per cent of the civil engineering and 63 per cent of the steel-making equipment were to be built or assembled by Indian firms. Moreover, the government intervened in 1969 to have the capacity of the first phase raised from 1·7 million to 2·5 million tons as a result of increased estimates of the future demand for flat products.

As to the HEC plants at Ranchi and Durgapur, we find a turnkey formula again. The Indian authorities stepped in during the discussion of the two preliminary reports, Russian and British, in 1957. Having decided in favour of Russian and Czech collaboration, basically because of the nature of the credit offered, they enjoyed once more the possibility of influencing the decisions taken on the basis of the detailed project reports drawn up for the four factories (1960–63).[6] This influence was of a very general

5. Herouville and Rollet (1965), p. 3.
6. Estimates Committee (1964), p. 51.

kind, since the assistance agreements had already been signed, but it did enable the Indian government to get the capacity of the FFP and HMBP projects raised from 45,000 to 80,000 tons per year.[7]

During the construction phase, it was the embryonic HEC which took on the ordering and supervision of the work of civil engineering firms from the public and private sectors. However, the Russians took responsibility for the engineering overall, including preparing the plans for civil works and for the internal organization of the new firms. They were certainly concerned about the success of the HEC projects, and sent advisory teams before the factories were completed to ensure that the capacity utilization rate was satisfactory for the plant supplied. The efforts put into training Indian staff, and the presence at Ranchi of Russian and Czech experts, were considerable.

## 3. *Valorization of heavy industry investments: the role of design and engineering consultancy*

Every engineering and metals industry creates a demand for equipment design and industrial drawing skills, first for the maintenance and repair of machines, later for modifying machinery and the production processes incorporating them to meet new demands, and finally for expanding existing installations and taking up new processes. As long as enterprises grow by successively adding new bits of plant or by partial modification of existing capital, they can generally make do with the services of their own research, development and design departments. A consultancy firm or a consulting engineer is only brought in when they need to set up an entirely new plant or start using highly specialized techniques unrelated to the experience which they have built up. The more advanced the industrial system becomes, the stronger the tendency to form, either within the firm or independent of any manufacturing firm, agencies studying new techniques and the setting up of new projects.[8] Usually the project planning is done by consultant engineers while machinery is designed by the staff of the equipment manufacturing firms.

In a developing country like India, where the aim is rapid industrialization by improving existing enterprises and by creating new ones, an important part is played both by equipment design and by modern consultancy techniques, and there is a strong tendency to try to grasp the methods of project planning and design before having fully mastered the older forms of research and development and innovation within the enterprise. The result, well

7. As far as the provisional production plans were concerned, which were drawn up on the basis of forecasts of the needs of future users, the Indians left matters to the Russians. This was sharply criticized later, on the grounds that it prevented Indian Plan officials from being able to coordinate and articulate different investment projects.

8. Judet, Perrin and Tiberghien (1970), p. 2.

illustrated in the Indian case, is a contradiction: the development of project planning and design depends on the mastery of techniques and innovations (often patented) developed by various enterprises for practical use; if the techniques are unknown or unused in its own country, the engineering consultants have to buy the rights from foreign firms; and the purchase of foreign 'know-how' leads to a potentially damaging domination over the developing country, first by the country being obliged to a greater or lesser degree to use foreign equipment or at least to perpetuate the use of a variety of technical norms within the country, and secondly by short-circuiting local R&D and making it still more backward relative to that under way abroad.

In India, the difficulties of maintaining a dialogue between equipment design and R&D on the one hand and project planning and design on the other can be seen in the relations between HEC, responsible for making equipment for the new steelworks, and the Central Engineering and Design Bureau (CEDB) of HSL.

HSL realized very early on the importance of having their own project engineering capability in order to be able to break out of the constraints imposed by the turnkey formula used in creating the first generation of factories. In 1959 they formed the CEDB to plan new installations, prepare preliminary feasibility studies and then make the plans and detailed drawings in order to take charge of the technical side of carrying out projects. This raises the question of why HSL decided not to use the experience built up already by M. N. Dastur & Co., which had specialized in the steel industry since its formation in 1952. The answer is probably to do with the Indian tendency to develop the public sector alongside, rather than out of, the private sector. The CEDB at first consisted of thirteen engineers working at Rourkela; in 1964 it was reorganized at Ranchi with HSL's central services. It was to take responsibility for extensions and new works in HSL's existing enterprises, apart from Bhilai where the Design Cell continued to collaborate closely with the Russian firm Gipromez; and it was equally able to undertake similar work for other companies. According to HSL's 1968–9 annual report, in March 1969 the CEDB had 857 employees of whom 377 were engineers. In 1967 the work-force included fourteen foreign experts.

The CEDB now has an impressive number of project reports and actual projects to its credit; it is clear that it has carried out operations located all along the chain of services which would be provided by consultant engineers already experienced in handling major projects, without being able just yet to provide all those services together.*

* CEDB has only developed a capability for detailed project engineering (i.e. detailed planning and drawing of installations and machinery within battery limits, as opposed to the simple specification of their major characteristics) since 1970.

(1) The CEDB prepared detailed project reports and plans for the first expansions to the Rourkela and Durgapur plants. It set out the specifications in broad terms, and supervised the construction and commissioning of new installations. It is now ready to do the same for the second planned expansions of these plants, and has already done detailed reports for this. Certain specific tasks have of course been sub-contracted to foreign firms: for example, Germans helped with the rebuilding of the fourth coke oven at Durgapur. It seems that in general the CEDB's original design work only covered the more straightforward aspects of the projects.

(2) It was responsible to some extent for setting up a rolling mill for special steels at Rourkela.

(3) It undertook the preparation of feasibility studies for the steel projects intended to begin during the Fourth Plan period (1969–73), including a cold rolling mill for silicon steels.

(4) It prepared the designs for some secondary installations in the Bokaro plant, and it has just been appointed principal consultant engineers for the expansion of Bokaro to 4 million tons, so that if other engineering firms (e.g. Russian ones) are asked to participate in the planning work, they will be regarded as sub-contractors.

(5) In 1965 it was involved in the work of an Anglo-American consortium carrying out a study for a fifth integrated plant.

(6) It undertook the study of a project for a billet-rolling mill at Singapore, and there was an idea that they might do a feasibility study for a rolling mill project in the UAR.

(7) Finally it took part in setting up a naphtha-reforming plant at Rourkela, a concentration plant at the Barsua ore mines and a fertilizer factory at Ranchi for the National Coal Development Corporation.

What is the basis for CEDB's pool of experience and of technical knowledge? One source of information feeding in from within HSL is the Central Research and Development Organization, an R&D group in the ferrous metals field which works on the improvement of steel products and the development of new product ranges. A further source is the much more longstanding work of the National Metallurgical Laboratory at Jamshedpur, whose experiments and pilot projects have concentrated especially on the preparation and sintering of local ores, on coal blends, and on the pretreatment of limestone for blast-furnace charges.[9] For the mechanical engineering aspects of the work, however, this was not enough. Without

9. As a result of the National Metallurgical Laboratory's work there were savings in fixed capital during the extension of the first generation plants. The specifications reached for washing, concentrating and sintering ores meant that the blast furnace output could be increased. The composition of the ore and the treatment methods would normally have been studied by consultant engineers given the job of adapting the production processes being used to local conditions.

really firm links with the mechanical engineering industry (we shall see later that HEC is not yet up to designing equipment in current use, let alone new developments), the CEDB had to make licensing or technical collaboration agreements with foreign owners of technical knowledge. For example, in September 1968 a licensing agreement was made with United Foundries Co. of Pittsburgh, USA, which granted CEDB rights to know-how and designs for rolling mills and related plant and for treatment plant for ferrous and non-ferrous ores which could be used, in the CEDB's work as consultant engineer, not only in India but also abroad. Another agreement made in November 1968 with Russia allowed CEDB to fill in further gaps in its experience. Through agreements of this kind, CEDB would be able to extend its already considerable body of know-how on blast furnaces to other sorts of plant: first rolling mills with the American licensees and then, according to HSL's 1968–9 annual report, coke ovens and LD converters. Once this process is complete, CEDB will in principle be ready to supply not only detailed plans for plants to be built but also specifications for the equipment to be constructed by the heavy engineering industry. However, there is always the problem of standardization of technical norms: it is natural that the CEDB engineers, having worked basically on the Rourkela and Durgapur extensions, would be most used to German and British specifications and would tend to recommend them for the plant and equipment they are in charge of. This is what has obstructed the merger of CEDB and the Design Cell at Bhilai, where the know-how is completely Russian, a merger which has been planned for several years and which logically should be carried through. This diversity of technical norms and equipment design practice, partly due to the absence of technical skills in the machinery industry, in turn makes it very difficult for the equipment designers at HEC who began work after those at HSL and are now trying to catch up and meet the new demands coming from a large steel industry embarking on a diversification programme.*

HEC, as we have noted, is still unable to provide the mechanical engineering support which CEDB needs in its project design work. Although each of HEC's factories has for several years had a design office where designs are prepared for equipment ordered from the firm, their work has basically involved, up to now, only making a few modifications to designs produced overseas, especially in Czechoslovakia and the USSR. HMBP's drawing office was, as the Committee on Public Undertakings of the Lok Sabha

* CEDB has also *benefited* from this diversity of background, which has given it access to technology from a variety of sources. Not only has it learned from its own successes and failures in the operations listed above: it has also acquired an archive of 250,000 technical drawings. Its drawing offices are now providing machine drawings for neighbouring HEC, making up for HEC's design limitations.

reported in 1968, the cause of a serious bottleneck in the unit's operations; this was a major weakness considering that, according to the Committee, the preparatory work for carrying out a major equipment order could last $1\frac{1}{2}$ to 2 years.[10] The equipment built for the Bokaro factory followed plans provided by the Russians to HSL and passed on to HEC.[11]

The conclusion is clearly that as long as HEC's design department and drawing offices are not able to originate, either by themselves or in collaboration with the CEDB, the designs for equipment ordered, they will remain enmeshed in the contradiction already alluded to, which in this specific case leads to the problem of non-standardization of the HSL equipment needing replacing or supplementing; the dialectic of mutual exchanges of knowledge between the equipment manufacturer and the engineering consultants could never become established, and the CEDB could remain the only reservoir of accumulated experience able to aspire to some autonomy.

## 4. *Engineering consultancy and technological independence*

The inability of HEC engineers to build heavy equipment without turning to designs and drawings supplied from abroad simply reflects a technical level, both in research and product development and in production management, too low to meet the needs of the technologies in use. Another sign of this is to be found in the slow decline in the number of foreign experts in the steel plants:

Number of foreign experts

| Factory | March 1966 | March 1967 | March 1968 | March 1969 |
|---|---|---|---|---|
| Bhilai | 74 | 65 (+10 in Design Cell) | 76 | — |
| Durgapur | 28 | 7 | 2 | — |
| Rourkela | 32 | 27 | 43 | — |
| Total | 134 | 109 | 121 | 112 |

10. Committee on Public Undertakings (1969), pp. 21, 28.
11. Despite all this, HEC's production of equipment for steelmaking is becoming more and more diversified. It has already met an order for designing, building and installing an iron-casting machine (of 160 tons per hour capacity) at Durgapur. This achievement, while of limited significance, is nevertheless interesting in that all the engineering right up to start-up was carried out by HEC teams. Other orders carried out or under way include a blast furnace built at Bhilai (the sixth), some complex handling equipment (along with a transport system) and rolling-mills for the Bokaro plant. On the basis of this experience HEC will be well placed to fulfil rather better its role in preparing detailed designs and machining plans for equipment which it constructs to specifications laid down by the units responsible for the engineering of future projects (see also note * opposite).

The commissioning of new installations (wiredrawing mill at Bhilai, galvanized sheet steel and tinplate rolling mills at Rourkela) always requires a new intake of foreign staff. The small number of foreigners at Durgapur reflects political sensitivity more than better management skills: the Bird Mission of 1967 in fact proposed that 70 to 80 British technicians be brought to Durgapur to eliminate the many technical problems that had arisen. This recommendation was rejected by the Indian government, which will probably be forced nevertheless to accept a system of visits by *ad hoc* teams to deal with specific problems.

Another symptom of the inadequate training of engineers and technicians is faulty maintenance work, which in several cases has been very serious: the case most often mentioned is the coke oven at Durgapur which had to be completely rebuilt.

Clearly a low technical level, even in the day-to-day management of the firm, is detrimental to the normal development of design and engineering functions: these depend for their success on a constant, accurate flow of information on the functioning of existing plant. It is vital, therefore, that the work of training managers, engineers and technicians which is under way at both HSL and HEC is continued and developed. This took the form at first of sending Indian engineers abroad for training; about 400 went to Britain, 600 to Germany and 650 from HEC alone to Russia and Czechoslovakia. A good point about this last example is that training began very early on, several years before the HEC plants were established. Now, training at HSL takes place in Technical Training Institutes attached to each steelworks for engineers and technicians, and at the Management Training Institute in the case of administrative staff. The MTI organized 19 sessions in 1968–9 involving 300 staff, and during the same period only 15 engineers were sent abroad for final training. HSL's annual report says that 4 high-level staff, 314 engineers, 150 technicians and skilled workers and 1,500 others were enrolled in its institutes in March 1969.

In order to make the work of the design and consultancy organizations easier and more efficient, an effort is now being made to standardize the processes used and the spare parts. Various committees have been set up to study the problem and it now looks as if, just when a programme of important plant replacements and repairs is under consideration, they are on the way to making a large number of spare parts in India, which in the long run is bound to help bring about greater uniformity of processes and plant.

## 5. *Perspectives for the Fourth and Fifth plans*

After a recession (1965–8) which led to a lowering of the demand projections for steel products, some new additions to productive capacity are now envisaged, most of which will not be finished until after the current five-year plan. To what extent will Indian engineering be able to take charge of these projects?

Clearly, even if the consultancy organizations had limitless abilities it would still be impossible to predict exactly the role they would play, especially because this role would vary according to the needs of the owners and the sort of services provided by the equipment manufacturers; the shape of the consultancy function is only determined once the other conditions necessary for carrying out the project have been met. However, past experience suggests the following scenario.

There will be one category of project involving investments using more or less the same technologies already in use, which can therefore be handled right up to the detailed design stage by Indian consultant engineering teams; these teams can basically manage without the foreign assistance they have needed up to now. Such projects include the new extensions to the first-generation plants (Bhilai expansion to 3·2 million tons, possibly Durgapur), and three plants planned in the south of India at Hospet (2 million tons), Visakhapatnam (2 million tons) and Salem (0·5 million tons).* These latter are especially interesting because they are at least in part being built in order to allow HEC's plants to reach production levels a lot nearer their theoretical capacities (in 1968–9 HMTP only managed to reach 2·2 per cent of capacity and HMBP only 11–22 per cent among its various workshops). M. N. Dastur & Co. has already prepared the detailed study for Salem. CEDB, using the experience it has gained on the Bokaro project, and the technology which will have been passed on to it by the Russian units collaborating with it there, should be able to go well beyond the stage of pre-project studies and general coordination to initiate the necessary dialogue with the equipment manufacturers about specifications for each bit of the project. Finally, HEC will be better placed than at present to provide essential equipment on schedule, as its capabilities will have specifically been taken into consideration by the consultant engineers in elaborating their proposals.

The second category of projects will include ones requiring, at least to some extent, new technologies which are either little known in India or only feasible for Indian engineers with foreign collaboration in designing the central processes. Likely examples are the expansion of the Durgapur steel alloys plant and the building of a special steel and alloys plant at Badravati,

* No expansion is at present (1973) under way at Durgapur. Among the options under consideration for the South Indian plants is a formula comprising substantial quantities of imported plant and equipment (for speed of delivery) corresponding to specifications to be laid down in detailed project reports, which would be drawn up after the 'Western' as opposed to the 'Soviet' manner, i.e. around the known characteristics of the products of Western equipment manufacturers. The alternative would be much more elaborate detailed project reports with item-by-item specifications and drawings intended for the guidance of indigenous equipment manufacturers.

Mysore (both these projects began in 1969), and also the seamless pipe project at Bhilai. The amount of investment devoted to these projects will be much less than that involved in the projects mentioned above: but the public and private engineering consultants are already certain of enough work, so long as the level of investment planned for the steel industry is actually reached. However, there is a strong likelihood that the contradiction discussed previously will persist. The role of engineering consultancy is to determine a system of machinery and a corresponding organization of work which meets the need of the project promoter and also embodies technical progress. Ideally, technical progress takes place in research laboratories or in the R&D activity of existing firms. In the case of developing countries, technical progress is taking place faster abroad than at home. Local engineering consultants then have to resolve a dilemma: either stick to techniques well-known locally, which will allow local manufacturers to supply most of the equipment but at the same time perpetuate the country's technological backwardness; or keep up with the new techniques invented and applied abroad, in which case engineering consultancy risks being reduced to a tool of technological dependence, acting as a transmission belt for foreign techniques and equipment. It is difficult not to conclude that consultancy work in a developing country, so vital for the accumulation of productive capital, may well remain entangled in a contradiction which it cannot overcome: the two elements in the contradiction being local capabilities in equipment manufacturing and the technical progress taking place abroad.

### Conclusion

The Indians are very well aware, at least in their public utterances, of the necessity of creating and strengthening consultancy services. The Fourth Five-Year Plan states:

A number of design and consultancy organizations have come into existence in both the public and private sectors. These organizations will have to be strengthened and their scope enlarged . . . An important requirement is that the maximum utilization of the technical consultancy services already built up should be ensured. The appointment of foreign consultancy services should not be resorted to except when unavoidable. Even when the need for foreign consultancy services is felt, the primary consultant should so far as possible be an Indian agency.[12]

In the opinion of the Parliamentary Committee on Public Undertakings, the era of turnkey contracts is definitely over, and soon the engineers and designers at HSL, together with their colleagues in the heavy electrical equipment industry, will themselves be undertaking turnkey contracts.[13]

12. Government of India (1969), p. 241.
13. Committee on Public Undertakings (1969), p. 31.

However, this optimism is surely premature given that engineering consultancy can only flourish if based firmly on a command over technology and over innovation in equipment design developed by the research groups in the firms themselves; without this, it falls back into dependence. Nevertheless, Johnson's (1966) pessimism is also unjustified, when he argues that India will take several more decades to master all the techniques needed in building steel plants, since there is plenty of determination among those in charge of heavy industry, at least at CEDB which seems to have achieved most in this respect.

## References

COMMITTEE ON PUBLIC UNDERTAKINGS (1969), 4th Lok Sabha, 14th Report, *Heavy Engineering Corporation*.

ESTIMATES COMMITTEE (1964), 3rd Lok Sabha, 51st Report, *Heavy Engineering Corporation*.

GOVERNMENT OF INDIA (1969), *Fourth Five-Year Plan 1969–73 (Draft)*.

HEROUVILLE, R., and ROLLET, C. (1965), *Les sociétés d'engineering en Inde*, Centre Nationale du Commerce Extérieur, Paris (mimeo).

JOHNSON, W. A. (1966), *The Steel Industry of India*, Harvard University Press.

JUDET, P., PERRIN, J., and TIBERGHIEN, R. (1970), *L'engineering*, IREP (mimeo).

# Epilogue

On 4 December 1972 Salvador Allende addressed the United Nations General Assembly as President of Chile (Reading 11). He attacked the US copper companies and their retaliation against nationalization, the financial blockade imposed by US and other interests, and the political machinations of ITT in Chile. He related these matters to under-development in Latin America and elsewhere.

Less than a year later Allende was dead and his government overthrown by a military *coup d'état*. His UN speech could hardly have had a more brutal proof than the speed with which the financial blockade was lifted and international firms and banks once more crowded round the debilitated Chilean economy like vultures round a corpse. Reading 12, by Terri Shaw of the *Washington Post*, reports the first stages of the return of capitalist freedom to Chile.

# 11 Salvador Allende

## Speech to the United Nations

Extract from Salvador Allende's speech to the UN General Assembly, 4 December 1972, printed in *Granma*, Year 7, no. 50, Havana, 10 December 1972, pp. 10–11.

I come from Chile, a small country but one where today any citizen is free to express himself as he so desires. A country of unlimited cultural, religious and ideological tolerance and where there is no room for racial discrimination. A country with its working class united in a single trade union organization, where universal and secret suffrage is the vehicle of determination of a multiparty regime, with a Parliament that has been operating constantly since it was created 160 years ago; where the courts of justice are independent of the executive and where the constitution has only been changed once since 1833, and has almost always been in effect. A country where public life is organized in civilian institutions and where the armed forces are of a proven professional background and deep democratic spirit. A country with a population of almost 10,000,000 people that in one generation has had two first-place Nobel Prize winners in literature, Gabriela Mistral and Pablo Neruda, both children of simple workers. In my country, history, land and man are united in a great national feeling.

But Chile is also a country whose retarded economy has been subjected and even alienated to foreign capitalist firms, resulting in a foreign debt of more than $4,000 million whose yearly services represent more than 30 per cent of the value of the country's exports; whose economy is extremely sensitive to the external situation, suffering from chronic stagnation and inflation; and where millions of people have been forced to live amidst conditions of exploitation and misery, of open or concealed unemployment.

Today I have come because my country is confronting problems of universal significance that are the object of the permanent attention of this assembly of nations: the struggle for social liberation, the effort for well-being and intellectual progress and the defence of national identity and dignity.

The outlook which faced my country, just like many other countries of the Third World, was a model of reflex modernization, which, as technical studies and the most tragic realities demonstrate, excludes from the possibilities of progress, well being and social liberation more and more millions of people, destining them to a subhuman life. It is a model that will produce a greater shortage of housing, that will condemn an ever-greater number of citizens to unemployment, illiteracy, ignorance and physiological misery.

In short, the same perspective that has kept us in a relationship of colonialization or dependency and exploitation in times of cold war, has also operated in times of military conflict or in times of peace. There is an attempt to condemn us, the underdeveloped countries, to being second-class realities, always subordinated.

This is the model that the Chilean working class, coming on the scene as protagonist of its own destiny, has decided to reject, searching in turn for a speedy, autonomous development of its own, and transforming the traditional structures in a revolutionary manner.

The people of Chile have won the Government after a long road of generous sacrifices, and it is fully involved in the task of installing economic democracy so that productive activity will operate in response to needs and social expectations and not in the interests of individual profit. In a programmed and coherent manner, the old structure, based on the exploitation of the workers and the domination of the main means of production by a minority, is being overcome. It is being replaced by a new structure – led by the workers and placed at the service of the interests of the majority – which is laying the foundations for a growth that will represent real development, that will include all the population and not cast aside vast sectors of the people and doom them to poverty and to being social outcasts.

The workers are driving the privileged sectors from political and economic power, both in the centres of labour as well as in the communes and in the state. This is the revolutionary content of the process my country is going through for overcoming the capitalist system and opening the way for a socialist one.

The need to place all our economic resources at the service of the enormous needs of the people went hand in hand with Chile's regaining of its dignity. We had to end the situation as a result of which we Chileans, plagued by poverty and stagnation, had to export huge sums of capital for the benefit of the world's most powerful market economy. The nationalization of basic resources constitutes an historic demand. Our economy could no longer tolerate the subordination implied by having more than 80 per cent of its exports in the hands of a small group of large foreign companies that have always put their interests before those of the countries in which they make profits. Neither could we accept the curse of the latifundium, the industrial and trade monopolies, credit for just a few and brutal inequality in the distribution of income.

### The revolutionary path that Chile is following

The change in the power structure that we are carrying out, the progressive leadership role of the workers in it, the national recovery of basic riches, the liberation of our country from subordination to foreign powers, are all crowning points of a long historical process; of efforts to impose political and social freedoms, of heroic struggle of several generations of workers and farmers to organize themselves as a social force to obtain political power and drive the capitalists from economic power.

Its tradition, personality and revolutionary awareness make it possible for the Chilean people to give a boost to the process towards socialism, strengthening civic liberties, collective and individual, and respecting cultural and ideological pluralism. Ours is a permanent battle to install social freedoms and economic democracy through full exercise of political freedoms.

The democratic will of our people has taken upon itself the challenge of giving a boost to the revolutionary process in the framework of a highly institutionalized state of law, that has been flexible to changes and is today faced by the need to adjust to the new socio-economic reality.

We have nationalized basic riches, we have nationalized copper, we have done so by a unanimous decision of Parliament, where the government parties are in a minority. We want everyone to clearly understand that we have not confiscated the large foreign copper mining firms. In keeping with constitutional provisions, we have righted a historic injustice by deducting from the compensation all profits above 12 per cent a year that they had made since 1955.

Some of the nationalized firms had made such huge profits in the last 15 years that when 12 per cent a year was applied as the limit of reasonable profits, they were affected by important deductions. Such is the case, for example, of a branch of the Anaconda Company, which made profits in Chile of 21·5 per cent a year over its book value between 1955 and 1970, while Anaconda's profits in other countries were only 3·6 per cent a year. That is the situation of a branch of the Kennecott Copper Corporation, which in the same period of time, made an average of 52·8 per cent profits a year in Chile – and in some years it made really incredible profits like 106 per cent in 1967, 113 per cent in 1968 and more than 205 per cent in 1969. In the same period of time, Kennecott was making less than 10 per cent a year in profits in other countries. However, the application of the constitutional norm has kept other copper firms from suffering deductions because their profits did not exceed the reasonable limit of 12 per cent a year.

We should point out that in the years just before the nationalization, the large copper firms had started expansion plans, which have failed in large measure and to which they did not contribute their own resources, in spite of the huge profits they made, and which they financed through foreign credits. In keeping with legal ruling, the Chilean state must take charge of these debts that reach the enormous figure of more than $727 million. We have even started to pay debts that one of those firms had with Kennecott, its parent company in the United States.

These same firms that exploited Chilean copper for many years made more than $4,000 million in profits in the last 42 years alone, while their initial investments were less than $30 million. A simple and painful example, an acute contrast: in my country there are 600,000 children who can never enjoy life in normally human terms, because in the first eight months of their existence they did not receive the elementary amount of proteins. My country, Chile, would have been totally transformed by these $4,000 million. Only a small part of this amount would assure proteins for all the children of my country once and for all.

The nationalization of copper has been carried out while strictly observing internal judicial order and with respect for the norms of international law, which there is no reason to identify with the interests of the big capitalist firms.

In short, this is the process my country is going through, and I feel it is useful to present it to this assembly, with the authority given to us by the fact that we are strictly fulfilling the recommendations of the United Nations and relying on internal efforts as the base for economic and social development. Here, in this forum, the change of institutions and backward structures has been advised, along with the redistribution of income, priority for education and health and care for the poorest sectors. All this is an essential part of our policy and it is in the process of being carried out.

### The financial blockade

That is why it is even more painful to have to come here to this rostrum to proclaim the fact that my country is the victim of grave aggression.

We had foreseen problems and foreign resistance to our carrying out our process of changes, especially in view of our nationalization of natural resources. Imperialism and its cruelty have a long and ominous history in Latin America and the dramatic and heroic experience of Cuba is still fresh. The same is the case with Peru, which has had to suffer the consequences of its decision to exercise sovereign control over its oil.

In the decade of the 70s, after so many agreements and resolutions of the international community, in which the sovereign right of every state to control its natural resources for the benefit of its people is recognized, after the adoption of international agreements on economic, social and cultural rights and the strategy for the second decade of development, which formalized those agreements, we are the victims of a new expression of imperialism – more subtle, more sneaky, and terribly effective – to block the exercise of our rights as a sovereign state.

From the very moment of our election victory on 4 September 1970, we were affected by the development of large-scale foreign pressures, aimed at blocking the inauguration of a government freely elected by the people and then overthrowing it. There have been efforts to isolate us from the world, strangle the economy and paralyze the sale of copper, our main export product, and keep us from access to sources of international financing.

We realize that when we denounce the financial-economic blockade with which we are attacked, it is hard for international public opinion and even for many of our compatriots to easily understand the situation because it is not an open aggression, publicly proclaimed before the whole world. Quite the contrary, it is a sneaky and double-crossing attack, which is just as damaging to Chile.

We find ourselves opposed by forces that operate in the shadows, without a flag, with powerful weapons that are placed in a wide range of influential positions.

We are not the object of any trade ban. Nobody has said that he seeks a confrontation with our country. It would seem that our only enemies or opponents are the logical internal political ones. That is not the case. We are the victims of almost invisible actions, usually concealed with remarks and statements that pay lip service to respect for the sovereignty and dignity of our country. But we have first-hand knowledge of the great difference that there is between those statements and the specific actions we must endure.

I am not mentioning vague matters, I am discussing concrete problems that affect my people today and which will have even more serious economic repercussions in the coming months.

Chile, like most of the nations of the Third World, is very vulnerable to the situation of the external sector of its economy. In the last 12 months, the decline in the international price of copper has represented a loss of about $200 million in income for a nation whose exports total a bit more than $1,000 million, while the products, both industrial and agricultural, that we must import are much more expensive now, in some cases as much as 60 per cent.

As is almost always the case, Chile buys at high prices and sells at low prices.

It has been at these moments, in themselves difficult for our balance of payments, that we have had to face, among others, the following simultaneous actions, apparently designed to take revenge on the Chilean people for their decision to nationalize copper.

Until the moment my Government took office, every year Chile received almost $80 million in loans from international financial organizations such as the World Bank and the Inter-American Development Bank. This financing has been violently interrupted.

In the past decade, Chile received loans from the Agency for International

Development of the Government of the United States (AID) totalling about $50 million a year.

We are not asking for those loans to be reinstated. The United States has the sovereign right to grant or not grant foreign aid to any country. All we want to point out is that the drastic elimination of those credits has resulted in important restrictions in our balance of payments.

Upon taking office as President, my country had short-term credit lines from private US banks, destined to finance our foreign trade, that amounted to $220 million. In a short period of time those credits were suspended and about $190 million have been deducted, a sum we had to pay, since the respective operations were not renewed.

Just like most of the nations of Latin America, because of technological reasons and other factors, Chile must make important purchases of capital goods in the United States. Now, both the financing of the supplies and that normally provided by the Eximbank for this type of operation has also been suspended for us, putting us in the irregular position of having to purchase goods of that kind by paying in advance. This puts extraordinary pressure on our balance of payments.

Payments of loans contracted by Chile with agencies of the public sector of the United States before my Government took office, and which were being carried out then, have also been suspended; so we have to continue carrying out the corresponding projects making cash in hand purchases on the US market, because, once the projects are in full swing, it is impossible to replace the source of the respective imports. That is why it had been decided that the financing should come from US Government agencies.

As a result of the operations directed against the sale of copper in the nations of Western Europe, our short-term operations with private banks on that continent, mainly based on payment of that metal, have been greatly blocked. This has resulted in more than $20 million in credit lines not being renewed, the suspension of financial negotiations for more than $200 million that were almost complete, and the creation of a climate that blocks the normal handling of our purchases in those countries and acutely distorts all our activities in the field of external financing.

This financial stranglehold of a brutal nature, given the characteristics of the Chilean economy, has resulted in a severe limitation of our possibilities to purchase equipment, spare parts, supplies, food and medicine. Every Chilean is suffering the consequences of those measures, which bring suffering and grief into the daily life of all and, naturally, make themselves felt in internal political life.

What I have described means that the nature of the international agencies has been distorted. Their utilization as instruments of the bilateral policy of any of their member states, regardless of how powerful it may be, is legally and morally unacceptable. It means putting pressures on an economically weak country and punishing a nation for its decision to regain control over its basic resources. It is a premeditated form of intervention in the internal affairs of a nation. This is what we call imperialist arrogance.

Distinguished representatives, you know this and you cannot forget it. All this has been repeatedly condemned by resolutions of the United Nations.

## Chile attacked by transnational companies

Not only do we suffer the financial blockade, we are also the victims of clear aggression. Two firms that are part of the central nucleus of the large transnational companies that sunk their claws into my country, the International Telegraph and Telephone Company and the Kennecott Copper Corporation, tried to run our political life.

ITT, a huge corporation whose capital is greater than the budget of several Latin American nations put together and greater than that of some industrialized countries, began, from the very moment that the people's movement was victorious in the elections of September 1970, a sinister action to keep me from taking office as President.

Between September and November of 1970, terrorist actions that were planned outside of my country took place there, with the aid of internal fascist groups. All this led to the murder of General René Schneider Chereau, Commander in Chief of the Army, a just man and a great soldier who symbolized the constitutionalism of the armed forces of Chile.

In March of this year, the documents that denounced the relationship between those sinister aims and the ITT were made public. This company has admitted that in 1970 it even made suggestions to the Government of the United States that it intervene in political events in Chile. The documents are genuine, nobody has dared deny them.

Last July the world learned with amazement of different aspects of a new plan of action that ITT had presented to the US Government in order to overthrow my Government in a period of six months. I have with me the document, dated in October of 1971, that contains the 18-point plan that was talked about. They wanted to strangle us economically, carry out diplomatic sabotage, create panic among the population and cause social disorder so that when the Government lost control, the armed forces would be driven to eliminate the democratic regime and impose a dictatorship.

While the ITT was working out this plan, its representatives went through the motions of negotiating a formula for the Chilean state to take over ITT's share in the Chilean telephone company. From the first days of my administration, we had started talks to purchase the telephone company that ITT controlled, for reasons of national security.

On two occasions I received high officials of the firm. My Government acted in good faith in the discussions. On the other hand, ITT refused to accept payment at prices that had been set in keeping with the verdict of international experts. It posed difficulties for a rapid and fair solution, while clandestinely it was trying to unleash chaos in my country.

ITT's refusal to accept a direct agreement and knowledge of its sneaky manoeuvres has forced us to send to Congress a bill calling for its nationalization.

The will of the Chilean people to defend the democratic regime and the progress of its revolution, the loyalty of the armed forces to their country and its laws have caused these sinister plots to fail.

Distinguished representatives, before the conscience of the World I accuse ITT of trying to provoke a civil war in my country – the supreme state of disintegration for a country. This is what we call imperialist intervention.

Chile now faces a danger whose solution does not only depend on national will, but on a whole series of external elements. I am talking about the action of the Kennecott Copper Corporation.

Our constitution says that disputes caused by nationalizations must be solved by a court that, just like all the others in my country, is independent and sovereign in its decisions. Kennecott Copper accepted its jurisdiction and for a year it appeared before that tribunal. Its appeal was not accepted, and it decided to use its considerable power to deprive us of the benefits of our copper exports and put pressure on the Government of Chile. In September, it went so far in its arrogance as to demand the embargo of the payment of these exports in courts in France, Holland and Sweden. It will surely try the same thing in other countries. The basis for this action cannot be more unacceptable from the judicial and moral points of view.

Kennecott would have the courts of other nations, that have absolutely nothing to do with the problems or the negotiations between the Chilean state and the Kennecott Copper Corporation, decide that a sovereign act of our Government – carried out in response to a mandate of the highest authority, like that of the political constitution, and supported by all the Chilean people – is null and void.

This attempt of theirs is in contradiction to basic principles of international law by virtue of which the natural resources of a country, especially those which constitute its livelihood, belong to the nation and it can dispose of them at will. There is no universally accepted international law or, in this case, specific treaty, which provides for that. The world community, organized under the principles of the United Nations, does not accept an interpretation of international law, subordinated to the interests of capitalism, that will lead the courts of any foreign country to back up a structure of economic relations at the service of the above-mentioned economic system. If that were the case, there would be a violation of a fundamental principle of international life: that of non-intervention in the internal affairs of a state, as was explicitly recognized at the third UNCTAD.

We are guided by international law repeatedly accepted by the United Nations, especially in resolution 1803 (XVIII) of the General Assembly; norms that have just been reinforced by the trade and development board, based itself on the charges my country made against Kennecott. The respective resolution reaffirmed the sovereign right of all states to freely dispose of their natural resources, and declared in application of this principle, that the nationalization carried out by states to regain control over those resources are an expression of their sovereign powers. Every state must set the standards for those measures and the disputes that may arise as a result are the exclusive concern of its courts, without prejudice to resolution 1803 of the General Assembly. This resolution allows the intervention of extra-national jurisdictions under exceptional conditions and as long as there is an agreement between sovereign states and other interested parties.

This is the only acceptable thesis of the United Nations. It is the only one that is in keeping with its philosophy and principles. It is the only one that can protect the rights of the weak against the abuses of the strong.

Since it could not be any other way, in the courts of Paris we have obtained the lifting of the embargo that had been in effect on the payment of a shipment of our copper. We will continue to ceaselessly defend the exclusive jurisdiction of Chilean courts over any dispute resulting from the nationalization of our basic resource.

For Chile, this is not only an important matter of judicial interpretation. It is a problem of sovereignty and, even more, of survival.

Kennecott's aggression inflicts grave damage on our economy. Just the direct difficulties imposed on the marketing of copper have resulted in the loss of many millions of dollars for Chile in the last two months alone. But that isn't all. I have already discussed the effects linked to the blocking of my country's financial operations with the banks of Western Europe. There is also an evident effort to create a climate of distrust among the buyers of our main export product, but this will fail.

The objectives of this imperialist firm are now going even further than that, because in the long run it cannot expect any political or legal power to deprive Chile of what rightfully belongs to her. It wants to bring us to our knees, but this will never happen.

The aggression of the big capitalist firms seeks to block the emancipation of the people. It represents a direct attack on the economic interests of the workers in the concrete case against Chile.

The Chilean people are a people that have reached the political maturity to decide by a majority the replacement of the capitalist economic system by a socialist one. Our political regime has institutions that have been open enough to channel that revolutionary will without violent clashes. It is my duty to warn this assembly that the reprisals and the blockade, aimed at producing contradictions and the resultant economic distortions, threaten to have repercussions on peace and internal coexistence in my country. They will not attain their evil objectives. The great majority of Chileans will find the way to resist them in a patriotic and dignified manner. What I said at the beginning will always be valid: our history, land and man are joined in a great national feeling.

## The phenomenon of the transnational corporations

At the third UNCTAD I was able to discuss the phenomenon of the transnational corporations. I mentioned the great growth in their economic power, political influence and corrupting action. That is the reason for the alarm with which world opinion should react in the face of a reality of this kind. The power of these corporations is so great that it goes beyond all borders. The foreign investments of US companies alone reached $32,000 million. Between 1950 and 1970 they grew at a rate of 10 per cent a year, while that nation's exports only increased by 5 per cent. They make huge profits and drain off tremendous resources from the developing countries.

In just one year, these firms withdrew profits from the Third World that represented net transfers in their favour of $1,723 million: $1,013 million from Latin America; $280 million from Africa; $376 million from the Far East; and $74 million from the Middle East. Their influence and their radius of action are upsetting the traditional trade practices of technological transfer among states, the transmission of resources among nations and labour relations.

We are faced by a direct confrontation between the large transnational corporations and the states. The corporations are interfering in the fundamental political, economic and military decisions of the states. The corporations are global organizations that do not depend on any state and whose activities are not controlled by, nor are they accountable to any parliament or any other institution representative of the collective interest. In short, all the world political structure is being undermined. The dealers don't have a country. The place where they may be does not constitute any kind of link; the only thing they are interested in is where they make profits. This is not something I say; they are Jefferson's words.

The large transnational firms are prejudicial to the genuine interests of the developing countries and their dominating and uncontrolled action is also carried out in the industrialized countries, where they are based. This has recently been denounced in Europe and in the United States and resulted in a US Senate investigation. The developed nations are just as threatened by this danger as the underdeveloped ones. It is a phenomenon that has already given rise to the growing mobilization of organized workers including the large trade union organizations that exist in the world. Once again the action of the international solidarity of workers must face a common enemy: imperialism.

In the main, it was those acts that led the Economic and Social Council of the United Nations – following the denunciation made by Chile – to unanimously approve, last July, a resolution that called for a group of world figures to meet and study the effects and function of transnational corporations in the process of development, especially in the developing countries, and their repercussions on international relations, and present recommendations for appropriate international action.

Ours is not an isolated or a unique problem. It is the local expression of a reality that overwhelms us, a reality that covers Latin America and the Third World. In varying degrees of intensity, with unique features, all the peripheral countries are threatened by something similar.

The spokesman for the African group at the Trade and Development Board a few weeks ago announced the position of those countries towards the denunciation made by Chile of Kennecott's aggression, reporting that his group fully supported Chile, because it was a problem which did not affect only one nation but, potentially, all of the developing world. These words have great value, because they represent the recognition of an entire continent that through the Chilean case, a new stage in the battle between imperialism and the weak countries of the Third World is being waged.

## The countries of the Third World

The battle in defence of natural resources is but a part of the battle being waged by the countries of the Third World against underdevelopment. There is a very clear dialectical relationship: imperialism exists because underdevelopment exists; underdevelopment exists because imperialism exists. The aggression we are being made the object of today makes the fulfilment of the promises made in the last few years as to a new large-scope action aimed at overcoming the conditions of underdevelopment and want in the nations of Africa, Asia and Latin America appear illusory. Two years ago, on the occasion of the 25th anniversary of the founding of the United Nations, the UN General Assembly solemnly proclaimed the strategy for a second decade of development. In keeping with this strategy, all UN member states pledged to spare no efforts to transform, via concrete measures, the present unfair international division of labour and to close the vast economic and technological gap that separates the wealthy countries from the developing ones.

We have seen that none of those aims ever became a reality. On the contrary, the situation has worsened.

Thus, the markets of the industrialized countries have remained as tightly closed as they ever were to the basic products – chiefly the agricultural products – of the developing countries and the index of protectionist measures is on the increase. The terms of exchange continue to deteriorate, the system of generalized preferences for the exportation of our manufactured and semi-manufactured goods has never been put into effect by the nation whose market – considering its volume – offered the best perspectives and there are no indications that this will be done in the immediate future.

The transfer of public financial resources, rather than reaching 0·7 per cent of the gross national product of the developed nations, has dropped from 0·34 to 0·24 per cent. The debt contracted by the developing countries, which was already enormous by the beginning of this year, has skyrocketed to between $70 and $75 thousand million in only a few months. The sums for loan services paid by those countries, which represent an intolerable drain for them, have been to a great measure the result of the conditions and terms of the loans. In 1970 these services increased 18 per cent, and in 1971, 20 per cent – more than twice the mean rate for the 1960 decade.

This is the drama of underdevelopment and of the countries which have not stood up for their rights, which have not demanded respect for their rights and defended, through a vigorous collective action, the price of their raw materials and basic products and have not confronted the threats and aggressions by neo-imperialism.

We are potentially wealthy countries and yet we live a life of poverty. We go here and there, begging for credits and aid and yet we are – a paradox typical of the capitalist economic system – great exporters of capital.

### Latin America and underdevelopment

Latin America, as part of the developing world, forms part of the picture I have just described. Together with Asia, Africa and the socialist countries, she has waged many battles in the last few years to change the structure of the economic and commercial relations with the capitalist world, to replace the unfair and discriminatory economic and monetary order created in Bretton Woods at the end of World War II.

It is true that there are differences in the national income of many of the countries in our region and that of countries on other continents, and even among countries that could be considered as relatively less developed among the underdeveloped countries.

However, such differences – which many mitigate by comparing them with the national product of the industrialized world – do not keep Latin America out of the vast neglected and exploited sector of humanity.

The consensus at Viña del Mar, in 1969, affirmed these coincidences and defined, pointed out clearly and indicated the scope of the region's economic and social backwardness and the external factors that determined it, pointing out the great injustices that are being committed against the region under the disguise of cooperation and aid. I say this because large cities in Latin America, admired by many, hide the drama of hundreds of thousands of human beings living in marginal towns that are the product of unemployment and sub-employment. These beautiful cities hide the deep contrast between small groups of privileged individuals and the great masses whose nutrition and health indexes are the lowest.

It is easy to see why our Latin American continent shows such a high rate of infant mortality and illiteracy, with 13 million people out of jobs and more than 50 million doing only occasional work. More than 20 million Latin Americans do not use money even as a means of exchange.

No regime, no government has been able to solve the great deficit in housing, labour, food and health. On the contrary, the deficit increases with every passing year in keeping with the population increase. If this situation continues, what will happen when there are more than 600 million of us by the end of the century?

The situation is even more dramatic in Asia and Africa, whose *per capita* income is even lower and whose process of development shows an even greater weakness.

It is not always noticed that the Latin American subcontinent – whose wealth potential is simply enormous – has become the principal field of action of economic imperialism for the last 30 years. Recent data given by the International Monetary Fund shows that private investment in the developed countries in Latin America shows a deficit against Latin America of $9,000 million between 1960 and 1970. In a word, that amount represents a net contribution of capital from our region to the wealthy world in one decade.

Chile is completely in solidarity with the rest of Latin America, without exception. For this reason, it favours and fully respects the policy of non-intervention and self-determination, which we apply on a worldwide scale. We enthusiastically foster the increase of our economic and cultural relations. We are in favour of the complementing and the integration of our economies. Hence, we work with enthusiasm within the framework of LAFTA and, as an initial step, for the creation of the Andean countries' common market, which unites us with Bolivia, Colombia, Peru and Ecuador.

Latin America has left the era of protest behind her. Needs and statistics contributed to an increased awareness. Reality has shattered all ideological barriers. All attempts at division and isolation have been defeated and there is an ardent desire to coordinate the offensive in defence of the interests of the countries on the continent and the other developing countries.

Those who make peaceful revolution impossible make violent revolution inevitable. These are not my words. I simply share the same opinion. The words are those of John F. Kennedy.

## Chile is not alone

Chile is not alone. All attempts to isolate her from the rest of Latin America and the world have failed. On the contrary, Chile has been the object of endless demonstrations of solidarity and support. The ever-increasing condemnation of imperialism; the respect that the efforts of the people of Chile deserve; and the response to our policy of friendship with all the nations of the world, were all instrumental in defeating the attempts to surround our country with a ring of hostility.

In Latin America, all the plans for economic and cultural cooperation or integration, plans of which we form part on both the regional and sub-regional level, have continued to take on strength at an accelerated pace. As a result, our trade – particularly with Argentina, Mexico and the countries of the Andean Pact – has increased considerably.

The joint support of the Latin American countries in world and regional forums in favour of the principles of free determination over natural resources has remained firm as a rock. And, in response to the recent attacks against our sovereignty, we have been the object of demonstrations of complete solidarity. To all of these countries, we express our most deep-felt gratitude.

Socialist Cuba, which is suffering the rigours of blockade, has always given us her revolutionary solidarity.

On the world scale, I must point out very especially that we have enjoyed the full solidarity of the socialist countries in Europe and Asia from the very beginning. The great majority of the world community did us the honour of electing Santiago as the seat of the third UNCTAD meeting and has welcomed with great interest our invitation to be the site of the next world conference on rights to the sea – an invitation which I reiterate on this occasion.

The non-aligned countries' foreign ministers meeting, held in George-town, Guyana, in September, publicly expressed its determined support in response to the aggression of which we are being made the object by Kennecott Copper.

The CIPEC, an organization of coordination established by the main copper-exporting countries – Peru, Zaire, Zambia and Chile – which met recently in Santiago, at the ministers' level, at my suggestion, to analyse the situation of aggression against my country created by Kennecott Copper, has just adopted a number of resolutions and recommendations of vast importance to the various states. These resolutions and recommendations constitute an unreserved support of our position and an important step taken by countries of the Third World in defence of trade of their basic products.

The resolutions will no doubt constitute important material for the second commission. But I would like to refer at this moment to the categorical declaration to the effect that any action that may impede or obstruct the exercise of a country's sovereign right to dispose freely of its natural resources constitutes an economic attack. Needless to say, the Kennecott actions against Chile constitute an economic aggression and, therefore, the ministers agreed on asking their respective governments to suspend all economic and commercial relations with the firm and state that disputes on compensation in case of nationalization are the exclusive concern of those states which adopt such measures.

However, the most significant thing is that it was resolved 'to establish a permanent mechanism of protection and solidarity' in relation to copper. Mechanisms such as this one, together with the OPEC, which operates in the field of petroleum, are the germ of what would be an organization which would include all the countries of the Third World to protect and defend all basic products – including the mining, petroleum and agricultural fields.

The great majority of the countries in Western Europe, from the Scandinavian countries in the extreme north to Spain in the extreme south, have been cooperating with Chile, and their understanding has meant a form of support to us. It is thanks to this understanding that we have renegotiated our foreign debt.

And, lastly, we have been deeply moved by the solidarity of the world's working class, expressed by its great trade union central organizations and demonstrated in actions of great significance, such as the port workers of Le Havre and Rotterdam's refusal to unload the copper from Chile whose payment has been arbitrarily and unfairly embargoed.

# 12  The 'Washington Post' – Terri Shaw

## Multinationals Queue for Post-Allende Credits

Article in the *Washington Post*, 2 November 1973, and in the *Guardian*, 2 November 1973.

*Washington, 1 November*

Less than a year ago, President Allende of Chile went to the United Nations to say that his country had been brought to the brink of civil war by an economic blockade that deprived his Government of the commercial credits and financial help needed to keep it going.

Now, with President Allende dead and his Government replaced by a right-wing military junta, the blockade shows signs of being lifted.

By 4 December, the first anniversary of President Allende's speech, representatives of several international financial institutions will have visited Chile to decide whether the country is eligible for new development loans, and goods bought with commercial credits will be flowing into the country again.

Towards the end of this year, the Inter-American Committee for the Alliance for Progress is to make a special review of the Chilean economy and draft recommendations on the type of aid that is needed.

Shortly after the review, Chile's major creditors will meet in Paris to discuss rescheduling the country's huge foreign debt, a problem that must be settled before full assistance can be resumed.

The military junta that deposed President Allende on 11 September has said that one of its priorities will be economic reconstruction; it will change from a centrally planned economy moving towards socialism, and will encourage private enterprise and foreign investment.

These promises have encouraged American businessmen and Government officials, most of whom say it was President Allende's policies, not an economic blockade, that bankrupted Chile.

To reassure international bankers, a high-level Chilean delegation visited Washington and New York in October and emphasized that the new Government's intention was to pay off all of Chile's debts and strengthen the economy.

This campaign has already begun to bear fruit: three weeks after the coup the United States Department of Agriculture granted Chile a credit of $24 millions, on commercial terms, to buy 120,000 tons of wheat.

Senator Edward Kennedy, who has criticized the Chilean junta for violations of human rights, said the wheat credit was 'eight times the total commodity credit offered to Chile in the past three years when a democratically elected Government was in power'.

As the wheat deal was being announced, however, New York bankers were meeting representatives of the new Chilean Government who asked for a reopening of lines of credit which had dwindled to one-tenth their previous level.

According to one knowledgeable source, Chile had lines of credit worth between $250 millions and $300 millions at the end of 1970, when President Allende took office: a year later, it had about $25 millions.

Early next month the International Monetary Fund and the Inter-American Aid Committee plan to send missions to Chile. The IMF is expected to give the junta technical assistance in preparing a new Budget and a standby loan providing the foreign exchange needed to buy food and spare parts to get the factories and farms functioning efficiently. A representative of the World Bank will accompany the IMF group.

This flurry of activity is no guarantee that funds will begin flowing to Santiago immediately. A major obstacle to credits from both private and international banks was the Allende Government's refusal to pay two major US copper companies for the mines it nationalized in 1970.

As a result of this action the US was unwilling to reach an agreement with Chile about renegotiating its debts to US agencies or to support loans for Chile in the international banks.

So far the US Government has made no public commitment on these issues, although the Chilean junta has promised to study the possibility of payment to Anaconda and Kennecott for the copper mines they lost.

# Further Reading

There has been such an explosion of literature on international firms in recent years that any list of further reading is bound to be highly selective. I have included works that are intrinsically significant, or representative, or useful sources of further references, or readily accessible; it is by no means a comprehensive guide. Numbers in brackets refer to the listed books of readings.

## A. General

*Introductory*

Behrman, J., *Some Patterns in the Rise of Multinational Enterprise*, North Carolina Graduate School of Business Administration, Research Paper no. 18, 1969.

Tugendhat, C., *The Multinationals*, Penguin, 1973.

Vernon, R., *Sovereignty at Bay*, Longmans, 1971 (Penguin 1973).

*Collections of readings*

1. Bernstein, H. (ed.), *Underdevelopment and Development*, Penguin, 1973.
2. Dunning, J. (ed.), *The Multinational Enterprise*, Allen and Unwin, 1972.
3. Dunning, J. (ed.), *International Investment*, Penguin, 1972.
4. Kindleberger, C. P. (ed.), *The International Corporation*, MIT Press, 1970.
5. Rhodes, R. I. (ed.), *Imperialism and Underdevelopment*, Monthly Review Press, 1970.
6. Tudyka, K. P. (ed.), *Multinational Corporations and Labour Unions*, SUN, Nijmegen, 1973.
7. US Congress Joint Economic Committee, Hearings, *A Foreign Economic Policy for the 1970s, Part 4, Multinational Corporations and International Investment*, US Government, 1970.

*Historical*

Plummer, A., *International Combines in Modern Industry*, Pitman, 1934.

Wilkins, M., *The Emergence of Multinational Enterprise: American Business Abroad from the Colonial Era to 1914*, Harvard University Press, 1970.

*Management and finance of international firms*

Brooke, M. Z., and Remmers, H. L., *The Strategy of Multinational Enterprise*, Longmans, 1970.

Robock, S. H., and Simmons, K., *International Business and Multinational Enterprises*, Irwin, 1973.

Zenoff, D. B., and Zwick, J., *International Financial Management*, Prentice Hall, 1969.

*Orthodox economics of international firms*

Aharon, Y., *The Foreign Investment Decision Process*, Harvard University Graduate School of Business Administration, 1966.

Caves, R., 'International Corporations: the Industrial Economics of Foreign Investment', *Economica*, February 1971, and in (3).

Hirsch, S., *Location of Industry and International Competitiveness*, Clarendon, 1967.

Johnson, H. G., 'The Efficiency and Welfare Implications of the International Corporation', in (3) and (4).

See also (2), (3) and (4).

*Marxist writings on internationalization of capital*

Altvater, E., 'Multinational Corporations and the Working Class', in (6).

Barratt Brown, M., *The Economics of Imperialism*, Penguin, 1974 (especially Ch. 9).

Bukharin, N., *Imperialism and World Economy*, Merlin, 1972.

Palloix, C., *Les Firmes multinationales et le procès d'internationalisation*, Maspero, 1973.

See also (5) and (6).

## B. Advanced countries

*Interpenetration of capitals and imperial rivalries*

Mandel, E., *Europe versus America?*, New Left Books, 1970.

Rowthorn, R. E., and Hymer, S., *International Big Business 1957–67: a Study of Comparative Growth*, Cambridge University Press, 1971; also their article in (4).

Servan-Schreiber, J. J., *The American Challenge*, Penguin, 1969.

*Impact on national economies*

Behrman, J., *National Interests and the Multinational Enterprise*, Prentice-Hall, 1970.

Dunning, J., 'Technology, United States Investment and European Economic Growth', in (3).

Levitt, K., *Silent Surrender*, Macmillan, 1970.

Murray, R., 'The Internationalization of Capital and the British Economy', in J. M. Samuels (ed.), *Readings on Mergers and Takeovers*, Elek.

Reddaway, W. B. (ed.), *Effects of UK Direct Investment Overseas: Final Report*, Cambridge University Press, 1968.

Steuer, M. (ed.), *The Impact of Foreign Direct Investment on the UK*, HMSO, 1973.

*Response of labour*

Gunter, H. (ed.), *Transnational Industrial Relations*, Macmillan, 1972.

Jennings, P., testimony to US Congress, in (7).

Levinson, C., *International Trade Unionism*, Allen and Unwin, 1972.

Trades Union Congress, *International Companies*, TUC, 1970.

Also (6).

## C. Less developed countries

### International firms and development/underdevelopment

Arrighi, G., 'International Corporations, Labour Aristocracies and Economic Development in Tropical Africa', in (5).

Kidron, M., *Foreign Investments in India*, Oxford University Press, 1965.

Murray, R., 'Underdevelopment, International Firms and the International Division of Labour', in *Towards a New World Economy*, Rotterdam University Press, 1972.

North American Congress On Latin America, *Yanqui Dollar – the Contribution of US Private Investment to Underdevelopment in Latin America*, NACLA, 1971.

O'Connor, J., 'International Corporations and Economic Underdevelopment', *Science and Society*, vol. 34, 1970.

Warren, B., 'Imperialism and Capitalist Industrialization', *New Left Review* no. 81, September–October, 1973.

### Technological dependence

Dos Santos, T., 'The Structure of Dependence', *American Economic Review Papers & Proceedings*, May 1970.

*Journal of Development Studies*, Special Issue on Science and Technology in Development, vol. 9, no. 1, October 1972.

### Raw materials exploitation

Beckford, G. I., 'The Economics of Agricultural Resource Use and Development in Plantation Economies', in (1).

Girvan, N., and Jefferson, O., 'Corporate vs. Caribbean Integration', in (1).

Mikesell, R. F. (ed.), *Foreign Investment in the Petroleum and Mineral Industries: Case Studies on Investor-Host Relations*, Johns Hopkins Press, 1971.

Penrose, E. T., *The Large International Firm in Developing Countries: the International Petroleum Industry*, Allen and Unwin, 1968.

### Manufacturing investments

Ádám, G., 'New Trends in World Business: Worldwide Sourcing and De-domiciling', *Acta Oeconomica*, vol. 7, 1971.

Baranson, J., *Automotive Industries in Developing Countries*, World Bank Staff Occasional Papers no. 8, IBRD, 1969.

Frank, A. G., 'On the Mechanisms of Imperialism: the Case of Brazil', in (5).

Helleiner, G. K., 'Manufactured Exports from Less Developed Countries and Multinational Firms', *Economic Journal*, March 1973.

### Class Structure and Labour Aspects

Amsden, A. H., *International Firms and Labour in Kenya, 1945–70*, Cass, 1971.

Arrighi, G., and Saul, J., 'Socialism and Economic Development in Tropical Africa', *Journal of Modern African Studies*, vol. VI, no. 2, 1968.

Cardoso, F. H., 'The Industrial Elite in Latin America', in (1).

# Acknowledgements

*for permission to reproduce the Readings in this volume,*
*acknowledgement is made to the following:*

2  Macmillan Publishing Co. Inc.
3  François Maspero
4  Artisjus and Mrs Adam
5  Robin Murray
6  *New Left Review*
7  Merlin Press Ltd
8  *New Left Review*
9  Constantine Vaitsos
10  John Roberts and Jacques Perrin
12  *Washington Post*

# Author Index

Ádám, G., 12, 82, 84, 89, 90n, 95n, 98n
Aharoni, Y., 124n
Aliber, R. Z., 14
Allende, S., 233
Altman, O., 130, 131n
Angell, N., 28
Azouvi, 83n

Balassa, B., 111, 129n, 130n
Baran, P. A., 16, 116, 152n
Barnard, C., 43n
Barratt Brown, M., 16, 16n
Barrio, S., 113n
Bauer, O., 32
Behrman, J. N., 67, 68, 69
Berle, A. A., 57
Bertin, G. Y., 64n, 66
Bettelheim, C., 86n
Blackburn, R., 10n
Borrelly, R., 81n
Bradshaw, M. T., 130n
Brash, D., 132
Brooke, M. Z., 66
Bruck, N. K., 128n
Bukharin, N., 14n, 15, 16, 23
Byé, M., 112

Chandler, A. D., 43n, 44, 48, 49
Chenery, H., 91, 94n, 96, 100n
Coase, R. H., 41n
Cooper, C., 189n, 213n
Coux, C., 67

Delilez, J.-P., 68n, 81n
Diaz, P., 212n
Diegger, J. A., 203
Dobb, M., 112n
Dunning, J., 12

Eatwell, J., 14n

Emmanuel, A., 16, 79
Engels, F., 111, 127n
English, H. E., 102n
Erbes, R., 112n

Fabra, P., 152n
Fallers, L. A., 51
Fanjzylber, F., 210n
Fanon, F., 37
Feis, H., 136n
Frank, A. G., 16, 17
Franko, L. G., 63, 64n
Furjot, D., 86n

Gates, T. R., 171n
Geras, N., 10n
Gervasi, S., 51n
Girvan, N., 59
Gruber, W., 196n

Harcourt, G. C., 14n
Harms, 28n
Hawkins, R. G., 102n
Hay, K. A., 102n
Helleiner, G. K., 100, 101n
Herouville, R., 220n
Hilferding, R., 15n, 33
Hirsch, S., 130n
Holman, M. A., 204n
Horst, T. O., 185n
Hughes, H., 91, 94n, 100n, 102n
Hunt, E. K., 14n
Hymer, S., 37, 38n, 45n, 47n, 64, 166

Jalée, P., 159
Janco, M., 86n
Jefferson, O., 59n
Johnson, W. A., 229
Jones, A., 15
Judet, P., 218n, 221n

# Subject Index

Eurodollar market, 128, 130, 131
European capital, 167–73
European Economic Community
(EEC), 111, 124, 135–7, 141
external relations of, 152–4
and international capital
concentration, 148–50
socialist position on, 154–6
and supranational state power,
146, 147
and US capital, 145, 175–9
European firms
growth, 47, 48
size, 151, 160, 161
worldwide sourcing by, 89, 91, 95,
97
Export processing zones, 100
External relations of capitalist
systems, 114

French industry, 63, 153
Finance capital, 27, 30, 33, 63, 113
Finance capitalism, 31

Globalism, 90, 98

Host countries, 12, 13, 122

Imperial rivalry, 159–63, 179–80
India
engineering consultancy
and heavy industry investment,
221–5
perspectives, 226–9
projects, 217–18
and technical independence,
225–6
types of contract, 218–21
Fourth Five-Year Plan, 228
shift of industry to, 92–3
technological innovation, 215,
228–9
Indonesia, 92, 185n
Inter-American Committee for the
Alliance for Progress, 248
International capital movements, 64n

International competition, 117, 125,
166
intensification of, 145
and size of firms, 151
International division of labour, 18,
23, 32, 60, 108
distortion, 35
and worldwide sourcing, 90–95,
100–102
International exchange, 23, 124–6, 132
International firms (IFs), 9n
see also Multi-national
corporations and
Multi-national enterprise
International investment trends, 11
International sub-contracting, 93, 94
International trade, 9
and investment, 164, 167
Internationalism, 12
Internationalization, 15, 16, 29, 128,
141
and financial independence of
multinationals, 132
of banking capital, 27
of capital, 18, 21, 26, 63, 85
as a social relation, 70–73, 79
process of expansion, 73–8
of self-expanded capital, 78–85
ITT in Chile, 239–40

Japanese capital, 161–3, 167–73
Japanese firms, 162, 166
growth of, 47, 48
worldwide sourcing by, 89–91, 95,
98
Joint ventures, 84, 99

Labour process, internationalization,
85–7
Law of uneven development, 17, 37,
48, 155, 160
exposition, 38
Law of increasing firm size, 37
Less developed countries (LDCs), 181
exports to, 99, 100
industrialization in, 18

Ultra-imperialism, 158
US firms, 47, 63, 95, 151, 159
  overseas investment, 47n, 165
  size, 161–3
US super-imperialism, 158
US Tariff Commission, 94

West German industry, 143, 147,
  148, 154

World economy
  definition, 23, 24
  development, 18
  growth, 24–6
  and national economies, 16, 17,
    23–33, 108
  organization forms, 27–9

# More about Penguins and Pelicans

*Penguinews*, which appears every month, contains details of all the new books issued by Penguins as they are published. From time to time it is supplemented by *Penguins in Print*, which is a complete list of all titles available. (There are some five thousand of these.)

A specimen copy of *Penguinews* will be sent to you free on request. For a year's issues (including the complete lists) please send 50p if you live in the British Isles, or 75p if you live elsewhere. Just write to Dept EP, Penguin Books Ltd, Harmondsworth, Middlesex, enclosing a cheque or postal order, and your name will be added to the mailing list.

*In the U.S.A.*: For a complete list of books available from Penguin in the United States write to Dept CS, Penguin Books Inc., 7110 Ambassador Road, Baltimore, Maryland 21207.

*In Canada*: For a complete list of books available from Penguin in Canada write to Penguin Books Canada Ltd, 41 Steelcase Road West, Markham, Ontario.

*Penguin Education*

# Modern Economics Readings

*Penguin Education*

# Modern Economics Readings

*Penguin Education*

**Law Library**

Constitutional and Administrative Law   *de Smith*
Family Law   *Puxon*
Government Contracts   *Turpin*
Labour Law 1: Employment, Welfare and Safety at
   Work   *Aikin/Reid*
Law and Practice Relating to Banking   *Perry*
Law of Nations   *Fawcett*
Local Government   *Buxton*
Negotiable Instruments   *Ryder*
Race and Law   *Lester/Bindman*
Remedies of English Law   *Lawson*
Sale of Goods and Hire-Purchase   *Lowe*

*Penguin Education*

## Education Library

*Penguin Education*

# Education Library

*Penguin Education*

# Education Library

Penguin Education

# International Firms and Modern Imperialism

Edited by Hugo Radice

Penguin Modern Economics Readings

*General Editor*
B. J. McCormick

*Advisory Board*
K. J. W. Alexander
R. W. Clower
P. Robson
J. Spraos
H. Townsend